Twayne's Theatrical Arts Series

Warren French
EDITOR

Sam Peckinpah

Sam Peckinpah

Sam Peckinpah

DOUG McKINNEY

BOSTON

Twayne Publishers

1979

Sam Peckinpah

is first published in 1979 by Twayne Publishers.
A Division of G. K. Hall & Co.

Copyright © 1979 by G. K. Hall & Co.

Printed on permanent / durable acid-free paper and bound
in the United States of America

First Printing, October 1979

Library of Congress Cataloging in Publication Data
McKinney, Doug.
Sam Peckinpah.

(Twayne's theatrical arts series)
Bibliography: p. 249-52
Includes index.
1. Peckinpah, Sam, 1926-
PN1998.A3P4256   791.43 '0233 '0924   79-4570
ISBN 0-8057-9264-3

Contents

About the Author

DOUG MCKINNEY has seen almost as many films as Peter Bogdanovich used to claim he'd seen. Though he began his college education as a Physics / Chemistry student, he created his own major program to graduate from Yale University with a B. A. in Film Study. For several years, he ran a comprehensive film program at Yale, in charge of the Yale Law School Film Society; he has lectured and taught film widely, and has written many film articles and reviews, including contributions to the Wadsworth Atheneum film program in Hartford, Conn. In addition, he served as Assistant Curator of the Yale Film Collection.

Currently working in film distribution, Mr. McKinney is also a professional entertainer, and like most people who love film and try to write, he is at work on a screenplay.

Editor's Foreword

THIS BOOK is unusual in this series, for it is about an unusual man who has tried to beat the system while working within it during a period when most people find the system too much to cope with. When an artist's career is over, evaluation of his achievement is essential; books about younger men who have attained some celebrity must clearly be marked "subject to revision." But Sam Peckinpah is an experienced artist with a considerable body of work—perhaps even his best—behind him whom we may as yet lack even adequate materials to understand fully.

The reason for this uncertain state of knowledge, as Doug McKinney stresses in this book, is that hardly anyone has seen Peckinpah's films as he intended them to be seen. Even though he is still alive and working, a "legend" has overwhelmed the man. McKinney avoids repeating or embroidering the legend, as most previous writers about Peckinpah have done, and, rather, questions it, tests it, explodes it where necessary, in order to provide us with accurate information about what any judgment of Peckinpah should be based upon.

We are as yet in no position to judge this work, because we hardly know what Peckinpah expected us to see. Several of his most important films, like *Major Dundee*, *The Wild Bunch*, and *Pat Garrett and Billy the Kid*, have been mutilated by producers and distributors; some of those that most accurately represent Peckinpah's intentions, like *The Ballad of Cable Hogue* and *Bring Me the Head of Alfredo Garciu*, have been misunderstood and poorly distributed; the recent *Cross of Iron* has been both altered and poorly circulated. This is surely a lamentable state of affairs if Peckinpah has been concerned—as McKinney maintains—with exploring in his films the complex subject of America's loss with its frontier of the "direct potential of individual survival."

In offering this first major study in print of Peckinpah's themes and artistry, we hope to compensate for some of the disservices of distributors and earlier reviewers and to call attention to the need for making Peckinpah's work available as he intended it to be seen. This book does not pretend to be the "last word" on its subject, but to make readers aware of what needs to be done so that justice may at last be done to a man who has doggedly attempted in the face of the very kind of opposition that his characters typically face to create moral tales about the loss of individual identity, stressing the themes of self-knowledge, dedication, and loyalty.

For the present, I confess that I have no idea what Peckinpah's place may be in the history of the development of our cinema; but I have found Doug McKinney's account enormously valuable in helping me find out how little I really knew about the director from what fragments I had been able to see of his work and what I had heard about him from the myth-makers.

W.F.

Preface

I HAVE presumed that the reader is probably familiar with at least a few of Peckinpah's films, or, failing that, has some impression of the man and / or his work through reputation. This book is intended to "correct" something of the implicit danger in opinions based on the latter. While it is hoped that this kind of reference may not be necessary to most readers, the fact that we do not approach Peckinpah's films in a vacuum justifies the acknowledgment of the critical and commercial climate Peckinpah's films have been subject to. There is a vitality in some forms of rebuttal that is not possible in initial debate. Meanwhile, it is hoped that this book will help fill the vacuum that now exists in print on Peckinpah and his work.

If you have the time, see Peckinpah's films first, before you read further. But, before or after the fact, I attempt here to act as a guide to those films. Obviously, you'll get more out of this if you've seen the films; but if you haven't, the hope is that something you read will perk your interest enough to seek out a film you otherwise might have missed. You probably would never have *heard* of Abel Gance today if you hadn't first *read* something about him.

I have not included plot synopses, for two reasons: if you are familiar with a film, you don't need it; if you are not familiar with a given film, no amount of synopsizing will be accurate enough to give you an impression of the film better than you'll get by reading the discussion of it, anyway.

A few words about the archaeological nature of film study are called for here, perhaps a warning. We must never take for granted the mere *existence* of films. Well-known, popular films are disappearing as you read this. Though admirable strides have been made in recent years to preserve films, it is a sad fact that we will lose more than we will save. Moreover, what will be saved in all likelihood will not always be the same as the original. Looking at second-generation, scratched prints of "old" films is related to reconstructing a Grecian urn from fragments: critical allowances *must* be made. The time is approaching when people will not be able to understand the differences among various color processes; the day will come when one cannot see *Ride The High Country* in Cinema-Scope. Therefore, a piece of advice: if you have an abiding interest in films, make your viewing choices with this in mind, that if an old film is still "around," chances are it will be for a while yet, so see the newer ones first—you may not get another chance. Learn to appreciate the physical fact of a film, and cherish the wide-screen experience. And, you haven't necessarily "seen" the film if you've only seen it on TV.

With the above in mind, I would like to indicate what this book is based on. With the exception of *The Deadly Companions*, I have seen all of Peckinpah's feature films theatrically as well as in other situations; in addition, I have seen all thirteen of Peckinpah's features and the teleplay "Noon Wine" during the writing of this book. Where relevant variances in film versions occur, I have indicated them in the text and in the filmography. Though this verges on the pedantic, I cannot underscore enough the importance of accuracy in this area. One may not always achieve it, but one should be able to depend upon it where possible. Peckinpah's films are steeped in too much myth as it is. A primary value of a book like this is hopefully to clear up some of that, at least in terms of the "facts."

I don't want to imply that there are no stones left unturned; for the moment, I have turned all that a book of this size allows room for. For reasons of length I have limited discussion in certain areas, choosing instead to point to those areas that in particular offer the promise of further fruitful investigation. Peckinpah's films offer that kind of inexhaustible richness. Though it may seem wishy-washy to allow certain ambiguities, there is no other honest choice; for it is often this very ambiguity of some of the elements of Peckinpah's films that provides the quality of richness, the feeling that the man is "on to something" about human experience, the ring of some truth. It is intended that this book be of immediate service to the novice and the intermediate student, but it is also hoped that the expert will equally enjoy the explorations.

Peckinpah is often thought of primarily in relation to the Western genre. But rather than discuss the films by grouping them according to themes and physical similarities, I have decided to deal with them chronologically. This procedure helps to account for an aspect of the artist's maturation while not sacrificing the interest of relationships among films in an *auteur* context. Conversely, grouping films thematically is a luxury that should only be undertaken after the films have been considered as single works.

At the outset, however, I have traced Peckinpah's career in a biographical sketch; for, giving some idea of how certain things came about will inform the discussion of the works themselves. (It is significant that film is a business where often the next project undertaken is the one that gets financed first.) The films can stand alone and, indeed, most do. But there is a point quickly reached in discussing individual works where knowledge of the artist himself is demanded to account for certain things. My last chapter deals summarily with Peckinpah's themes and includes a few words about the peculiar nature of his reputation, at the expense of which his work has often suffered.

For further "hard" information about Peckinpah and his films, I heartily direct the reader's attention to Louis Garner Simmons's scrupulously researched doctoral dissertation (see the Selected Bibliography). Hopefully it will be published, but as yet this major critical biography is not; in the meantime, the work is available in its original form and is invaluable. I have relied heavily on the wealth of documented information it contains, especially in my first chapter, on Peckinpah's background and career development. Simmons talked to literally everybody.

All dialogue quoted in the book is transcribed directly from the soundtracks of the films.

For their help with stills, I would like to acknowledge Carol Cleary of the Museum of Modern Art Stills Archive, Jerry Ohlinger's Movie Material Store, Movie Star News, and The Memory Shop. I would also like to particularly acknowledge the gracious assistance of Rhonda Bloom, Don Rosen, Jerry Cadwallader, Emily Green, Jack Hurd, Pat Diehl, Susan

Goldberg of the Tucson Public Library, Dorothy Schechter of UPA, Twyman Films, Phil Foley, Lon Feldman, Allen Meitchik, and Angela Scalpello, for special help in obtaining research materials.

My deepest gratitude is extended for the invaluable encouragement and aid given me by Annette Insdorf, Garner Simmons, Ricardo Mendez, Gregory Nicoll, Jeanine Basinger, Warren French, and Lynda McKinney, and a special warm note of thanks goes to Mr. and Mrs. Jason Robards, Jerry Fielding, Katy Haber, and Sam Peckinpah, for their kindness.

DOUG McKINNEY

Dobbs Ferry, N.Y.

***

For Lynda.

Chronology

1925 David Samuel Peckinpah born in Fresno, California, February 21. Raised on family's land.

1943 Enlists in Marine Corps; tour of duty includes most of a year in China.

1947 Introduced to theater at Fresno State College; marries Marie Selland.

1949 Daughter Sharon born; graduates with B.A. in Drama.

1950 Masters Degree in Drama at University of Southern California; thesis was a film from a Tennessee Williams one-act play.

1950-1951 Director-Producer in Residence, Huntington Park Civic Theatre.

1951-1953 Works as propman / stagehand at KLAC-TV; assistant editor at CBS; daughter Kristen born.

1954-1957 Hired by Walter Wanger to work as an assistant on *Riot in Cell Block 11*; works for director Don Siegel on four more films; approximately a dozen films as an assistant; writes TV scripts for various Western series, including "Gunsmoke"; daughter Melissa born.

1957 Hired to do feature script (after many revisions by others eventually becomes *One-eyed Jacks*, directed by Marlon Brando).

1958-1959 Directs episode of TV series "Broken Arrow"; writes and directs pilot for "The Rifleman," and other series episodes.

1959-1960 Writes more feature scripts, and television work; oversees series production of "The Westerner," writing and directing several episodes as well.

1961 Directed first feature, *The Deadly Companions*; son Matthew born; divorced from Marie Selland.

1962 *Ride the High Country*; produced and directed teleplays "Pericles on 31st St." and "The Losers" for "Dick Powell Theater."

1963 Receives awards in Europe for *Ride the High Country*; works on scripts at Walt Disney Productions.

1964 *Major Dundee* filmed; marries Begonia Palacios (one child, daughter Lupita, from this marriage); fired from directing of *The Cincinnati Kid*.

1965 *Major Dundee* released; Arnold Laven's *The Glory Guys*, based on his script, released.

1966 Writes and directs "Noon Wine," from Katherine Anne Porter's novella, for ABC-Stage 67.

1968 *The Wild·Bunch* (released 1969); Buzz Kulik's *Villa Rides!*, based on his script, released.

1969 *The Ballad of Cable Hogue* (released 1970).

1971 *Straw Dogs*.

1972 *Junior Bonner*; *The Getaway*; marries third wife, Joie Gould (later divorced).

1973 *Pat Garrett and Billy the Kid*.

1974 *Bring Me the Head of Alfredo Garcia*.

1975 *The Killer Elite*.

1976- *Cross of Iron*.
1977

1977- *Convoy*.
1978

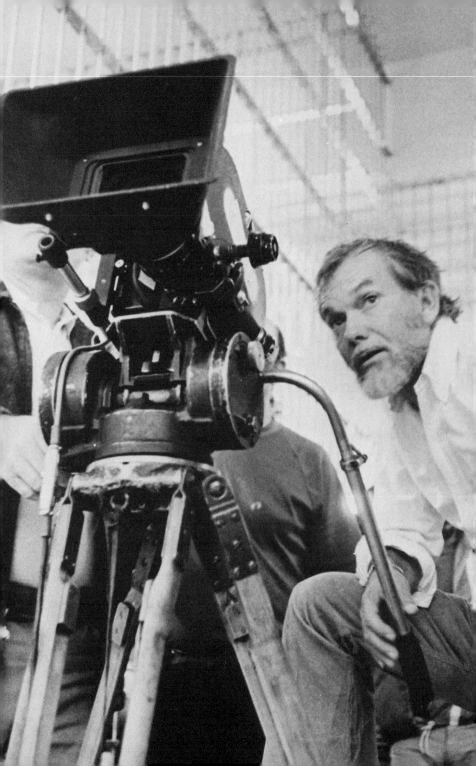

1

Sam Peckinpah's Life and Career

SAM PECKINPAH is a man whose roots are a conscious influence on his work. His background includes an especially American heritage, indelibly linked to the pioneer history of California. Sam saw the "Old West," saw the passing of an era, growing up amidst traditions and attitudes that belonged more directly to the nineteenth rather than to the twentieth century. "Progress' eclipsed that way of life, but for Sam there would always be things from it worth hanging on to.

He was born David Samuel Peckinpah on February 21, 1925, in a Fresno hospital, named for his father and maternal grandfather. Both the Peckinpahs and the Churchs (his mother's family) had been in the area for more than seventy years, both families having migrated west in the 1850's.[1]

Sam's grandfather Charles Peckinpah hauled borax out of Death Valley until he had enough money to buy timberland and then ran a successful saw mill from the 1880s to just after the turn of the century on Peckinpah Mountain. After selling the mill, the family maintained a general store and way station they had built nearby.

His grandfather Denver Samuel Church was named after a Union general, to celebrate the Union victory at Antietam. Denver's uncle Moses Church had driven sheep into the Fresno area in 1868, and, after defeating the Cattleman's Association in a range war, built a 1,000-mile irrigation canal system which attracted more settlers to the area. Moses sent for Denver in 1875 to help with a land survey for the Temperance Union he had also established.

Denver went to college, went on to study law, and began a law practice in Fresno in 1893, the same year Sam's mother, Fern Church, was born. In 1905, the family moved to a ranch

17

Peckinpah on location for The Getaway, *at Huntsville Prison in Texas, 1972.*

in Crane Valley near Peckinpah Mountain, and raised cattle. But while they kept the ranch, Denver was elected District Attorney of Fresno County, and in 1912 was elected to Congress, where he served three terms, deciding not to run again after opposing U.S. entry into World War I in 1917.

Meanwhile, Sam's father David had gone to work as a cowboy on the Church ranch, where he met Fern in 1914. They were married a year later; Denver was pleased with his son-in-law's desire to become a lawyer, and made it possible for David to go to law school in Washington.

After law school, David went into practice in a partnership with his brother-in-law and Denver. This lasted until 1924, when Denver was elected to a Superior Court judgeship, and David went into practice with another lawyer in Fresno.

It was into this combination of law, ranching, and a tradition of pioneering independence that Sam Peckinpah was born; having the same first name as his father, he came to be called "D. Sammy." A major part of the responsibility for the looking-after of "D. Sammy" in his childhood was delegated to his older brother Denny (born in 1916, named after his grandfather). Denny took Sam along on visits to his Church grandparents, and it was during this time of riding through the country, fishing, learning to cowboy at the Church ranch, and hunting that Sam had some of the formative experiences which are his fondest memories. He has referred to it as the finest time of his life and acknowledges that there will never again be another time like it.

His grandfather Denver Church had a marked influence on Sam. Denver was a man of principle, and he taught by example as much as by instruction. Though he went broke a number of times as a rancher, ranching was his first love. He ran for Congress again in 1932 in order to raise money for his ranch, but although he was assured of reelection in 1934, he decided against further public office out of his deep opposition to Franklin D. Roosevelt. It was his belief that too much governmental control was the nation's biggest problem. Another illustration of the man is that, although he was an abstainer himself, he voted against Prohibition before leaving Congress in 1919.

Grandfather Church taught his family and Sam that you hunt to eat, not for fun, and that what nature offered was not to be wasted. The family lived off the land in many ways during the Depression, and it was strictly followed that you ate what you killed. It was also imperative that you were committed to the animal in a respect for what that animal provided in the way of survival. In interviews with Garner Simmons, Sam relates several incidents that illustrate this tenet, including a moving recollection of a deer hunt where he felt a profound anguish at the deer's death, out of that commitment to and respect for the animal he had chased. This idea was not limited to hunting wild animals: Sam's father David founded the Humane Society of Fresno.

Grandfather Church also taught a respect for firearms, and a necessity for accuracy in their use. He would send Sam out with two shells for the shotgun and the admonition not to bother coming back without two quail. Sam learned to hunt this way; the point was never skill for its own sake, but to obtain meat.

Likewise, the family had a traditional attitude toward the importance of self-reliant survival. Denver demanded that Sam learn to be observant, as it could mean the difference between starving in the woods and making it back. If Sam couldn't relate the details of an outing, Denver would give Sam a good kick in his butt. The lesson was learned quickly. It was perhaps the beginning of the training of the boy's visual sense that would later inform his work as an adult.

Sam attended elementary school in Fresno with a variety of kids of other races and cannot recall witnessing any racial prejudice in that period of his life. Indeed, Sam's father and uncles had been raised with two adopted Indian girls, and in their high-school days had started the rumor of Indian blood in their family. But Sam's uncle Mortimer Peckinpah maintains as family historian that there is no Indian blood in the family; the name Peckinpah is of German-Dutch origin.

Sam loved the outdoor life, but enjoyed reading a lot as well, from Edgar Rice Burroughs to *Moby Dick*. A particular family influence brought about his familiarity with the Bible: he read it cover-to-cover, including some passages of the Book of Judges and Song of Solomon often enough to commit them to memory. He also enjoyed seeing as many movies as he could.

One other point bears mentioning here, that the Peckinpahs were a musical family. But when Sam and his brother demon-

strated a knack for noise rather than melody, they were re-
lieved of contributing to this tradition. This certainly has an
impact on Peckinpah's work, for he is concerned with the
music in his films, but needs someone like Jerry Fielding to
guide the fruition of his ideas for the soundtrack.

By the time Sam finished his freshman year at Fresno High
School, the aggressive spirit that served him well on the foot-
bal team had become visible enough off the field for his parents to enroll him at another high school for his sophomore
year; but his behavior as a sophomore was similar, so that he
was transferred back to Fresno for his junior year. When his
temper remained undisciplined, his parents sent him to San
Rafael Military Academy for his senior year. He did well
enough there and would have graduated with honors had it
not been for the fact that he had also managed to accumulate
more demerits than anyone else in the school's history.

Surrounded by judges and lawyers—his father, grandfather,
uncle, and finally his brother Denny—at home, Sam had a special opportunity to learn that the "simple truth" as such didn't
exist. With dinner discussions generally turning to law, the
ambiguity of "the Truth" became apparent. Justice was acknowledged as something relative as opposed to a fixable constant.

Sam's father, David, had, like Grandfather Church, a direct
influence in many ways. He wanted to foster a belief in
humanitarian causes in his children. During the Depression,
his legal fees were often of bartered food and laundry rather
than money; but no client was refused if his cause was just. He
taught his sons that you earned what you got. The nickname of
"the Boss," by which his sons knew him, was one of affectionate respect. All David Peckinpah wanted to do was to "enter
his house justified," knowing that he had always tried to do
the right thing.

Taken as a whole, this atmosphere in which Sam Peckinpah
grew up tells a lot about the man and his work in films. It
affords insight into many later developments in his career, particularly when it comes to getting a sense of the man, his pride
about his integrity, his stubbornness, his methods of working,
and in reading "between the lines" of aspects of his public
reputation. The connection to the "Old West" and respect for
the environment go hand in hand with a sense of the violence

inherent in the natural order and in man, an eye for visual accuracy in detail, and ideals of truth and justice, knowing that they are both unknowable and relative.

After graduating from military school in 1943, Peckinpah enlisted in the Marines. He took college courses at Arizona State College and Louisiana State Teachers' College while stationed nearby awaiting assignment. He was sent to Officers' Candidate School, but washed out as a result of returning late from a New York City reunion with his brother Denny, then in Air Combat Intelligence. This was apparently fortunate, for the OCS class Sam would have graduated with went on to have a 70 percent casualty rate.

He continued to accumulate college credits until he was sent to China in the summer of 1945; but the war was soon over and he saw virtually no combat action during his tour of duty. He did see another marine hit seriously by sniper fire, remembered as "one of the longest split-seconds of my life."[2] Spending eighteen months in China, he grew to love the Far East, but his request for a discharge there was refused, and he was released from the Marines back in the United States.

With all the lawyers in his family, about the only thing Peckinpah knew he surely didn't want to be was a lawyer, much as his family would have liked him to be. He enrolled at Fresno State College, where in 1947 he met his future wife, Marie Selland. She wanted to be an actress and introduced Sam to theater when he tagged along after her one day to acting class. It took him immediately; he claims Tennessee Williams as a particular influence, and a major project for him was an adaptation of *The Glass Menagerie*, which he also directed. He graduated with a B.A. in drama in 1949; his first child, Sharon, was born the same year. Pursuing a Master's Degree at the University of Southern California, he filmed an adaptation of a one-act Williams play. It served as his thesis; he is glad that the film no longer exists.

After that, Peckinpah became a director / producer in residence at the Huntington Park Civic Theatre. He was successful there for a year and a half, with a summer spent in Albuquerque doing summer stock. He enjoyed a measure of control over productions, in exchange for long hours at low pay. From there he went to station KLAC-TV in Los Angeles, where he worked as a stagehand, floorsweep, and propman for

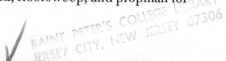

about two years, until he was fired after an argument with a studio executive. (During that stint he was fired from the Liberace TV show for showing up in jeans instead of a suit.) While there, however, he managed to put together some short films on his own time, which led to his being hired as an assistant editor at CBS in 1953. This job didn't last long. CBS fired him when he failed to report for work when his wife was in labor with their second child, Kristen.

A short time later, Sam decided to crack the film industry. Through a friend of his brother's, he landed an opportunity to wait in the office of Walter Wanger, who was then head of Allied Artists Film Corp. After he held out three days, Wanger gave him a job as third or fourth assistant casting director: a gopher. The first picture he was assigned to was *Riot in Cell Block 11* (1954); the director was Don Siegel. Working for Siegel was a fortunate association that taught Peckinpah a good deal. He has since referred to Siegel as his "patron" (Spanish).[3]

Becoming Siegel's personal assistant, Peckinpah served the director well from the start. In his book *Don Siegel: Director,* Stuart Kaminsky relates the story as recalled by Siegel of how he and his crew were first ushered in to meet the warden of Folsom Prison, where the film was to be shot. There was an air of guarded hostility, as the warden, without looking up from his desk, asked how long they would be at the prison. Siegel answered, "Sixteen days," to which the warden responded, "You're full of shit." Siegel replied, "Maybe you have a point there, but with your cooperation we can get the picture done in sixteen days." The grunting warden, still not looking up from his work, was next introduced to Peckinpah as Siegel's assistant. With that, the warden looked up and asked if he was related to the Peckinpahs of Fresno. Peckinpah said yes, and the warden, who knew Sam's father, stood up, put his arm around the director's assistant, smiled, and became cooperative.[4]

Peckinpah was impressed with the shooting of the film on actual location, feeling that the best things in the film were primarily due to the atmosphere of realism afforded by Folsom Prison. Siegel was impressed with Peckinpah and hired him for four other pictures while at Allied Artists. Peckinpah worked as "dialogue director" (mainly as personal assistant to

Siegel) on *Private Hell 36* (1954), *An Annapolis Story* (1955), *Invasion of the Body Snatchers* (1956), and *Crime in the Streets* (1956).

One of the few things Siegel remembers pleasantly about *Private Hell 36* is Peckinpah's loyalty and diligence as his assistant. The film was plagued by set tensions, arguments, and alcohol, and was a rough experience for those involved.[5] Siegel recognized Peckinpah's talents, and often got him to tackle problems that he would have to figure a way out of himself.[6] Peckinpah recalls this affectionately, allowing that Siegel was usually "kind enough not to laugh openly while watching me run about with both of my feet in my mouth and my thumb up my ass."[7] In any case, Peckinpah learned. (It is noteworthy that Siegel is also a filmmaker noted for action).

On *Invasion of the Body Snatchers*, Peckinpah also played a bit part as an actor, appearing as Charlie the meter-reader, who later becomes one of the pod people leading the chase after Kevin McCarthy and Dana Wynter. He also was given an opportunity to do a minor rewrite on perhaps two short scenes. Although not the major rewrite he is sometimes credited with, it was his first try at screenwriting.[8]

Peckinpah recalls having worked on roughly a dozen pictures while at Allied Artists. In addition to those with Siegel, he worked on at least three films as dialogue director for director Jacques Tourneur: *Stranger on Horseback* (1955), *Wichita* (1955, also in a bit part), and *Great Day in the Morning* (1956).

Television: Writing and Directing

In 1955, Siegel turned down an offer to become involved in the television series "Gunsmoke," but passed on several of the submitted scripts to Peckinpah, who then spent several months writing his own. After he was accepted by the producer, Peckinpah more or less became a full-time writer for television. In 1955-56, he wrote twelve scripts for "Gunsmoke" and an episode for the "Broken Arrow" series. Ten of the "Gunsmoke" scripts were produced, all adaptations of "Gunsmoke" radio scripts. One of the remaining two original scripts later became the pilot for "The Rifleman." In 1957-58, Peckinpah added to his television-writing credentials with scripts sold to "Tales of Wells Fargo," "Blood

Brother," "Have Gun–Will Travel," "Trackdown," "Tombstone Territory," and "Man Without a Gun."[9]

Also in 1957, Peckinpah was hired to write his first feature, based on the book *The Authentic Death of Hendry Jones*, by Charles Neider. This was in turn loosely based on Pat Garrett's book, *The Authentic Life of Billy the Kid*, and eventually, after many changes and alterations culminating with those of the director, the script became the film *One-eyed Jacks* (1960), starring and directed by Marlon Brando.[10] The amount of research Peckinpah put into the project was not to be wasted, though, and would later be used for his own film, *Pat Garrett and Billy the Kid* (1973).

Finally, in early 1958, Peckinpah was given a chance to direct, on an episode of "Broken Arrow" called "The Knife Fighter."[11]

After reworking an original script rejected by "Gunsmoke," Peckinpah submitted and sold it and himself to Dick Powell at Four Star Productions. The story was originally aired on "Dick Powell's Zane Grey Theater"; it received an excellent response, quickly found a sponsor, and "The Rifleman" series was set for the fall 1958 schedule. The story was drawn directly from Peckinpah's youth and utilized the names of places he grew up with. His contract guaranteed him a chance to direct, and during 1958 and 1959, he directed four episodes. He left the show in 1959 when he felt that the producers had sufficiently corrupted his initial concept–by not letting the boy in the show grow up, among other things. The producers maintained they were doing the show for children.[12]

Peckinpah thereafter worked on two projects he hoped to make himself, one on Pancho Villa and the other based on a book by Fred Gipson called *Hound Dog Man*. The Gipson book appealed to the same ideas Peckinpah wanted to feature in "The Rifleman," involving the story of a young boy's rites of passage through his hunting experiences with a backwoodsman.[13] But the film was made by Don Siegel, who later regretted it as it came to be used as a vehicle for teen-idol Fabian. Siegel allows that Peckinpah should have done a picture from the book, that Peckinpah would have done it "the way it should have been done, small."[14]

Meanwhile, Dick Powell had commissioned Peckinpah to

write and direct a pilot for airing on "Zane Grey Theater," which, if successful, was to be done as a series to be called "Winchester." Peckinpah wrote a story which again drew on his background, creating a self-sufficient drifter named Dave Blassingame who had a mongrel dog called Brown and a special Winchester rifle. The pilot ("Trouble at Tres Cruces"), as well as the eventual series, starred Brian Keith and was well received though it found no immediate sponsor.[15]

Following this, Peckingpah was hired by ZIV Productions to direct a pilot (which he also cowrote) for a series called "Klondike." Finding the production situation unsatisfactory, Peckinpah went back to Four Star. But he had met David Levy, then head of NBC-TV, who liked his work and told Sam that if he could put a series together he'd try to get it for NBC. Peckinpah had Dick Powell show "Winchester" to Levy; NBC picked up the series for the fall of 1960, with the title now changed to "The Westerner." In an interview with Garner Simmons, Peckinpah states: "Don Siegel, Dick Powell, and David Levy—those were the three gentlemen who really made it possible for me to get the background I needed to make the move into features."[16]

From late 1959 through 1960, Peckinpah produced the thirteen episodes of "The Westerner." He also directed five of the episodes and cowrote four.[17] Involved from start to finish, this producing experience certainly helped to round out Peckinpah's basic knowledge of total film production.

But "The Westerner" had strong competition that fall, going against "The Flintstones" and "Route 66," both new that season. In addition, there was some resistance from some of the rural network affiliates to the relatively adult content of the series. The premiere show, inspired by a couple of people Peckinpah had met,[18] dealt with "a guy who goes to take this young whore, who he knew as a kid, home."[19] More significant was the fact that this was the season when television audiences displayed a marked preference for hour-long shows; "The Westerner" was a half-hour show. Though the premiere received an extraordinarily rave review in the trade paper the *Hollywood Reporter* (at a time when it was rare to review TV shows) and received praise elsewhere, "The Westerner" was canceled after thirteen shows. But the series had a measurable benefit for Peckinpah: it won a Producers Guild Nomination for Best Filmed Series and, more important to Sam, it won his father's approval.[20]

The Move into Features

After "The Westerner," Brian Keith was hired to star in a film to be called *The Deadly Companions* (1961). It was a low-budget, independently produced Western project put together by Maureen O'Hara, her brother Charles FitzSimons, and writer A. S. Fleischman. In addition to a male lead, the star, producer, and writer needed a director; Keith suggested Peckinpah. But FitzSimons as producer had very definite ideas about the film, having worked on it with Fleischman for more than two years. Peckinpah chafed at some of these notions, feeling that interpretive control should reside with the director. The resulting conflict contributed problems to the production, some visible in the finished film, as well as those caused by bad weather and the low budget. *The Deady Companions* performed adequately, even though its distributor, Pathé-America, went out of business shortly thereafter. Peckinpah received good personal notices, and learned the importance of script control. But as he said later, "Sometimes even that is not enough."[21]

Following *The Deadly Companions*, Peckinpah continued with television briefly, directing an episode of "Route 66" ironically one of the shows which had helped cancel "The Westerner." Then Richard Lyons, a new producer at MGM, approached Peckinpah to direct *Ride the High Country* (1962). Contrary to some rumors, Lyons found Peckinpah through a friend at the William Morris agency and did not offer it to others first. The film was to be a low-to-modest-budgeted feature; the script was an original by N. B. Stone, Jr., seriously rewritten by William S. Roberts. The two principal actors, Joel McCrea and Randolph Scott, had already been signed when Peckinpah was hired.

Peckinpah did a significant rewrite on the script, enough so that Lyons later tried to get Peckinpah a share of the writer's credit on the film. Peckinpah was also responsible for a large part of the casting beyond the two principals. But the project became something of a pawn in an MGM power struggle between Sol Siegel, head of production, and Joseph R. Vogel, head of MGM's parent company. Problems arose in production, including an incident where the studio moved the company from one location to another without telling the director. When the film was ready to be edited, MGM's editor-in-chief, Margaret Booth, disliked the rushes, while Sol Siegel did. Siegel gave Peckinpah the chance to edit the first cut himself, which he did with editor Frank Santillo. Siegel was impressed with the first cut and told Peckinpah to prepare the final cut with his backing. But soon Vogel removed Siegel from the company and Peckinpah was thrown off the lot, barred from the studio. Fortunately, it was mainly up to producer Lyons and Frank Santillo to finish the film, and they did it pretty much in line with Peckinpah's wishes. Rather than spend any more money on it, Vogel let it go, but buried the film as the bottom half of a double bill in its first release.

To MGM's embarrassment, the film received excellent reviews and became a real "sleeper" success, including *Newsweek's* calling it the best picture of 1962. When released in Europe in 1963, the film won a number of awards, including the Belgian International Film Festival Grand Prix. But the most significant praise for Peckinpah came from two sources: his sister, Fern Lea, cried over it, as the Joel McCrea character reminded her so much of their father, who had died the previous year; and Sol Siegel wrote to Peckinpah after seeing the film at a theater, saying, "Who ... do you think you are ... John Ford?"[22]

Waiting for *Ride the High Country* to find an audience, Peckinpah returned again to television, to produce and direct two hour-long shows for "The Dick Powell Theater." The first was called "Pericles on 31st Street," for which Peckinpah cowrote the script with Harry Mark Petrakis, who had written the original story. The second was "The Losers," cowritten by Peckinpah and Bruce Geller, who had written several episodes for "The Westerner." "The Losers" was basically a contemporary update of the Brian Keith "Westerner" character and a Geller character creation from the series, Burgundy Smith, played by John Dehner originally. Like the "Westerner" episodes in which the Smith character appeared, "The Losers" was a comedy. Garner Simmons records that Peckinpah used slow-motion for the first time in a "violent" scene here, as well as utilizing fast-motion and stills in the show. It starred Lee Marvin in the Dave Blassingame role; and though it was well received enough to be repeated half-a-dozen times in prime time, the possibility of a series with Peckinpah as producer fell apart with the death of Dick Powell and a change of management at Four Star Productions.

Peckinpah next went to Walt Disney Productions as a writer-director, working on a script from a novel called *Little Britches*. He soon switched to another script more in keeping with his thematic ideas, based on Ralph Moody's novel *The Boy and the Gunfighter*. Among other things, it once again involved a young boy's initiation to "manhood" (which should more accurately be read to mean "life" or "maturity"), but a disagreement with the project's producer caused a delay; the producer went abroad and Peckinpah moved on.

In late summer of 1963, producer Jerry Bresler hired Peckinpah to direct *Major Dundee* (1965), based on a story by Harry Julian Fink. The film proved a watershed experience for Peckinpah; the problems involved in its production and release have unfortunately assumed legendary proportions. It was a three-sided affair between Peckinpah, who naturally wanted to do the film his way, Bresler, who disagreed with Peckinpah's handling of the two main characters and the length of the film, among other things, and Columbia, the financing distributor, who liked what they were seeing but who grew increasingly anxious as costs mounted and the film began to run over budget. While Peckinpah was not wholly "innocent" in the affair, he must be seen as the underdog, in what seems to have become for Bresler (admittedly under pressure from the studio himself) a test of authority. It "culminated" with Bresler issuing ultimatums and threatening Peckinpah with ruination, saying that he'd have Peckinpah blackballed out of the business. Columbia wasted a lot of money through their own short-sightedness. It even got to the point where Charlton Heston offered to return his salary if it would help allow Peckinpah to do the film he wanted. Columbia accepted; Heston did the film for nothing. But it hardly altered the outcome.

One way or another, *Major Dundee* was finished, but the scars it left on Peckinpah represented bitter lessons on the notion of control over a project. After the filming, Peckinpah married Begonia Palacios (an actress in the film; he would marry her a total of three times), but the editing of *Major Dundee* provided a continuation of the struggle. According to Bresler, the film ran a million dollars over budget (Peckinpah maintains this is "bullshit") and ran 4 hours and 36½ minutes in first cut. Peckinpah left the film at a cut of "approximately" 2 hours and 36 minutes; Bresler says that Columbia cut the film further to its release length of 134 minutes. Consequently, discussion of the film has centered around the film that "might have been." The last "laugh" was Peckinpah's: after the success of *The Wild Bunch* (1969), Columbia invited Peckinpah to reedit and rework the film into his own version. He refused; he didn't have the time.

But he would have had the time then, for Bresler's threat came true for all practical purposes. Peckinpah was signed to direct *The Cincinnati Kid* (1965) for producer Martin Ransohoff, and in October 1964, he began work on it, including some script revision. But Peckinpah and Ransohoff did not "get along" very well; Ransohoff didn't agree with some of Peckinpah's ideas; and although Peckinpah made several compromises in the casting, Ransohoff closed the production and fired Peckinpah after four days of shooting. The "official" reason for the firing was the filming of a sequence involving Ann-Margret nude under a raincoat, which Ransohoff had forbidden, but apparently Peckinpah (and anyone else seen as his friend) was fired out of spite more than anything else. The film was given to Norman Jewison, who shot it in color; Peckinpah had been shooting in black-and-white. It should also be noted that Spencer Tracy, originally set for the film, also disagreed with Ransohoff's conception, and had withdrawn from the project. Tracy, however (and Katharine Hepburn), liked Peckinpah's work.

Peckinpah was now truly out of work, and the truncated *Major Dundee*'s release in April of 1965 only served to confirm the rumors of his "unhirability" and "uncooperative" nature. A French producer, Jacques Bar, tried to sell two of the many Peckinpah scripts written in this period over the next two years, to no avail; one was called *Ready for the Tiger*, an international drug-traffic adventure set in the Caribbean, and the other was *Caravans*, based on the James Michener novel. Peckinpah sold his rights on "The Westerner" to Four Star Productions; the series was repackaged and reissued.

But the only screen credit Peckinpah would receive for three years after the *Cincinnati Kid* firing, apart from *Major Dundee*, was as screenwriter for *The Glory Guys* (1965), a cavalry film based on a novel by Hoffman Birney called *The Dice of God*. Peckinpah's script dealt with a fictionalization of the basic Custer massacre, focusing on the "lack of under- standing between white man and red and the fatal megalomania of the Custerlike "General McCabe."²³ But the film itself bears little resemblance to Peckinpah's conception, though providing some ironic contrast to themes of friendship and camaraderie Peckinpah would later develop further; the film as made centers on a love triangle. It is also of interest that the film company used some of the same cast of *Major Dun- dee*, including Michael Anderson, Jr., Senta Berger, and Slim Pickens, hoping to take advantage of what they thought would be a good box-office response for *Major Dundee*.

Daniel Melnick, then a producer with Talent Associates, hired Peckinpah in 1966 to adapt and direct Katherine Anne Porter's story "Noon Wine." As Melnick recalls, as soon as Peckinpah's hiring was announced he received a number of calls, even from strangers, telling him not to do so. But Mel- nick refused to accede to this, to his credit and, later, satisfac- tion. Peckinpah visited with Porter over branch water and bourbon, and after her wholehearted approval of his adapta- tion, the project went ahead as an hour-long show for ABC's "Stage 67." The reviews were ecstatic, singling out Peckinpah among others for his work. "Noon Wine" garnered Peckinpah two award nominations from peers, for Best Television Screenplay Adaptation from the Writer's Guild and for Best Television Directing from the Director's Guild.

Another television job followed, where Peckinpah directed a Western drama for "Bob Hope's Chrysler Theater" called "That Lady Is My Wife." Indeed, his own wife, Begonia Palacios, played the second female lead.

Peckinpah's script on Pancho Villa was reworked and finally sold to producer Ted Richmond in April 1967. It became *Villa Rides!* (1968), but Peckinpah's script was substantially rewrit- ten by Robert Towne and, as with *The Glory Guys*, the film bears little resemblance to the original conception, significantly in the matter of Villa's characterization. Peckinpah taught writing and directing for film and TV at UCLA in the fall of 1967, but finally was beginning to find work in films again.

Kenneth Hyman, vice-president in charge of worldwide production at Warner Brothers-Seven Arts at the time, hired Peckinpah to write a script based on a story by Hyman and writer David Chandler. Peckinpah had met Hyman in Europe in 1965; Hyman had produced Sidney Lumet's *The Hill* (1965) and Robert Aldrich's *The Dirty Dozen* (1967) and impressed Peckinpah. The script for Hyman was called *The Diamond Story*, a caper adventure set in Africa. But Peckinpah also submitted a script he had rewritten from a story by his longtime friend, stuntman Roy Sickner, and a script of that story by Sickner and Walon Green. It was decided to make this second script, *The Wild Bunch* (1969), instead of *The Diamond Story*. Peckinpah had been set to direct in either case.

Production began in late 1967; the shooting lasted from late March through July 1968. It was a major production in all ways, with all the major headaches arising from such a production, but, for once, Peckinpah had a studio that was at least initially as excited as he was over the project. When the film was first released domestically in June of 1969, it met with the kind of reactions that would typify the film's reception, extremely pro or violently (!) con. By this time Peckinpah had already completed photography on his next film, *The Ballad of Cable Hogue* (1970), when Warner Brothers called him to tell him they were going to cut *The Wild Bunch* further. They did not feel the film was performing up to expectations; they pulled it and cut some ten (critical) minutes from the film. To help understand the "reasoning" behind this, one should consider the money saved in print costs by multiplying the cut footage by the hundreds of prints made. More to the point, Warner Brothers had undergone a change of management, and Ken Hyman was out.

This led to similar problems with *The Ballad of Cable Hogue*. The script by John Crawford and Edmund Penny had been brought to Peckinpah by Warren Oates. It was designed as a small-budget film and set for production while Hyman was still with Warner Brothers. Shot in the early months of

1969, the filming ran into grueling difficulties on location. While the cast and crew were there, it rained in Nevada's Valley of Fire more than it had in the previous thirty years *combined*.[24] People were sick, strung out, and exhausted. Peckinpah was no exception, but the film was finished through the efforts of a lot of determined participants. Enough people had been fired, however, so that more than forty surviving members of the cast and crew took out a full-page ad in the *Daily Variety* as a testament to Peckinpah, in order to belie the Hollywood rumors about the film's troubles. But Warner Bros.-Seven Arts, minus Hyman by the time of the film's release, either didn't know what to do or didn't *want* to do much with the film, and it was buried domestically, without a first-run booking.[25]

During Cable Hogue's production, Dan Melnick approached Peckinpah with a project based on a Gordon Williams novel called *The Siege of Trencher's Farm*. Meanwhile, other projects under Peckinpah's consideration included doing *Deliverance*, by James Dickey; work on a script from a story by friend Frank Kowalski (which later became *Bring Me the Head of Alfredo Garcia*); and a project called *Summer Soldiers*, cowritten by Peckinpah, Lee Pogosin, and Robert Culp. This last was pretty close to being set for production at Warner Brothers, but after the treatment of *Cable Hogue* and a "falling-out" with the other participants, Peckinpah withdrew from it. Melnick had by that time put together a first-draft screenplay and financing through ABC Pictures for *The Siege of Trencher's Farm*. Peckinpah accepted this offer, and the project became *Straw Dogs* (1971).

Once again Peckinpah enjoyed Melnick's support, as well as that of Martin Baum, president of ABC Pictures. Although Peckinpah fell seriously ill with flu and pneumonia during filming, the producers stuck by him and shut down the production (an expensive proposition) while he recovered. Shooting lasted from January through April 1971; when the film was released in London in December of that year, it met with a storm of vociferous condemnation in the British press. Also released domestically in late December 1971, *slightly* cut to avoid an X rating, *Straw Dogs* divided American critics into extreme positions, either for or against. However, the film was Peckinpah's first to show a firm profit not long after its initial release.

Dustin Hoffman, Daniel Melnick and Peckinpah on location in Cornwall, England with *Straw Dogs*.

During *Straw Dogs*'s production, Peckinpah was approached by Martin Baum for another film, *Junior Bonner* (1972). It was a case of the right place at the right time: Steve McQueen was very interested in doing it, and Peckinpah for similar reasons wanted to do a film less violent than those he was getting a reputation for. Both were extremely impressed with the script by Jeb Rosebrook. But a centerpiece of the film was to be the Prescott, Arizona, annual rodeo celebration; timing was critical in order to be ready to shoot. As a result, Peckinpah began work on it while simultaneously editing *Straw Dogs*, narrowly giving up a significant tax break by returning to the United States early.

Everyone was satisfied with the finished film, but it died a premature death at the box office. McQueen was convinced that the marketing strategy was completely wrong, that the film should have opened "small" and been given a chance to quietly but surely find its audience. The last film produced by ABC Pictures, *Junior Bonner* did not meet audience expectations of a McQueen-Peckinpah action film, but nobody has blamed the film for that.

As *Junior Bonner* was finishing, Peckinpah turned to what he hoped would be his next film, a pet project called *Emperor of the North Pole*. (The film, eventually made by Robert Aldrich, was released in 1973). Peckinpah took the script, rewritten by him, to Ken Hyman, then working as an independent producer, to arrange backing for the project. Hyman set up a meeting with Paramount's head of production, Robert Evans. Evans, however, wanted Peckinpah for *The Getaway*, a project Peckinpah was already familiar with. Evans agreed to do *Emperor of the North Pole* if Peckinpah would first do *The Getaway*. Then, in a double turn-around, Hyman dismissed Peckinpah from *Emperor* and Paramount decided against *The Getaway*. Out both films, Peckinpah was particularly angered by the loss of *Emperor of the North Pole*.

But Steve McQueen, who had agreed to *The Getaway* as it was brought to Paramount, took the film to First Artists (a partnership of his and several other stars), where it was set for production. *The Getaway* (1972) would indeed after all be Peckinpah's next film.

David Foster, the producer on the film who had initiated the whole project (and who had worked with Peckinpah previously on publicity for *Ride the High Country*), told Peckinpah to choose whomever he wanted for the crew, in order to avoid as many hassles as possible in that area. It worked, and production went smoothly despite some major moves from one location to another. Although Steve McQueen made some relatively minor changes in the final release version (which was his ultimate right, contractually), Peckinpah was fairly satisfied with the film as a whole. The only change of significance was the replacement of the music score by Jerry Fielding with a score by Quincy Jones. It would be difficult for Peckinpah to be *too* unhappy with the film: it had grossed over $25 million by late 1974, a certifiable box-office hit that would mean a lot to Peckinpah's market value.

In 1970, MGM producer Gordon Carroll commissioned Rudolph Wurlitzer to write a screenplay on Billy the Kid. Originally scheduled for director Monte Hellman, MGM canceled the project; Carroll tried to take it elsewhere, but to no avail. After a Wurlitzer rewrite, Peckinpah was approached and agreed to direct. As *The Getaway* was being completed, *Pat*

Garrett and Bill the Kid (1973) was set for filming in late 1972, with MGM backing after all.

The problems encountered during production in Mexico made the experience a nightmare. Cast and crew had to live with a flu epidemic which killed many that winter; Peckinpah's health was constantly in jeopardy; Bud Hulburd, who had done special effects for *The Wild Bunch*, visited the set, caught the flu, and later died from it. At the same time, a situation developed that can best be described as a state of open warfare between Peckinpah and MGM, exemplified by its then-president, James Aubrey, known in the trade as "the smiling cobra" for his reputation in dealing with creative people. There were technical problems which were aggravated further by studio impositions, frustrating Peckinpah enormously. The film ran over schedule and over budget; and, in a further insult, MGM insisted that the film be edited in record time to meet booking plans. Moreover, MGM didn't care how Peckinpah wanted the film cut; after allowing him his contractual obligation of first and second cut, the studio recut it to suit their own "tastes," removing whole scenes and people, drastically altering the film in a situation reminiscent of the hacking-up of *Major Dundee*. Furious with the way MGM (Aubrey) gutted the film, Peckinpah sued the studio for damages in what he felt was a necessary gesture. In his version, the film ran some fifteen to twenty minutes longer, and he referred to it then as his best film to date. Ironically, after a management change and complete reorganization taking them out of film distribution, MGM offered Peckinpah the opportunity to recut the film "back" to his version, again recalling what happened with *Dundee*. With Dan Melnick as head of MGM, Peckinpah did some more work on it; but the "director's cut" has yet to be released and, as a practical matter of time and economics, probably won't be. The version of *Pat Garrett and Billy the Kid* shown on television does have some scenes originally cut by MGM; but as such, with other cuts, it is no more definitive than the theatrical version.

Peckinpah next took up the script for *Bring Me the Head of Alfredo Garcia* (1974), the idea for which had been brought to him by friend Frank Kowalski during the making of *Cable Hogue*. Production was arranged with Martin Baum, who had gone independent after ABC Pictures folded, and who had an arrangement with United Artists. Shooting began in Mexico in late September 1973, lasting until just before Christmas. Completion of the picture took place in early 1974. By and large, the production went smoothly; problems which arose were solved. But upon its release in August 1974, critics blasted the film almost everywhere except Chicago, for reasons unknown. It was censored in Germany and Sweden. United Artists got cold feet and wanted to cut their losses; the film's distribution dried up quickly. Nevertheless, Peckinpah remarked at a film festival retrospective late that year: "I did *Alfredo Garcia* and I did it exactly the way I wanted to. Good or bad, like it or not, that was my film."[26]

Peckinpah then considered or was considered for several projects, including an espionage thriller for 20th Century-Fox called *The Insurance Company*, but his next film came to be *The Killer Elite* (1975). Based on the novel by Robert Rostand, the first script by Reginald Rose went through several revisions including one by Stirling Silliphant. One significant alteration by Silliphant was in the locale of the action: the novel takes place in England with the main character protecting Africans, while Silliphant's rewrite shifted the action to San Francisco, where Orientals are protected. Peckinpah would have preferred England, as it would have allowed him to again use John Coquillon, his photographer on *Straw Dogs* and *Pat Garrett*, among others. *The Killer Elite* was shot from April to June 1975 and released that December, produced by Martin Baum and Arthur Lewis. Figuratively speaking, Baum may have wanted another *Getaway*; there was some friction between him and Peckinpah in production, and a few minutes were cut from the film over Peckinpah's objections to secure a PG rating instead of an R. In any case, the film at least broke even.

Peckinpah's next film, *Cross of Iron* (1977), developed financial troubles during production. In addition to other technical problems and friction with the producer, the filming encountered a significant language problem on location in Yugoslavia. The film was buried in its release domestically, hardly marketed at all. Once again a Peckinpah film was cut seriously for American theaters, supposedly in part to avoid an

X rating; the European version is some eleven to fifteen minutes longer.[27]

In May 1977, shooting began on *Convoy* (1978). Loosely "based" on a 1975 hit song by C. W. McCall, producer Robert M. Sherman bought the script by Bill Norton and hired Peckinpah to direct. The film was financed through EMI, a European production company (which had also bought *Cross of Iron* for European distribution). On location in the deserts and on the highways of Arizona, New Mexico, and Texas, the production became bogged down with enormous difficulties: the grueling heat, logistics problems with trucks and machinery, and a script whose changes many could not keep up with. There was also a fire which destroyed a large set, possibly a case of arson.[28] EMI became increasingly nervous as the film almost doubled its budget; Peckinpah "finished" the filming but left the production in the early stages of editing, in what has been described to me as a "mutual backing off." Needless to say, the release version does not conform to Peckinpah's designs; the director's "version" has been placed at roughly 2½ hours, while the film as released runs about 112 minutes. Opening widely in late June 1978, *Convoy* performed reasonably well in some areas (including a strong showing in Japan) but was rudely dismissed by the press with few exceptions.

In a brief phone conversation in July 1978, Peckinpah referred to "obligations" that he would attend to; hopefully, these obligations include doing another film soon.

2

The Deadly Companions (1961)

THE ONE THING I learned was never to agree to direct a picture unless you have script control—since then, I've learned that sometimes even that is not enough," Sam Peckinpah said in 1973.[1]

His first feature as director was initially a fortunate coincidence, as many directorial jobs have always been. Brian Keith's recommendation, based on their association with the TV series "The Westerner," brought Peckinpah to the film. Peckinpah's directorial control of "authorship" was an extremely limited one, with Peckinpah leaving the film after its first cut and being expressly prohibited by the producer from making any major changes in the script he was hired to direct.

As a director, Peckinpah strives to make films "his way"; he is involved wherever possible in every aspect of production; he is consistently open to suggestions from all corners, but the decision to use those suggestions is his. Ultimately, however, the film the public gets to see is in the hands of whoever holds the purse strings; this can make an enormous difference between the film that was "made" and the film that gets shown. Therein, in profoundly ironic ways, lies the rub.

Such was the case with *The Deadly Companions*. Peckinpah was initially under the impression he had been hired partially to help fix the script; this impression was proved wrong, as producer Charles FitzSimons resisted Peckinpah's attempts to change anything significantly. Consequently, Peckinpah was not "in control," but accepted the job (after all, it was a chance to direct a feature), making what alterations he could despite FitzSimons's refusal of his ideas. He does not regard the finished film with much esteem.

Set in the 1870s, *The Deadly Companions* is an odd West-

39

ern, full of irregularities that begin with the psychological aspects of the script. Its principal interest apart from simple genre considerations lies in its marking the impressive debut of a director. In this manner, the film is of interest in retrospect; it will be recalled by later films more than it relies on its own merits. Ignoring its place in Peckinpah's work, the film does not stand up too well.

As a revenge story, it provides a contrast later when considering *The Ballad of Cable Hogue*. Brian Keith's Yellowleg is an obsessive character, the first of many such characters in Peckinpah's features. But Yellowleg's quest for revenge, his desire to catch up with the Confederate soldier who tried to scalp him during the Civil War, has reached a climax at the opening of the film: in the first scene, Yellowleg finds his man. At the outset, Yellowleg is considering a mechanical problem of how to actually take his revenge; we join him at the end of his five-year search. For a man who has been motivated for that length of time by revenge, he sublimates it rather well in the presence of its object. It is almost laid aside for the body of the film, figuring as an element of background which will *eventually* be resolved. Yellowleg's thirst for revenge is replaced quickly by the combination of guilt and attraction he feels toward Kit, the dance-hall girl whose son Yellowleg has accidently killed.

The premises of plot wear thin rapidly. The film depends on enough coincidences to make Charles Dickens proud: the doctor in Gila City who knows all about (and explains to us) Yellowleg's scalping; the hold-up of the Gila City bank by an anonymous gang just before Yellowleg, Billy, and Turk are prepared to do the same; Yellowleg's shooting of Kit's son Mead during that hold-up; the convenient appearance of drunken Apaches whose horses are ripe for stealing, enabling Kit and Yellowleg to press onward; the reappearance of Billy and Turk at Siringo, enabling the use of a single setting to resolve the whole story at the end.

Arguing with the contrivances of plot is finally beside the point, though. Events are presented. Even if they strain credibility in terms of their "realistic" likelihood (an impression of the viewer's, anyway), once the possibility of their occurrence is granted, they are fair to use as storytelling devices, as long as they remain consistent within the story's frame of reference.

None of the above plot devices is "impossible," and most are accounted for in one fashion or another, but a plot flaw develops, for example, where it is not indicated that a corpse in the hot sun for several days doesn't get difficult to live with. Peckinpah acknowledged this last point and tried to work around it as best he could. You'd hardly know what they are carrying if you came in the middle.

But the story itself certainly figures in the offbeat realization of the film, beginning with the main characters. We are involved with four very striking figures. Besides Keith's Yellowleg, psychologically wounded by his "scalping" scar and physically wounded with a crippled shooting arm, there is Maureen O'Hara's Kit Tildon, a beautiful woman marooned in a desolate landscape, a dance-hall hostess with a son, who must bear the psychological burden of social ostracism as a result of having lost a husband whom no one has ever seen and whose one-time existence is doubted by most. She, too, becomes an obsessive character, vowing to bury her son next to his father in the desert ghost-town of Siringo, reachable only by going through hostile Apache territory. Her commitment to this act is important to spite her rejection by the proper townspeople of Gila City. But there is some doubt throughout the film whether in fact she really had a husband or if she has come to believe a protective lie she has told herself.

Turk (sometimes Turkey) is the object of Yellowleg's revenge. As played by Chill Wills, he is something of a grotesque, a bear in a buffalo robe with a bowler. The non-Western hat is a nice touch, an out-of-place element that contrasts to the rest of his appearance, which is summed up more than once by his rubbing himself like a large animal against solid objects, including a cactus at one point. Turkey is a Reb deserter who hides a Union officer's cap in the voluminous confines of his robe; it is a token of eccentricity which finally overtakes him. Crazy by degrees, Turkey dreams of an army of Comanchero bandits, with himself as general. By the time of his final confrontation with Yellowleg, he is raving irretrievably, lost far beyond the comprehension of Yellowleg's simple revenge.

Turkey, lost if alone, has attached himself to an exaggerated stereotype of a free-wheeling gunslinger named Billy. He is cock-sure and full of bravado, a little boy in a cowboy outfit with two six-guns, bursting with self-confidence displayed most readily by his animal sexuality. He professes to be his own man, yet he allows Yellowleg to give the orders as long as Yellowleg doesn't push his luck too far; Billy expresses a curious fascination for him, following him as long as it looks interesting. In the saloon / church scene, when the parson calls for those who are going to Hell to stand, Billy jumps up proudly, tired of the service and eager to reestablish himself in the room.

If these characters are not expressly Peckinpah's creations, they are nonetheless placed resolutely in a Peckinpah landscape, allowing for the contrivances of the script in delivering a film of angular, subdued tensions, somewhat skewed within the confines of the genre. It is perhaps premature to speak here definably of the Peckinpah "landscape." Nevertheless, the qualities which make *The Deadly Companions* work at all are those which resonate freely in Peckinpah's later work.

A particular quality noticeable here (especially with regard to the limitation of a relatively low budget) is Peckinpah's concern for realism, as evidenced by a combination of on-location photography and attention to small detail. The location realism is the result of a fortunate coincidence, as producer FitzSimons was equally interested in the economical aspect of shooting on location. The film was shot entirely in and around Tucson, Arizona, in a few weeks. Peckinpah was pleased with the locations; his sense of the physical landscape, shaped to a degree by his childhood experience, is demonstrated repeatedly by the placement of the camera to include specific details of the environment which heighten the tensions between characters and their surroundings. When Yellowleg goes to wait in the rocks to ambush the lone Apache who stalks Kit and himself, the camera pans an expanse of rock and desert which ends with Yellowleg as the lone object in that landscape. Yellowleg scans the horizon as the camera has, searching for the invisible figure whom we cannot see, either; the irony is that while both Yellowleg and the viewer expect the Apache to be out there somewhere, the Indian has meanwhile outwitted both and is on the verge of ambushing Kit. Likewise, when Kit, Billy, Turk, and Yellowleg make camp after fixing the wagon, we see Turk lounging like some great beast on a low-lying tree limb. There are many other examples in this respect, including one breath-taking shot of the stalking

Apache atop a butte, silhouetted against the night sky, alone with the moon in the background. This shot is all the more remarkable for its irony: it suggests a stereotypical "noble" and independent savage at one with his environment, recalling a famous image of Burt Lancaster in Robert Aldrich's *Apache* (1954); but this Apache is stalking Yellowleg out of revenge: he was drunk and ignominiously knocked cold as Yellowleg stole horses from his party.

Indeed, it is the harsh nature of the environment as shown which forces Yellowleg and Kit into a position where they can begin to acknowledge their growing attraction for each other. At the outset of the journey, Yellowleg follows to assist Kit out of guilt; Yellowleg as the murderer of her son is the last person Kit wants any help from. But by the time they arrive in Siringo, each has come to accept the other in spite of the surface conflicts. Siringo is a dried-up ghost-town, hardly an oasis. They stand in front of the church, a particularly desolate token of affirmation, but in the middle of a graveyard. They need each other more than ever; it is Yellowleg who finds Kit's husband's grave, even as she is about to give up looking for it. No sooner have they solved Kit's problem than they must face Yellowleg's problem with the reappearance of Billy and Turk; it is now Kit's turn to "save" Yellowleg, stopping him from his revenge scalping of Turk in the church. In every situation, the environment acts as an additional character. It is Peckinpah's doing that this environmental presence is so keenly felt throughout.

Peckinpah's interest in the realization of small background detail follows from the larger aspect of environmental realism. One example is indicative: Peckinpah refused to hire a blue-eyed extra to play an Apache. But details often carry more significant weight. In the saloon in Gila City, two nudes hanging behind the bar have roll-down drapes; the lowering of the drapes to cover the nudes signals the conversion of the room into a church, completed by the entrance of the parson.

The Deadly Companions is successful to a degree, based on Peckinpah's approach to some awkward material. Despite the prohibitions of the producer, Peckinpah and Brian Keith surreptitiously altered some of the more stilted dialogue in scenes with the men; the scenes with Maureen O'Hara are stiffer, where the prohibition was stricter, and suffer greatly by comparison. For all practical purposes, Peckinpah was not allowed to "direct" her as much. But for all the limitations, Peckinpah does evoke the individual character conflicts, and through the course of the desert journey, a love story, one finally of affirmation, emerges between Kit and Yellowleg.

When Kit strikes Yellowleg with a whip, as he has allowed the possibility that there is no husband's grave at Siringo, he responds by saying, "You don't know me well enough to hate me that much," and proceeds to explain his own hatred-revenge motivation in a round-about way. It is the beginning of the replacement of individual anger with love based on mutual necessity. By the end of the journey, they know each other well enough to express that need.

Throughout the journey, they are shadowed by forces which push them together, first by Billy and Turk, then by the Apache. Turk is the symbol of Yellowleg's past; Billy, who wants only to rape Kit, is the symbol of her dance-hall "past." Billy is first seen with two women at the opening of the film, coming out to aid Turkey, who is being hanged for card-cheating, as they meet Yellowleg. As Yellowleg takes Billy and Turk to Gila City ostensibly to rob the bank, Billy hopes the town has pretty women; he reiterates that as soon as they get there. When he first sees Kit at the church service, he steals a kiss for which he is slapped, then crosses the street easily to entertain himself with the other dance-hall girls. He attacks Kit with a grin when the wagon breaks down; she holds him off with a rock. And later, at a night camp, he attacks her again—a scene which Peckinpah develops explicitly with shots of Billy slowly undoing the straps to his holsters, then unbuckling his gun belt. Without actually taking off his pants, he is naked. Yellowleg stops this attack and Billy is kicked out of camp. (During the fistfight we see that Yellowleg does have his hair when his hat is knocked off, and we begin to wonder whether his "scalping" is only imaginary.) When they all meet again in Siringo, Billy's object is *still* the pursuit of Kit, hoping to have it out with Yellowleg, winner take all. Cataloguing Billy in this way makes clear and a bit ludicrous his single-minded lust and main function in the story. But at the same time, albeit without subtlety or nuance, Peckinpah allows Billy to be rather charming in his gleefully forthright manner.

The lone Apache replaces Billy and Turk during the journey. As much a personification of the hostile environment as an individual danger, the Apache wears Kit and Yellowleg down just as Billy and Turk had kept them wary. And, as Yellowleg had protected Kit, it is Kit who finally kills the Apache.

If *The Deadly Companions* is seen as an outgrowth fundamentally rooted in Western genre conventions, a particular departure from those conventions is all the more revealing toward Peckinpah's attitudes. After Billy and Turk are gone, Kit and Yellowleg spot a stagecoach being chased by Indians. Seen at first in long-shot, it is difficult for us as well as Kit and Yellowleg to tell exactly what's going on. What is gradually revealed is that the Indians have *already finished* the stagecoach attack and are celebrating by reenacting their victory. It is a drunken parody of a classic Western moment; the final shot of the scene is of an Indian up-ending a bottle. Being after the fact, it has no immediate relevance for Kit and Yellowleg; it is an element of background, a complete turnaround of genre expectations for the audience. As such, it is an early example of the conflict between appearance and reality, of the ambiguity of our perceptions, an essential Peckinpah concern which will be seen much more in later works. Completing that turn-around of expectations, Yellowleg makes an easy job of stealing horses from the Indians, who are all passed-out stone-drunk, hardly the wily and watchful Apaches of Western iconography. The sequence ends on a comic note: after decking the one Apache who woke up, Yellowleg removes a scalp from the Indian's belt and lays it on his chest; when the Apache again comes to, his first thought is that the scalp could have been his own, and it is this insult he must avenge.

The film is marred by the ending which indicates the disagreement between Peckinpah and FitzSimons, the producer. As Peckinpah shot it, Billy shoots Turk because Yellowleg has trouble with his aim (his crippled arm); then Billy squares off to have it out with Yellowleg. But Yellowleg is determined to get to Turk, and has no time for Billy; Yellowleg shoots Billy as he stands in his way, continuing to march past Billy as he falls. Peckinpah's ending would have made the resolution between Kit and Yellowleg more ambiguous. Kit says she couldn't love a man who would kill in cold blood (if Yellowleg kills Turk), and the killing of Billy out of initial expedience would have clouded this, even as it would have completed the symmetry (another recurring Peckinpah construct) of necessary bloodshed when coupled with Kit's killing of the Apache. But FitzSimons wouldn't buy Peckinpah's ending, thinking it too coldblooded of Yellowleg, and recut the scene so that it appears that the wounded Turk shoots Billy in the back as Yellowleg walks past. This is difficult to accept because, although Billy has turned on him, Turk earlier could not bring himself to shoot Yellowleg in the back at several opportunities. ("It ain't no fit way to kill a man—not even a Yankee," as he says at one point.) If he couldn't do that to someone he *didn't* like, it is hard to accept that he could so quickly do it to Billy, whom Turk still wants to depend on. In FitzSimons's ending, Kit and Yellowleg ride off into the sunset, something else which Peckinpah was averse to.

It is important to note that Peckinpah gives a great deal of credit for good things in the film to photographer Bill Clothier. Working under conditions of bad weather and a tight budget, Clothier's expertise and professionalism were of great aid to Peckinpah; he accords whatever satisfactory color quality there is in the film to Clothier particularly.[2]

As Peckinpah's first feature, *The Deadly Companions* is an auspicious introduction to themes Peckinpah will explore more fully in later films, as well as to his engaging visual style. Significantly, it is the story of a quest for redemption and identity, seeming to be finally more optimistic than other Peckinpah films. But due to the altered nature of the ending, some ambiguity about the results is lost, an ambiguity which will become more apparent as Peckinpah develops his treatment of a world where morality is less a matter of recognizably fixed propositions than of individual circumstances. Peckinpah makes decidedly moral tales, but the ultimate objective moralities are difficult for human beings to live up to, let alone understand. He has sympathy for those who try, and pity for those who cannot. We are all sinners, and when we try to perceive morality in clear terms of black versus white, we must be reminded of the vast gray areas.

3

Ride the High Country (1962): "All I Want Is to Enter My House Justified"

RIDE THE HIGH COUNTRY is an enduring classic of film. In times when the phrase is used loosely, Sam Peckinpah's second feature is, even for such an apparently modest film, completely deserving of the description. Indeed, it is that modesty, that quality of unpretentious straightforwardness, that enables the film to yet play so well. I would heartily urge anyone who hasn't seen the film recently to do so, in CinemaScope and color; its virtues are so easily remembered, yet so easily underestimated. As the film's producer, Richard Lyons, describes, Peckinpah was handed a diamond in the rough, but he knew how to cut that diamond to bring out its brilliance.[1]

It is certainly not designed as a "message" film, yet there is plenty to take home from it. The film has resonance. The simple story line at first hides the depth of sincerity behind its execution; it is first and foremost a moral tale. The two aging friends are figures cut from the same cloth who have taken different paths for survival. The contrast and conflict of the pair creates the setting for the moral lessons: the value of self-respect, and the importance of loyalty to one's friend as a part of that self-respect.

It is also a story of individuals who have lived beyond their immediate usefulness to society. They have unfortunately outlived their jobs; they must cope with a society which has outgrown the need for their expertise and abilities; the problem for them is to maintain their dignity, their self-respect. While this has a lot to do with the particular time and place, it is also a universal problem of aging which we have yet to solve in any meaningful (or practical, for that matter) way.

Beyond this, the time and place are relevant. It is the West at

49

the time of the appearance of the automobile. Never in American experience have the symbols of two opposing centuries faced each other in symbolic confrontation so dramatically: the Age of the Horse has been met by the Age of the Auto. The single appearance of the motor-car in the opening scenes of the film locates us precisely. It is not the legendary, figurative West of 1860-1890; we recognize the beginning of the end of more than an era—it is also the end of a state of mind. Of course, the change did not take place overnight, but the aging individual in the context of a changing society is of different concern than one growing old in familiar surroundings. If Steve Judd and Gil Westrum could die marshalling there would be no problem in their dying with dignity; but the needs of the frontier have been supplanted by the needs of growing civilization. "The days of the '49'ers are past, and the days of the steady businessman have arrived," as Steve is told at the bank. Society has less use for rugged individualists, though it has plenty of room for cooperative builders and entrepreneurs. With the change of life-style comes a change of attitude; the traditions that supported the frontier are no longer primary to a successful society. But this is not to condemn the encroachment of civilization *per se*. The tragedy lies in the loss of esteem for traditional self-reliance, and the difficulty the frontier individual finds in making the transition with dignity.

Steven Judd rides into town to the shouts of people on the street and takes the noise as a greeting; his mistake is both comic and poignant as he tips his hat in passing, only to be told literally and figuratively to "get out of the way" of the carnival camel-horse race. As a figure from rougher days, he does not belong in this town; as his former partner Gil Westrum has found, their kind has been relegated to the status of sideshow attraction. Steve narrowly avoids being hit by the car.

Strangely, with the passing of the "Old West," we fear the loss of values we have never been able to satisfactorily identify. Simple communion with nature has its limits; the "freedom" of the wilderness is only a man-made association. The excitement of the struggle for survival as a test of the individual is a value for some. Perhaps the idea of change alone, a whole new ballgame to get used to, is enough cause for anxiety; or the idea that men will not be as "tall' in the new, "civilized" society. The loss of individual identity can serve to a point—at least, it is this loss of identity which makes a problem of maintaining self-respect for Steve Judd.

Finally, in addition to considering realistic levels, one can enjoy the fact that this is a movie, a Western movie at that, with a unique opportunity to enjoy the *form* as well as the content of the film. *Ride the High Country* works well in a vacuum outside of other films, but it has increased dimension as a genre film. This is a key factor in the film's artistry: while the topography and props are all familiar, the delivery and conception are completely original—the film has no *cinematic clichés*. Separating parts from the whole makes comparison to similar situations in other Westerns easier; we have seen hundreds of shoot-outs and have seen Randolph Scott riding to the rescue before—but never before in quite the same way, and certainly not in the same context. Scott's "ride to the rescue" in particular is an especially heroic, cheered scene, in that we can bring to the scene the memory of other gallant rides by Scott. But the cliché image truly does not exist: Cary Grant never said, "Judy, Judy, Judy," and Humphrey Bogart did not say, "Play it again, Sam." *Ride the High Country* might have worked with other lead actors, but the presence of Joel McCrea and Randolph Scott in the main roles adds a continuity of response from earlier Western films that deepens the impact of this particular story. The two *veteran* Western movie actors are playing *veteran* Western figures; they bring a unique set of baggage to the film. Indeed they are, as *actors*, Western genre icons as familiar as horses and six-guns. There is a vague possibility that even they themselves may have sensed this: originally, McCrea was cast as the "bad guy," Gil Westrum, while Scott had the Steve Judd role. But in an almost simultaneous and, as the story goes, independent change of heart, each actor felt he should play the *other* role.[2] The switch was made to their mutual satisfaction.

This kind of film self-reference is rarely so successful. Particularly in the Western genre an actor comes to stand for something. The ultimate example is probably John Wayne in *The Shootist* (1976), a film self-consciously inseparable from its main actor, and marvelously so. The fact is we can identify McCrea's Steve Judd readily from our experience with him in other situations. *Ride the High Country* doesn't depend, by any means, on one's having seen McCrea before; but it certainly adds another level of depth to the film, whether by design or not. There is more poignance to McCrea's death, for there is more potentially at stake than the passing of Steve Judd. It is one of the last glimpses of a kind of movie as well. There is a twinge of regret when one watches Errol Flynn imitate himself in *The Master of Ballantrae* (1953); Joel McCrea as a Western hero died with dignity. *Ride the High Country* was Scott and McCrea's "last" film.

Even aside from the actors, *Ride the High Country* is a significant page in the development/treatment of the Western film. It is easy to think of John Ford as being *before* everyone else, but 1962 saw the release of both *Ride the High Country* and Ford's *The Man Who Shot Liberty Valance*, a particularly bitter vision of the "end" of the West *and* the Western, and what has been seen as a marked departure for the director whose name had become synonymous with the form. The fact that Peckinpah and Ford address the "end of the West" simultaneously from different directions is of interest when the case is made for Peckinpah's being the thematic successor to Ford. Peckinpah doesn't repeat Ford, but he later explores ideas in the Western that Ford was approaching in the late stages of his long career. To label these films as revisionist, a term more relevant to political history (i.e., "reality"), can be misleading when one considers that the Western film is not realistic documentary, but a representation of how we see ourselves and how we like to think of ourselves. The *factual* history of the West can be of comparative interest in considering cinematic treatments, but it can also be irrelevant to the Western film.

The magic of *Ride the High Country* lies in the precision of Peckinpah's execution. The film's characters and environment are very close to home. The mining camp of Coarsegold was inspired by the real town of Coarsegold, not far from where Peckinpah grew up. He knew the people and the country well. In the film, what was always an expression of his background also became a tribute: Steve Judd's line, "All I want is to enter my house justified," is a direct quotation from Peckinpah's father.

Accuracy of observation, a value fostered by Peckinpah's grandfather, is witnessed in this film in hundreds of "little things." Peckinpah's striving for realism in the setting for his drama is of inestimable value to the film's impact, realized by countless small details. The hole in his boot, the frayed cuffs, the touching way he goes to the john to take out his glasses, telling Heck not to litter: all details which humanize Steve Judd, add dimension, make him real. Likewise, the pain Gil Westrum gets in his back from riding and the fact that he "doesn't sleep so good anymore" are small touches of age which add flesh to the character. Coarsegold, Kate's place, the slovenly quality of the Hammond's camp, and the Knudsen farm are triumphs of detail: the snow on the bedraggled miners' tents, the tattered red velvet and whores with a bit more mileage on them than customary in Westerns up to this time, the mud and disarray of the Hammond's capped off with Henry's pet crow, the inscription on Hester Knudsen's grave and the biblical plaque on the wall in the Knudsen house are but a few items which bring considerable depth to the enjoyment of the film. Even if Kate, the grotesque madame, is seen as an exaggeration, she is a grotesque completely in tune with the rest of the presentation; her most vivid "grotesquerie" is at the wedding, seen primarily from Elsa's point of view.

Peckinpah's attention is not limited to physical detail, however. His characters are often "rounded out" by elements which have little or no plot significance, such as the way the Hammond brothers sing together on their way to the wedding, or their bathing and shaving scene preparing for the wedding; Elsa's quick change from male to female clothing when she sees visitors approaching the farm; her father, Joshua's, biblical chapter-and-verse quotations, as well as Steve's biblical response and Gil's comic "coda," "You cook a lovely hamhock, Miss Knudsen, just lovely—Appetite, Chapter One."

Moreover, Peckinpah did a dialogue rewrite on the script that shows the same careful attention to detail in the speech rhythms and vocabulary of the individual characters. The dialogue in no small way contributes to the whole: the stories Steve and Gil reminisce over on the trail are important details of character which have a "ring" to them which must be recognized as a major accomplishment. The film plays to the eyes *and* ears. (It should be noted that the music for the film was initially producer Richard Lyons's responsibility, Peckinpah having been kicked off the MGM lot by that time. George

Bassman's score is in harmony with the rest of the film; the main title theme and its reprises, particularly during the shoot-out and end of the film, contribute pointedly to the experience. The theme variation played as the showdown begins adds to the "legendary-one-last-stand" dimension of the scene; the full orchestra chord as the theme rises over Steve Judd signals his death and last gaze at the high country in the background. The score is a bit of a tribute itself; it is, in a very real sense, "monument" music.)

At the time of *Ride the High Country,* Peckinpah's cinematic technique was still evolving; he had "learned" much by his second feature, and he was learning and developing his skills conscientiously, applying and adapting technical suggestions with expert facility. He gives a lot of credit to people who have helped him in this respect, and in the making of *Ride the High Country* Peckinpah defers substantial credit to photographer Lucien Ballard and editor Frank Santillo.

Ballard had worked with Peckinpah on several episodes of "The Westerner," and as Bill Clothier had aided Peckinpah on *The Deadly Companions*, Ballard was instrumental in achieving many of the effects Peckinpah wanted in *Ride the High Country*.[3] Apart from providing solutions to several serious technical problems, one of Ballard's ideas was the use of a Chapman crane. Peckinpah discovered that the use of the crane, the elevation it gave, provided visual support to the notion of the character's vertical motion as they ride up into the high country of Coarsegold and descend from it, as Ballard had suggested. The particular "crane shot" which begins at the stream (after Steve has spoken of the hole in his boot) and rises as they mount and ride away from the camera (into the frame) encompasses a great deal of information: in one shot we see the splendid variety of the environment, from the stream bank, through the trees, over the trees to the grassy plain, beyond to the foothills, and finally to the tall mountains in the background. Remarkably, we also see the figures in that landscape, as Steve points the way, his leadership accentuated physically by the composition of the shot. Peckinpah would use the crane to similar advantage in future films, notably *Major Dundee* and *Pat Garrett and Billy the Kid*.

If Peckinpah is careful with detail in his characters and "props," he is also careful in his composition of scenes, distinctly adept in choosing his camera angles and in arranging the balance of figures within a shot. This is a key talent in itself, not to be underestimated in its importance: it is one of the prime attributes of a masterful cinematic artist. It has been widely discussed that a camera angle can have political and moral implications, but it isn't necessary to go that far to acknowledge the emotional, perceptual effect of shot composition. Examples can be broadly fundamental, as in many of the great Russian films of the 1920s, or as in quintessential bits of Hitchcock, but it must be recognized that it is a quality of *any* cinematic frame to affect the viewer's relationship to what is "happening" on the screen. Knowing what those effects can be, intuitively more than intellectually, is a prerequisite to successful filmmaking (and I don't mean "successful" in financial terms). This is wonderfully imprecise, but it is indeed a significant part of what is referred to as a "visual sense."

For example, a "low" camera angle which forces the viewer to look up to a character has a different effect than does a straight-on or "higher" angle (looking down), in the same shot context. When we first meet Steve Judd as he rides into the town of Hornitos, the camera is slightly below him. An immediate effect of this is that the character by *visual means alone* becomes more imposing; in context, he will seem more authoritative. We see Steve Judd in this manner often in the film; looking up to him adds to his dignity, framed by the sky; he is seen to be on a level "above" others. By contrast, the same use of a low camera angle has a contrapuntal effect in *Major Dundee*: shots looking up to the Major present him as an imposing figure, but Dundee is a character whose self-identity is in question, and the "epic" figure presented by the camera is an image Dundee must live up to for his own benefit. Steve Judd justifies our image of him by his actions. The irony here is *after* the fact of the image, for the other people in the film do not see him with the same respect, i.e., from the same angle, that we do.

This idea carries through in the scene where Steve accepts the bank-guard job. The bank officers are indeed "smaller" men: while Steve dominates the right side of the frame, chest-high looking down, the left side of the frame has barely the shoulders and heads of the bank officers. We see the shot on a level with Steve; we look down on the bank officers. Finally, with Gil and Steve bedding down in the Knudsen's barn, they speak as old friends, equals; we are invited to share this, shot straight-on at their level.

Peckinpah also knows that selective angle and composition can increase tension. When Gil tries to steal the gold, the scene is "told" by feet initially: the horses' hooves hobbled, Gil's and Heck's boots among them, then a pan in the direction of Gil's movement to another pair of boots, Steve's, moving up to Steve's waist, where he holds his gun, then to Gil's reaction and finally climaxed by Steve's grim face in close-up. (The boot images recall the opening shot of *The Deadly Companions*: Yellowleg is introduced by a shot of his boots and yellow-striped Union army trousers).

The final showdown between Gil and Steve and the Hammond brothers is also significant with regard to illustrating Peckinpah's composition technique. By cinematic means, Peckinpah elicits the archetypal context of the Western gunfight to a point where Gil and Steve are aided by the mythic dimensions of the scene. In the ditch, they agree to "meet 'em head-on — half-way, just like always," immediately setting up the archetype. After taunting the Hammonds into agreement, they rise to the yard, the theme music starts, and they begin their walk. Both sides are seen first in long-shot. The Hammonds are stationary, a limit to their dignity which puts them on the defensive. As Steve and Gil begin walking, the camera shifts to an *overhead* view; once again, it is the archetype which becomes framed and emphasized, and the camera moves in as Steve and Gil do, accentuating the link between our point of view and theirs. The Hammonds are cut to straight-on; Steve and Gil are shot from *below* as they continue their pace, increasing their stature: they have become heroic. We see the Hammonds next as a group from Steve and Gil's point of view, then see Steve and Gil from an even lower angle than before, with only the sky, a tree-top, and the mountain in the background: they are now heroes of mythic proportions. The Hammonds are hopelessly outclassed. Thematically, it can be recalled as Steve said it on the trail earlier, talking about a time he was punished: "He was right — I was wrong — that makes the difference." When Gil asks, "Who says so?" Steve responds: "Nobody — that's somethin' you just know." Right makes might. So does careful camera placement.

Ride the High Country proved to be a training ground for Peckinpah in another key area: editing. In making the first cut on the film, Peckinpah worked closely with editor Frank Santillo. Santillo had worked with Slavko Vorkapich, the renowned montage expert and theorist, and consequently knew the potential value of single-frame edits and the effect of pace through editing. Peckinpah took to these ideas quickly, as the shoot-out with the Hammonds bears witness: some of the shots are only a few frames long, and pace is established by *not* strictly following a shot-reaction shot sequence. This "flash-cutting," which Peckinpah credits Santillo for teaching him, combined with other montage ideas which derive from or are at least sympathetic to Vorkapich's theories, develop into a unique editing style readily apparent in most of Peckinpah's later films. It is this editing aspect which gives such power to scenes in *The Wild Bunch* and *Straw Dogs* in particular.

Ride the High Country is often spoken of as a lyrical film which Peckinpah turned away from thematically in subsequent works. But it is precisely this "gentler" appearance of the film which makes it a key to understanding the later films. Themes which are of primary importance to Peckinpah are self-knowledge, dedication (the spirit of the professional), the subjectivity of the Truth and the Law, and loyalty to one's principles and, significantly, to one's friends. This last is often the measure of the others (mostly matters of honor), as Peckinpah examines the nature of friendships. That he deals more in apparently male-dominated settings than female arenas is an indication of background and familiarity, not necessarily strictly of sympathy. But this will be addressed more directly later on.

Ride the High Country is clear on many subjects which carry straight through Peckinpah's other films. The importance of self-respect, that which Gil has evaded and which Steve pursues, is an aspect of self-knowledge which can be seen as the fulfillment of the individual on his own moral terms, to feel that he has "done the right thing," so that he may "enter his house justified." Betrayal of principles (and of friends) is the sin which blocks self-respect. Peckinpah shows that maintaining self-respect is not easy, but it is what one must do if one is to find justification. Steve Judd compromises his idea of self-respect by surviving with jobs which lack principle: stick-man, bouncer, etc. Gil Westrum, a man with the same background, sacrifices his by parodying himself as the Oregon Kid in a rigged carnival game. (This is also demeaning, as it mocks the Western hero—Wyatt Earp would never resort to it!) But Gil "consciously" trades his self-respect further for material gain, convincing himself and trying to convince Steve that principles should be damned and life demands taking. "The clothes of pride" are all a poor man has, he says, and they're not very warm. But Steve retains his principles despite the suffering they cause him: he accepts the loss of Sara Truesdale, the girl he might have married but didn't because of his commitment to his job as marshal. He is redeemed by this acceptance, as well as by his ability to resist all of Gil's temptations to join him and steal the gold. Heck Longtree is likewise redeemed by his ultimate following of Steve rather than Gil, living up to his *word* by returning the gun after the first shooting encounter with the Hammonds. Heck is rewarded with the love and respect of Elsa.

All of Gil's materially oriented logic which denies principle is given the final blow in his humiliation by Steve as he attempts to steal the gold. Steve bitterly rebukes Gil, slaps him (an insult more painful than a fist), and dares Gil to draw his gun. Gil is practically defenseless; he has been confronted with his own lack of self-respect. More significant is the idea that Steve is hurt most not by Gil's wanting to steal the money, which belongs to the bank, but by the fact that this represents a betrayal of Steve by his friend. "What they don't know won't hurt 'em—not them, only *me!*" Steve roars. When Elsa asks if Steve will testify in Gil's behalf, Steve replies, "No, I won't . . . cause he was my friend." The last of Gil's dignity is gone as he fumbles his coffee cup with tied hands, and asks to be cut loose because he "doesn't sleep so good anymore."

Gil must at last ride to the rescue to redeem his self-respect and redeem himself in the eyes of his friend. The accent in the showdown is on partnership reestablished, and the final scene is moving because we can celebrate this friendship, even as Steve dies. Steve, with modest dignity and courage, says, "I'll

go it alone," to spare the youngsters the indignity of death. Gil tells him, "Don't worry about anything—I'll take care of it—just like you would have." Steve forgives his friend: "Hell, I know that—I always did—you just forgot it for awhile, that's all." There is incredible tenderness in this last moment; tough Gil Westrum has tears in his eyes as he bids his friend, through whom he has *regained* his self-respect, goodbye. Steve's last words are, "So long, *partner*." Gil replies, "I'll se ya later."

Peckinpah is especially responsible for the quality of this last scene. As originally written, the Gil Westrum character had been the one to die. In a brilliant alteration, Peckinpah changed this to the "good guy" dying, working against the Hollywood moral tradition. Gil Westrum is therefore redeemed by his act of loyal friendship, not by death. Steve Judd, meanwhile, makes his peace and prepares to enter his house, justified. For Peckinpah, it is a matter of honor that a character "plays his string out to the end."[4] Steve did, and we accept that Gil will.

After the attempt to steal the gold, Elsa says to Steve, "My father says there's only right and wrong—good and evil—nothin' in between; it isn't that simple, is it?" Steve's reply is a concise example of Peckinpah's background surrounded by lawyers: "No, it isn't; *it should be*, but it isn't." There is an ambiguity of circumstance in matters of Truth and Law, providing room for human frailty and forgiveness. Joshua Knudsen struggles with this in his rigid self-denial, and dies without understanding. There is danger in overrighteousness, as Joshua fights his human failings (and his own compassion) with strict scripture. The epitaph on the grave of his wife is unyielding; Elsa runs away in emotional self-defense. It is interesting to note here that the main action of *Ride the High Country* pivots on the woman: Elsa's dependence on Steve, Gil, and Heck as escorts leads them all into the confrontation with the Hammonds. But it is the choice of the men which completes this plot motivation: Steve responds to Elsa's need through a sense of chivalry, i.e., that it's the "right thing" to do; Heck responds from love, and Gil must follow or lose the chance at the gold. Action instigated by the woman will recur pointedly in several later Peckinpah films, most notably in *Bring Me the Head of Alfredo Garcia* and in *Straw Dogs*.

The Hammond brothers (L. Q. Jones, John Anderson, Warren Oates, and John Davis Chandler).

The Hammonds are a pristine group of Peckinpah rascals. They are finally the "villains" of the film, but they are only acting according to their idea of the rules, and beyond that with rather limited tools. Indeed, Billy is "cheated" out of his bride by Gil, who threatens the judge and takes the marriage license. Ironically, Steve's scruples prohibit him from this kind of expedient action. The situation is marked by a double standard, as we sympathize with Elsa, although it is Billy who has the law in his favor initially. Ultimately, everyone suffers through Elsa's naiveté about what she was getting into, though one can hardly blame her. If the stern repression by her father isn't enough, the wedding in the brothel and the greeting over the wedding bed should be: "For the bride *and* groom," it reads. The "and" is underlined with a winking leer. (She should have known something was wrong as *we* did, however, in the way Sylvus is offended by Billy's kicking him out of his and Elsa's tent). The Hammonds respond to Elsa's desertion the only way they know how. That they outnumber and are younger than their enemies serves to make it a contest.

But the Hammonds are
own limited sense of self-
the wedding party is an i
tially. Beyond that, the
Hammonds' pride. Steve
cepting the challenge of
Billy to hold on, that the
Billy's answer is the key
honor?" Even the Hamm
dom judges his character
even be loathsome, but t
ence and complexity rath
guys" have failings; his "
than evil. The worst one
cynically dismiss princip
play both sides without
monds, meanwhile, are th
in *The Wild Bunch*, and
Major Dundee (includin
"bad," really, as they are
design. On the other hand
derers—bad enough for S
ing them.

If the world is harsh in
world also possesses grea
the High Country is a pro
degree, supported by the
the characters. In additio
countless touches of origi
tle direct attention to them
cinematically, bring dime
The chickens interrupted
ning the last scene were n
"touches," his direction
tween a "diamond in the r

Youth is instructed by t
sed in older hands. *Ride th*
human beings need guida
may be an imposition, bu
one. People are defined b
what they do.

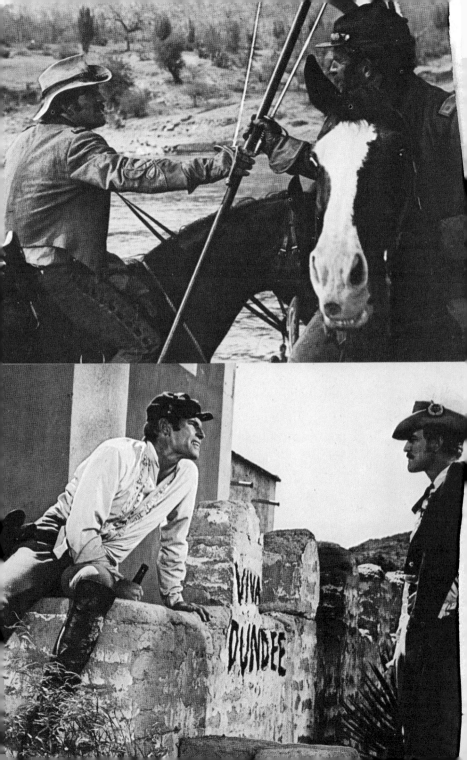

But the Hammonds are not without their own pride, their own limited sense of self-respect. Steve's removal of Elsa from the wedding party is an insult which must be answered, initially. Beyond that, the showdown itself *depends* on the Hammonds' pride. Steve and Gil goad the Hammonds into accepting the challenge of a straight-up duel. But Elder tells Billy to hold on, that they'll "get them when they rise up." Billy's answer is the key: "Ain't you got no sense of family honor?" Even the Hammonds respond to it. Peckinpah seldom judges his characters in simple terms. His villains may even be loathsome, but they are drawn from human experience and complexity rather than out of metaphor. His "good guys" have failings; his "bad guys" are often more pathetic than evil. The worst ones are those who either side-step or cynically dismiss principles, the users of people, those who play both sides without a commitment to either. The Hammonds, meanwhile, are the forerunners of the bounty hunters in *The Wild Bunch*, and the rag-tag band of Confederates in *Major Dundee* (including two of the same actors), not as "bad," really, as they are just not "equipped," by nature or design. On the other hand, however, the Hammonds *are* murderers—bad enough for Steve and Gil to find honor in defeating them.

If the world is harsh in the way it deals with humans, the world also possesses great beauty. The lyrical quality of *Ride the High Country* is a product of this scenic beauty to a great degree, supported by the foundation of empathy we feel for the characters. In addition, Peckinpah fills the picture with countless touches of originality, genuine things which call little direct attention to themselves but which, dramatically and *cinematically*, bring dimension, tone, and depth to the film. The chickens interrupted by Henry Hammond's crow beginning the last scene were not in the original script. Peckinpah's "touches," his direction of the film, mark the difference between a "diamond in the rough" and a gem of luster.

Youth is instructed by the lessons of experience, as witnessed in older hands. *Ride the High Country* is a hymn to values; human beings need guidance and values to live by. Morality may be an imposition, but Peckinpah sees it as a necessary one. People are defined by what they stand for, as well as by what they do.

The Hammond brothers (L. Q. Jones, John Anderson, Warren Oates, and John Davis Chandler).

The Hammonds are a pristine group of Peckinpah rascals. They are finally the "villains" of the film, but they are only acting according to their idea of the rules, and beyond that with rather limited tools. Indeed, Billy is "cheated" out of his bride by Gil, who threatens the judge and takes the marriage license. Ironically, Steve's scruples prohibit him from this kind of expedient action. The situation is marked by a double standard, as we sympathize with Elsa, although it is Billy who has the law in his favor initially. Ultimately, everyone suffers through Elsa's naiveté about what she was getting into, though one can hardly blame her. If the stern repression by her father isn't enough, the wedding in the brothel and the greeting over the wedding bed should be: "For the bride *and* groom," it reads. The "and" is underlined with a winking leer. (She should have known something was wrong as *we* did, however, in the way Sylvus is offended by Billy's kicking him out of his and Elsa's tent). The Hammonds respond to Elsa's desertion the only way they know how. That they outnumber and are younger than their enemies serves to make it a contest.

go it alone," to spare the youngsters the indignity of death. Gil tells him, "Don't worry about anything—I'll take care of it—just like you would have." Steve forgives his friend: "Hell, I know that—I always did—you just forgot it for awhile, that's all." There is incredible tenderness in this last moment; tough Gil Westrum has tears in his eyes as he bids his friend, through whom he has *regained* his self-respect, goodbye. Steve's last words are, "So long, *partner*." Gil replies, "I'll se ya later."

Peckinpah is especially responsible for the quality of this last scene. As originally written, the Gil Westrum character had been the one to die. In a brilliant alteration, Peckinpah changed this to the "good guy" dying, working against the Hollywood moral tradition. Gil Westrum is therefore redeemed by his act of loyal friendship, not by death. Steve Judd, meanwhile, makes his peace and prepares to enter his house, justified. For Peckinpah, it is a matter of honor that a character "plays his string out to the end."[4] Steve did, and we accept that Gil will.

After the attempt to steal the gold, Elsa says to Steve, "My father says there's only right and wrong—good and evil—nothin' in between; it isn't that simple, is it?" Steve's reply is a concise example of Peckinpah's background surrounded by lawyers: "No, it isn't; *it should be*, but it isn't." There is an ambiguity of circumstance in matters of Truth and Law, providing room for human frailty and forgiveness. Joshua Knudsen struggles with this in his rigid self-denial, and dies without understanding. There is danger in overrighteousness, as Joshua fights his human failings (and his own compassion) with strict scripture. The epitaph on the grave of his wife is unyielding; Elsa runs away in emotional self-defense. It is interesting to note here that the main action of *Ride the High Country* pivots on the woman: Elsa's dependence on Steve, Gil, and Heck as escorts leads them all into the confrontation with the Hammonds. But it is the choice of the men which completes this plot motivation: Steve responds to Elsa's need through a sense of chivalry, i.e., that it's the "right thing" to do; Heck responds from love, and Gil must follow or lose the chance at the gold. Action instigated by the woman will recur pointedly in several later Peckinpah films, most notably in *Bring Me the Head of Alfredo Garcia* and in *Straw Dogs*.

4

Major Dundee (1965)

... HOW EXACTLY do you see yourself, Major Dundee?"

The cavalry Western is a subset of the genre, with traditional images and settings which carry a number of social and / or political concerns often beyond the "regular" Western in immediate implications. An army is automatically associated with an idea of broad sociopolitical consequences, although the army of a conqueror may be only a personal tool, initially. In particular, the U.S. Army is a national enterprise. Likewise, the scope of the events open to a cavalry Western lend themselves to epic treatment. It is also impossible to consider the form with any significance without invoking the cavalry films of John Ford. Ford, in many ways, sets the standard, defines the territory. But, to a great extent, Ford concerns himself with the enterprise and its function, showing individuals as they perform in that context. In *Fort Apache* (1948), *She Wore a Yellow Ribbon* (1949), and *Rio Grande* (1950), things are seen primarily from *within* the cavalry; only later, in *Two Rode Together* (1961) and *Cheyenne Autumn* (1964), do we see an important viewpoint *outside* the army. *The Horse Soldiers* (1959), as a Civil War cavalry film, provides something of a bridge.

Peckinpah's *Major Dundee* relates to all of these variations, and, if viewed as a Western, can be seen as a diversion rising out of familiar territory. It "jumps off" from many individually recognized dramatic and genre conventions. But the pieces form a complex whole which is original in its accomplishments, forcing genre expectations aside in a story which is at once a national epic and a personal search for identity. In Peckinpah's hands, what begins in the original script as an action film of events becomes as well a character study of indi-

63

Questions of identity: Tyreen and Dundee rescue the colors (top); "a military genius or a damned fool" (bottom).

viduals who through their position have the power to produce large-scale consequences out of personal concerns—what could be viewed as the forging of a national identity. Major Dundee's war is a personal war. The problem is in determining who the enemy is.

In assessing *Major Dundee*, one must be mindful of the difference between the film-that-is and the film-that-might-have-been. The debate over the editing of the film provides a lot of room for the film's champions as well as its critics. There is not enough left in the released version for the film to stand as a masterpiece; yet there is too much of apparent value to call it a wasted effort. By nature of the history of its completion, *Major Dundee* is difficult to appreciate "cold." But when what's *in* the film is examined in conjunction with what we are told was *supposed* to be there, there is sufficient evidence found to support the idea that *Major Dundee* is indeed a masterpiece at least of conception. As Jim Kitses remarks in his book *Horizons West, Major Dundee* is "one of Hollywood's great broken monuments."[1] Like the ruin of an ancient temple, it is fair to imagine what it "originally" looked like. Indeed, most of the criticisms of the released film are answered by what was cut out.

The original release print ran 134 minutes; Peckinpah has spoken of the film he "made" as being at least 156 minutes.[2] Subsequent to initial release, the film was shown even in versions running just under two hours. Explaining several key scenes which were filmed and cut out will serve to better approximate Peckinpah's conception: 1) the opening Halloween party at the Rostes ranch, climaxed by Charriba's attack and the massacre (whose aftermath now opens the film); 2) a scene where Tyreen and the others, trying to escape, are recaptured by Dundee as he returns from the Rostes ranch, in a stream not far from the prison; this scene would also have established Sgt. Gomez as having lived with the Apaches after he had been stolen by them as a boy; 3) a scene following Jimmy Lee Benteen's insulting of Aesop and fight with Rev. Dahlstrom where whiskey is broken out and alternate toasts are raised, underlining the conflicts within the command; 4) following the ambush at the river, a scene where Dundee struggles to get a mule he is mounted on to move, which unites the command in laughter; 5) more of the night of the fiesta, where a mock-serious knife-fight between Potts and Gomez (recalling their Christmas Eve wrestling) is broken up by Dundee, revealing his position as an outsider in misunderstanding the nature of the fight; 6) significant parts of a montage of Dundee's breakdown and drunken delirium in Durango, which highlight Dundee's impressions of himself and all that has happened, as well as his refusal to return to the command with Gomez because the French are watching him.[3] In addition, small pieces were clipped throughout the film which resulted in an overall loss of bits of character insight—a loss which damages our understanding of those characters. But with the altered nature of the film in mind, we can better assess the conception of the work.

Major Amos Charles Dundee is a man with a complex identity crisis. He is torn between an obsessive image of heroic leadership and a lack of the self-knowledge to find a means to fulfill that image. As a result, his outward mien is a series of poses dictated by his position in relation to that imposed image, while the inner man struggles with the confusion of who he "really" is and what his role should be. Punished for fighting his "own war" at Gettysburg, Dundee bridles at the relative ignominy of his position as jailer. It is because of this notion of having to prove himself, to identify and redeem himself, that he seizes upon the pursuit of the Apache as a means to his personal resolution. Capt. Waller, terming the pursuit foolhardy, asks Amos pointedly if he is pursuing the Apache or a promotion. Amos is really pursuing himself.

But it is not that simple. Sierra Charriba is hardly a "noble savage," and whatever his motivation he is a destructive force that due to circumstances of time, place, and manifest destiny must be stopped. That his enmity for the white man is taken for granted in this story stops us short of considering *Major Dundee* as a parable of the pitfalls of the Indian Wars. It may be an element in finally recognizing the moral confusion inherent in American politics of the nineteenth century, but for this film it is only a fact of life. Hostile Apaches were something the cavalry was assigned to deal with. Pursuing Sierra Charriba is, in a way, the "MacGuffin"[4] of the story, an object as such.

Recognizing the backdrop of the Civil War, described as a fight of brother against brother, adds yet another element to the confusion of national as well as personal identity. Dundee is a Southerner fighting for the North; before he is "through" he will fight the Indian and the French. Even as Dundee's command of Union, Confederate, and civilian troops unites to fight the "common enemy," it is scarcely surprising to find confusion of individual purpose at a time when the notion of being an "American" is a tenuous one. By the time Dundee demands the French garrison's surrender, all thoughts of clear national mission are gone. As the French commander decries the infraction of "international law," Mr. Potts's reply is succinct: "Sonny, the Major ain't no lawyer." That Dundee's incursion into Mexico is illegal hardly matters. (He goes by the "book" only *within* the command.) The Indians' threat to domestic security was something of an excuse to allow Dundee to follow in the first place. Dundee knows he could be shot for what he has done as an official; as long as his "mission" is successful, he feels he will be vindicated. Indeed, the fact that Dundee is at least no worse than his opponents is vindication enough of his ends justifying his means.

The problem in following a man of Dundee's confusion is one of survival. The Confederates do so to avoid being hanged; it will also provide a means of eventual escape. The Union "coloreds" serve to prove themselves as soldiers, the civilians, to get out of jail; the other volunteers are there for personal reasons. But whatever the reasons for their presence, they are all trapped in Dundee's crusade. Jim Kitses suggests that Dundee's forebear in *Ride the High Country* is Joshua Knudsen.[5] The comparison is apt, for the act of trying to live up to an ideal image leaves behind a path full of wreckage and destruction for both. Dundee's, because of its scope, is certainly more severe. The hope is that the individual can achieve self-knowledge through his struggle, and recognize human limitations; Joshua Knudsen dies before achieving it, while Dundee survives back across the river, though it is not confirmed that Dundee really *has* learned anything at the end of the film. Hopefully, however, the viewer has.

The fortunes of war and storytelling have placed Dundee in the company of Benjamin Tyreen. Tyreen is for Dundee a bit like Gil Westrum was for Steve Judd, another side of the same human coin. Tyreen, an Irishman who owes his allegiance to the Confederacy, is also a former Union officer; he had even scouted Mexico with Grant in '47. But, after killing another officer in a "duel of honor," he was cashiered, with Dundee casting the "deciding" vote. As former friends from West Point, Dundee and Tyreen play upon each other's choice of outlook, Dundee out of a need to confirm his own choice, and Tyreen reluctantly accepting the rivalry first by circumstance, and later to back up his outlook versus Dundee's. Tyreen has the same confusion of identity, but he has accepted his position out of a primarily romantic set of ideals apart from those of professional duty. He prides himself as a man of honor, but the contradictions of his particular position become traps which Dundee helps to spring. Tyreen agrees to fight for Dundee and the Union flag "until the Apache is taken or destroyed." The irony of this litany, which is repeated as a face-saving device indicating where and why Tyreen's initial responsibility lies with Dundee, becomes profoundly clear after the Apache *has* been destroyed. After Charriba's death the French arrive, and Tyreen again fights the common enemy to the point where he is wounded saving the flag he had damned earlier, and dies in a gallant effort to stall the French and help Dundee and the survivors escape to Texas.

Tyreen's final gesture is in keeping with the rest of his character, a man full of gestures which make him both charming and tragic as he tries to follow the consequences of those attitudes. He relishes romantic gesture, as noted in his plumed hat and formal gentility with the woman Teresa (whom he later categorizes as a woman of "rather doubtful virtue" in humiliating Dundee), and tends to use a flourish where Dundee would be pragmatic. Dundee allows at one point to Teresa that Tyreen has "style." In prison, Tyreen stands as a martyred figure, even as he considers the practical significance of Dundee's intention of hanging him.

Dundee and Tyreen test each other repeatedly. At one point in explanation, Dundee says of Tyreen that "he is corrupt, but I will save him." Dundee cannot reconcile himself to the fact that he and Tyreen have a lot in common. As they are about to enter Mexico, Confederate troops appear on the horizon, and Dundee tempts Tyreen to escape. But Tyreen cannot escape without accepting Dundee's implication that Tyreen's word is no good; and thus he continues into Mexico, after repeating the limits of his allegiance to Dundee, "until the Apache is

taken . . ." etc. Tyreen also helps to avert an ugly fight in camp
after Jimmy Lee Benteen taunts Aesop, a gesture which Dundee thanks Tyreen for but doesn't fully comprehend. The up-
shot of that incident has Dundee jealous of Tyreen's apparent
grace under pressure. Finally, after O. W. Hadley deserts and
is captured, Tyreen is "forced" to *allow* Hadley to be killed
and then to kill Hadley himself, rather than let Dundee do it
and have the command fall apart completely, a further reflection on Tyreen's ability to keep his word that the Confederates
will serve "until the Apache . . ." etc. At that point Tyreen
swears to kill Dundee when circumstances permit (i.e., *when*
the Apache is caught), which they never do, finally, because of
the French.

Tyreen has his limited revenge on Dundee, however, as
Dundee is caught violating his own rules, going outside the
picket lines with Teresa, where he takes an arrow in the leg. It
is a moment of humiliation which initiates Dundee's retreat
into self-pity and his breakdown in Durango. After Dundee is
wounded, Tyreen catalogues his incompetence as an officer,
finally adding, "Just what the bloody hell are you doing here

Emotional risk: Dundee is wounded for violating his own "perimeters."

in the first place, Amos?" Dundee doesn't answer. When Dundee drunkenly asks Tyreen why he has come to save him, Tyreen replies it is so he can have the pleasure of killing Dundee himself. But when Dundee refuses to move, Tyreen agrees finally that Dundee is "not worth killing anyway," and Dundee rises, reprising the "until the Apache . . ." line himself this time.

After the main actions, plot incidents of the film dwell on character, indicating the secondary characters in ways which comment on the central figure of Dundee. The film is rich with these character vignettes, with figures such as the scout Potts, Sgt. Gomez, Rev. Dahlstrom, Lt. Graham, the Hadley brothers, and Sgt. Chillum incorporated to give balance to the imposing articulated figures of Dundee and Tyreen. Criticism of the film which sees *Major Dundee* as simply an action picture takes issue with some of these secondary characters as digressions, but they are pieces important to the whole tapestry of the complex range of human behavior embodied in the film.

This is particularly true of the woman, Teresa Santiago. It is probably less of a coincidence to find someone like her in the Mexican village than it is to find Tyreen in Dundee's prison, and she is explained as the German wife of the village doctor (killed by the French). Peckinpah agrees, however, that the casting of the voluptuous Ms. Berger was a mistake.[6] Through Teresa, we see a glimpse of the interior Dundee, coming to the surface briefly to reach out for some sympathy. Peckinpah's characters tend to suppress their inner feelings, and Dundee's moments with Teresa are revealing. In their first conversation, Dundee makes apparent his loneliness and his jealousy of Tyreen's apparent facility with the woman. In their next encounter, after the death of O. W. Hadley, Teresa acknowledges the effect of Hadley's death on Dundee; they had all died a little with Hadley, but Dundee had died most of all. When she says Dundee is concerned about how the men feel about him, he responds with the pose of the stalwart leader that he is concerned with how they fight, not how they feel toward him. Dundee also betrays his envy of the simple soldier as he explains why men fight: "Men can understand fighting. I guess maybe they need it sometimes. Truth is, it's easy. Forget about your problems, responsibilities; just let someone feed ya', tell

ya' what to do . . ." But when Teresa asks, "Whom do you answer to?" Dundee has no answer. (The first part of his statement marks an early hint about a quality of human nature
which Peckinpah will confront more directly in subsequent
films.) Dundee reaches out tentatively, asking Teresa if she
has ever thought about living in the United States, when he is
hit by the arrow. Finally, in Durango, when Teresa comes
upon Dundee with the Mexican girl, Dundee pleads that "the
war won't last forever"; to which Teresa replies, at this point
for everyone, "It will for you, Major." Dundee's relationship
with Teresa is much more than a mere romantic interlude.

Whatever the need for romance, Peckinpah recognizes the
need for comic relief. But moments of comedy come in relation to character, too. Lt. Graham is drawn in this way. For
most of the film, no one takes Graham seriously; Dundee
winces at the necessity of using him. But as the situation demands, Graham proves himself repeatedly. Graham uses the
"book" which Dundee purportedly goes by, and what at first
appears comic turns out to be right. When Dundee chastises
Graham for deserting his post to rescue him in Durango,
Graham corrects him, saying Dundee gave him a command,
not an order. Graham, despite his antics, is a professional.

Where Graham is the professional of inexperience, the
scout, Mr. Potts, is his counterpart, the professional of experience. Potts functions as a contrast to Dundee, and is the only
man whose judgment Dundee respects. In addition, Dundee
values Potts's opinion of himself. As Dundee is crippled emotionally, Potts is crippled physically, yet ironically he is a
stronger man than Dundee. Because of Dundee's respect,
Potts is the only man who can easily teach Dundee a lesson;
but because of his professionalism, Potts merely speaks his
own mind and lets Dundee make the inference. When Dundee tells Potts to have the murdered Indian scout Riago cut
down, Potts tells Dundee to do it himself, Dundee having
doubted the Indian's sincerity. As a professional, Potts tends
not to get involved outside the limits of his responsibility.

Tim Ryan, the bugler whose narration leads us through the
film, has a dual purpose. He is a contrived character who is
successfully interrelated with the others in the film, yet he
also functions as our witness, whose observation colors the
way we perceive Dundee. The entire film is framed by the

opening and closing of his journal. Narration as a technique is normally a risky cinematic device, but the narrative quality here forces the viewer to be distanced, a step removed from the action. This is important when one realizes that we are considering Dundee and his story *after* the "fact"; Ryan's diary reminds the viewer of dates and circumstances, altering our judgment away from an omniscient view or from a view entirely *within* the situation. Indeed, Ryan records directly at one point that he is "not fit to judge" the major. He also records, as the Civil War recedes for us in the background, that the war has faded for *the men*, as well. Finally, it is he who kills Charriba, an act of accidental revenge symmetry as he was the lone survivor of the Rostes massacre.

Peckinpah enriches his film with these and other characters, and in *Major Dundee*, as in his other works, there is a level of ensemble acting achieved which has his cast function as an integrated unit. This is a result in large part of Peckinpah's sympathy for his characters, involving an attitude of identification with *all* of his characters. His technique is exhausting as a director, but his actors respond to this sort of encouragement, receiving direction on and *off* the set. In *Ride the High Country*, Peckinpah had the actors playing the Hammond brothers stay apart from the rest of the cast, thinking of themselves as a unit. In *Major Dundee*, Charlton Heston lived in his uniform, spending hours in attitudes intentionally in keeping with his character; James Coburn, asking Peckinpah about his portrayal of Potts, says Peckinpah just told him to give "less," that the character was "drier" and simply "didn't care."[7] This sort of advice is especially vague intellectually, but it is exactly the sort of direction which has an actor respond *internally*, in the manner Peckinpah desires. There is a particular parallel between Peckinpah and the experience of the production, and the character of Dundee: both went through hell, but they *continued*, in spite of everything.

The effort toward behavioral ensemble acting is in keeping with Peckinpah's desire for a sense of visual realism. As in *Ride the High Country*, there is an abundance of detail which serves beyond set decoration. Dundee's cloak, his officer's great-coat, is a badge of office, which he alternately tries to fill and shrug off. His uniform becomes a symbol of the image he tries to justify. But he is most at ease without it, when he attempts to put aside the responsibility of position by taking the cloak off. Similarly, Peckinpah finds means to have his characters (and his actors) suggest through appearances what they are undergoing emotionally. By the time they are forced to fight the French, they have lost the distinctions of their different uniforms; they have lost their original identities and have come to be realized as a group, as they unite to defeat the French. As R. G. Armstrong describes the shooting of the final fight, "We all . . . looked like the wrath of God; I think Sam planned it that way!"[8] This grueling physical deterioration, as others have recognized, is a significant visual metaphor for what happens to Dundee and his command: in order to succeed in destroying the Apache (as well as in defeating the superior French force), Dundee and his men have become more like the savages they pursue. This technique also recalls the journey of Kit and Yellowleg in *The Deadly Companions*, where they come to resemble the Indians they're avoiding, breaking up the wagon to use a travois instead, etc.

If one considers everything in the discussion thus far as elements within the cinematic frame, Peckinpah's brilliance is further demonstrated by giving attention to the completion and selection of the frame itself.

The value of scenic realism, the irony of epic grandeur in a hostile environment, is of paramount importance to the execution of the film. Peckinpah is precise in his choice of locations and camera placement. Dundee and his command are at all times located as figures in their surroundings, often in longshot, minimizing their stature and accentuating their position. From the functional, relative comfort / security of Fort Benlin, the command moves through an increasingly forbidding landscape, a difficult, arid, desert terrain which humans enter at their own risk, and which because of its nature the Apache takes as a refuge. The terrain itself is another challenge to Major Dundee's authority, as he must assert himself and the command over the rigors of the territory. The Mexican village blooms in fiesta celebration over Dundee's one generous act, sharing the French garrison supplies. And the temporary oasis of the river camp, made cruel by the execution of O. W. Hadley, tempts Dundee into violating his own perimeter, literally and figuratively with Teresa, which he is punished for by the arrow from the ever-present Indian. As events signify, Dundee pays for letting his vigilance slip, at both the river camp and the earlier river-crossing ambush.

As the environment becomes a narrative presence, so does Peckinpah's composition. Dundee in particular is a character whose contradiction is elicited by his location in the frame. In the first half of the film, he is shot almost uniformly from below, increasing his stature in epic proportions beyond those mentioned in the previous discussion of *Ride the High Country*. In addition, Dundee's posture and costume suggest an angularity which increases the character's rugged dynamism and ambivalence of outlook: he never sits straight and tall in the saddle, his cap at an angle always opposite to the slope of his shoulders, as if he is imitating the craggy terrain behind him. Indeed, due to the angle of such shots, Dundee is a lone mountain against the sky.

Dundee's position in the frame is dictated by his relation to the rest of the scene. There is marked emotional contrast in shots which Dundee shares with another character: with Potts, he is often with him as an equal, in the same part of the frame; with Tyreen, the two are at opposite edges of the frame. Moreover, as the situations imply, Dundee appears more and more as the sole occupant of shots. At Hadley's death, he occupies the frame by himself, while Tyreen shares it with others of the command. As Dundee becomes isolated in the command, so does he become singled out by the camera.

This isolation is stressed similarly in other instances. At the prison in Fort Benlin, Dundee confronts the mass of Confederates "by himself," with several overhead views underscoring the tension between the mass and the solitary figure. As Dundee finishes his say, he moves to assert his authority further, by walking through the Confederates, who make a path despite their hatred. This is a curious test of pride on both sides, as if Dundee is daring them to strike him and they alternately are realizing that such action would only diminish themselves.

The composition of Dundee's first solitary moment with Teresa has a surreal quality, suggestive of Dali; the isolated ruin stands at an angle to the small, lonely image of Dundee with his back to us, the only elements in an otherwise featureless horizon. As the interior Dundee first tentatively surfaces, he and Teresa are framed by the ruin, somewhat symbolic of the incompleteness of the character and the encounter, which is broken off.

In another visually dramatic reference, Dundee stands alone at the rim of the canyon, gazing down upon the command enjoying themselves in a needed bath. Trapped by his position, Dundee is again the outsider, apart from the group literally and spiritually. Finally, at the river battle with the French, Dundee finds himself holding his bloodied sword and the flag, the colors of national pride and identity, and is at a momentary loss as to what to make of what he finds, save that indeed this image is what it all comes down to.

What *Major Dundee* is "about" is finally less an answer than an examination of the process one undergoes in looking for that answer, the complex, tangled web that an individual may weave in seeking self-knowledge. Dundee's pursuit of the Apache becomes an obsession which is finally a test of will and determinate resolve, through which Dundee hopes to define himself. If he learns anything, it is about the cost of the rigidity of his opinions. In a larger frame of reference, Dundee's command represents an aspect of the foundation of the United States as a national entity, a jumble of individuals at cross-purposes finally united by a shared experience against a common enemy. In human terms, there is grave doubt about the nature of the victory, except that the cost has been significant.

During the fiesta, Dundee sits on top of a wall prominently marked with the cheer "Viva Dundee." With the slogan in between them, Tyreen assesses Dundee as either a military genius (if successful) or a damned fool. His commentary is, "You haven't got the temperament to be a liberator, Amos," who replies, "I don't?" indicating the celebrating, liberated peasants. Perhaps there is the suggestion in Peckinpah's vision of a relevance to modern day generals such as Patton or Montgomery, both in part driven by ego. There *is* the indication that our history is often written by those who are driven as opposed to those who are secure. And we need to be aware of those drives, as they appear in all of us, in order to prepare for their consequences. Major Dundee is a dangerous, human character.

5

Noon Wine (1966) and *The Wild Bunch* (1969)

Noon Wine

BECAUSE OF ITS NATURE as a work for television, discussing "Noon Wine" may be seen as something of a digression in a study of Peckinpah's film work. Certainly, further investigation of his television work would be fruitful, if only to consider the precedents and development of Peckinpah as he learns his craft. Unfortunately, the scope of this study does not permit such exhaustive treatment.

But, coming as it does between major feature films, "Noon Wine" becomes an exception to the division between film and television (perhaps the division is artistically only an arbitrary one, anyway). It is, after all, the main piece of work which got him back into features, after the production debacles of *Major Dundee* and the aborted *Cincinnati Kid*, and it marks his first association with producer Dan Melnick as well as his first work with Jason Robards, composer Jerry Fielding, and editor Lou Lombardo—relationships which would prove to be of major significance in Peckinpah's following work.

At the same time, "Noon Wine" fills a gap in the development of Peckinpah's picture-making career, of thematic consistency with his concerns and of technical interest in the growth of his mastery over the visual media. Pointedly, it demonstrates Peckinpah as a craftsman in a production both written in adaptation and directed by him, but also with the wholehearted support of the original author. While it may be virtually impossible to pinpoint his motivations in doing the job (save for the fact that he needed it), it is probably safe to say that Peckinpah shows in "Noon Wine" that he can be faithful to another's conception, if he is in agreement with that

77

The Starbuck ambush and the final battle: "under the gun" (top), and "behind the gun" (bottom).

conception in the first place. It is perhaps an even more significant demonstration of his talent for brilliantly cutting a
"diamond in the rough" visually. As stated earlier, a committed professional like Peckinpah will try to make any project
his own, but his treatment of "Noon Wine" underscores his
professionalism to the extent of exemplifying the primacy of
the work itself. "Noon Wine" is remarkably and indisputably a
Peckinpah realization of a *story* by Katherine Anne Porter.
God bless Dan Melnick for offering it to the right director at a
critical time.

"Noon Wine" is set on a small South Texas farm at the turn
of the century. The farmer, Royal Earle Thompson, makes
enough to get by but never works the place to its potential,
never being sure that the routine chores and labors are fit for a
man like himself. He excuses himself in a number of ways,
including that his frail wife is for all practical purposes an in-
valid. He hires a withdrawn farmhand, Olaf Helton, under
whose quiet diligence the farm prospers. The title of the story
refers to the song that Helton plays on his harmonica constantly, a song about feeling so good in the morning you drink
up all the "likker" you were saving for the noon lay-off.

Years pass, until a Mr. Hatch appears one day looking for
Helton. Helton, it seems, is an asylum escapee, who had killed
his own brother over the loss of his harmonica. In defending
Helton from Hatch, Thompson accidentally kills Hatch; Helton runs away and is killed by a posse. Thompson, confused
about how he could come to do such a thing, though acquitted
of Hatch's killing by a jury, can't convince his neighbors of his
innocence; his wife, not an actual witness, can't live the lie
that would support her husband. When Thompson sees that
his sons think the worst of him as well, he leaves the house,
writes a note swearing his innocence before God, and blows
his head off.

As Katherine Anne Porter says, "There is nothing in any of
these beings tough enough to work the miracle of redemption
in them."[1] Elements of the story are clearly in line with major
Peckinpah themes: the ambiguity of the "truth," of apparent
"good and evil," and the morality which follows from that ambiguity, the inability of human beings to comprehend the manifestations of violence and the urge to be at peace or "right"
with the world, and the capability of violence in all people.

Both the story and the teleplay present an open-ended tragedy of the inability of individuals to come to terms with these ideas.

Peckinpah was completely faithful to the spirit and the letter of the original work. (Porter was so pleased by the teleplay that she would have been happy to have had Peckinpah film *Ship of Fools*.) A large part of the dialogue comes directly from the novel; but Peckinpah's craftsmanship and sensitivity as a writer / director are highlighted by his successful adaptation of descriptive and expository passages of the story into teleplay visuals and dialogue. The "blossoming" of the farm under Helton's stewardship and the struggle of Thompson to convince his neighbors of his innocence are two examples of Peckinpah's using a combination of visual and sound montage to capture the spirit of the original. This technique of exposition is in line with a development through *Ride the High Country* and *Major Dundee* to *The Wild Bunch* and *Cable Hogue*, in which Peckinpah uses the technique with increasing insight and excellence, until the special value of its use becomes evident in *Cable Hogue*.

There is another "alteration" worth mentioning, in that the story ends with Thompson's suicide, but the teleplay has one additional "shot": the camera cuts from an exterior of the farmhouse over which is heard the report of the shotgun, to a last shot of Mrs. Thompson in an expression of anxious uncertainty. The shot, of the woman's head to the left of the frame and the rest in total darkness, devoid of background, recalls a similar shot in *The Deadly Companions*, where Kit rides out of town and Yellowleg is left staring after her, uncertain of his feelings. In "Noon Wine," it reiterates the tragic nature of Thompson's anguish by "bringing it back" to the survivor.

Peckinpah also expertly combined the use of film and videotape in the production. (The filming was a particular matter of conviction, as union and financial restrictions made it necessary to accomplish it on the sly.) The film pieces brilliantly match the tape sections in an overall excellent color quality; it should be noted that in 1966 this achievement would not be as taken for granted as it might be today. The production was done on location and was rehearsed intensively as if it were a live television show. The amount of rehearsal shows in the virtually flawless performances of all of the cast, a cast which Peckinpah helped to choose and which includes his "stock company" friends Ben Johnson and L. Q. Jones. In particular, Jason Robards's performance demonstrates remarkable depth; if he is famous for his O'Neill interpretations, he deserves equal praise for his portrayal of Royal Earle Thompson. And with Peckinpah, it indeed led to his performance as Cable Hogue.

Once again, as in all of Peckinpah's work, the attention to realistic detail and to every aspect of production is of subtle yet immeasurable importance to the success of the work. One rarely expects in a television production such completeness of physical detail from the variety of farm implements to the dirt on the costumes. An excellent example of Peckinpah's total involvement in this regard can be found in the soundtrack. Jerry Fielding's carefully crafted score incorporates the harmonica motif of the narrative, but Peckinpah also went after sound details which would enhance the visuals: the creaking of the butter churn, the water dripping in the cooling shed, the sounds of buckboards and horses, the killing blow to Helton and his chilling scream, and the final explosive report of the shotgun as Thompson kills himself. To give more direct power to the axe-killing of Hatch (in the head), Peckinpah used the sound of a watermelon being split open by such a blow; but he cut the scene visually from the *beginning* of Thompson's swing to Mrs. Thompson's reaction to the sound, which was used as a bridge exactly at the visual cut. Thus the moment is dramatized without actually seeing the blow, a fact important to the problem that develops over Thompson's innocence or guilt in the killing.

Perhaps the principal significance of "Noon Wine" in relation to Peckinpah's films is the reminder it offers of a quality of sympathy for and sensitivity to people and their internal predicament which consistently informs Peckinpah's work, even at its most apparently violent. The signal aspect of violence in Peckinpah's films is that it is a part of life that we ignore at our peril. This idea is perhaps most visible in *Straw Dogs*, but the important idea to remember, which underlies *everything* of Peckinpah's, is this primary sensitivity to the complexities of human behavior. Peckinpah is not famous for his sentimentality – at times even he seems to be embarrassed by it – but it underlies all of his work and is the key element in understanding his use of, depiction of, and concern with violence. It is a testament to his cinematic skill that violence in his films can be so overpowering—an impact increased by his editing style—that it is easy to account for the variety of misinterpretations based on this one aspect of his work. But a misreading of Peckinpah is guaranteed without an appreciation of his sympathy for human beings as the generative influence on all of his attitudes.

The Wild Bunch

"When you side with a man you stay with him, and if you can't do that, you're like some animal; you're finished—we're finished—*all* of us."

There was a sense among the participants during the making of *The Wild Bunch* that they were making something important, that they were on to something significant. It was and is hard to put into words, which is finally how it should be with a great film, a film of emotional power that is ultimately fulfilled by interaction with its audience. That it has provoked a variety of strong reactions, pro and con, is a testament to its depth of impact. *The Wild Bunch* is, indeed, a film experience.

There are those who would prefer more "clarity" in intellectual film statements, but *The Wild Bunch* would not be as complex in its ability to challenge an audience were it not for the fact that Peckinpah does not "intellectualize" consciously in his films. It is an important factor of the vitality of his films that Peckinpah's cinematic sense is an intuitive achievement, a quality insufficient for greatness by itself, but a prerequisite without which a filmmaker cannot be "great." To the more cynical, the inability to "explain" one's work may give rise to suspicion, but the films finally speak for themselves. The problem is that we don't always understand the language, or appreciate the limits of our "literal" understanding of what's happening on the screen. We may think more in visual terms today, but we are a long way yet from sharing identically received images, especially since we are reluctant to acknowledge that we "see" differently the "same" things.

If this is a bit of a tease, so is *The Wild Bunch*. After one is "through" with the film, there is the fear that more may have been going on than one realizes; and days afterward one may perceive something else in one's reaction to the film. *The Wild Bunch*, at the very least, is overwhelming; and yes, you should question yourself and your sensitivity if you are *not* overwhelmed in some way by it.

What begins as "a simple adventure story" according to an open-ended Peckinpah description,[2] becomes first, as most good stories are, a story about people. But the people that we are primarily engaged with are criminals. There is never any equivocation about this—the "Bunch" are thieves and killers. We are seized by Pike's early declaration at the end of the opening credits: "If they move, kill 'em." Crazy Lee asks in the same scene if he should "kill 'em now" or wait; Freddy "did his share of killin' and more"; wanted posters proclaim their crimes. However, as "antisocial" as they are, they are human beings, not animals; they respond as human beings in ways which testify to basic possibilities found in all of human nature. It is an evasion of the issue, Peckinpah implies—indeed, wishful thinking—to regard them as less than human. Casting William Holden as their leader makes it all the more challenging: it is "easy" to side with William Holden.

This is important to keep in mind, for most of *The Wild Bunch* is seen from the "outlaws' " point of view. It has led to the film's being described as an "anti-Western" in a traditional sense. While in some ways it is, the film is not quite "anti" anything. Peckinpah points resolutely in certain directions, but the ultimate moral judgment is in the hands of the viewer, as it is in most of Peckinpah's films. The most "realistic" thing about the film is that the question as presented is not an easy one to decide. And if we are too quick to judge, we will only wind up "condemning" ourselves.

As *Ride the High Country* is a "last Western" about "good men," *The Wild Bunch* is a "last Western" about "bad men." Wanted for murder and train robbery (at least), the Bunch finds that the country is running out of room and finally out of tolerance for their way of life. "We gotta start thinkin' beyond our guns; those days are closin' fast," Pike says as they assay the results of the Starbuck ambush. It is circa 1913; and while civilization has a World War brewing, the frontier and the freedom it allowed the bandit are narrowing rapidly. The Starbuck job was to have been the Bunch's last; but their way of life does not permit them the insight to read the writing on the wall, so that they must look to the possibility of one more "last" score. What develops is a case of running out of room physically and emotionally, at the same time.

For the members of the Bunch are not intelligent men; it is presumptuous to expect any *conscious* eloquence from them, as it is to expect them to recognize the futility or the immorality of their occupation. That Dutch differentiates between themselves and Mapache is ironic, when he says in defense of the Bunch, "We don't *hang* nobody," *even* if the distinction is important from their point of view. (And it does become that: the idea that Mapache is worse is a prime factor in allowing the viewer to be caught up in the final shoot-out on the Bunch's side.) But limited as they are intellectually, the Bunch does respond to certain ethical ideas on a personal level. Pike and Dutch in particular try to make some sense out of their attitudes, to bring some ideas of principles into their understanding of how life should be lived. There is evident the idea of a "code" of loyalty, honor, and of the ethical responsibilities of friendship; it is equally apparent that the understanding is limited, but the basic response is there.

Pike holds the group together with various "appeals" to solidarity, mainly based on an idea of loyalty. It is, though, only a very tenuous hold. When Tector and Lyle dispute the sharing of the Starbuck spoils (in an argument based on "fairness"), Pike asserts the necessity of leadership: "All I know is I either lead this bunch or I end it right now." Solidarity was already threatened when Pike shot Buck on the trail, to put him out of his misery—made necessary by Buck's realization that he would hinder the group in not keeping up because of his wounds. When Freddy's horse stumbles in the sand, forcing them all to tumble down the dune, Tector is ready to kill Freddy and is stopped by Pike's rebuke: "We're gonna stick together just like it used to be; when you side with a man you stay with him, and if you can't do that, you're like some animal; you're finished—we're finished—*all* of us." Strained as the group's solidarity may be, by staying together they do attain a measure of respect, ours and their own, out of that appeal to principle. Pike's repeated order, "Let's go," achieves a significance when finally it is that idea that is all they have left.

In a way, the men of the "Wild Bunch" are a "sophisticated" version of the Hammond brothers of *Ride the High Country*. The Hammonds' final move is a response to "family honor"; Pike and Dutch have a bit more insight and experience, but not that much—while the Gorch brothers are first cousins to the Hammonds (including one of the same actors).

It is likewise the Bunch's attention (in the ethical leadership of Pike and Dutch) to a "code" of loyalty that is its final undoing. It is Pike's failure and his betrayal of his friendship with Deke Thornton that prevents him from allowing a confrontation with Thornton; Thornton is a constant shadow over Pike, a reminder of conscience, as it was Pike's fault that Deke was caught and is now forced to chase them. Similarly, it is the feelings of conscience they have with regard to Angel's capture that make the final shoot-out necessary, even as it seems to be the only thing left to do.

There is also a new wrinkle in the notion of the importance of giving one's word, a matter of integrity for Peckinpah that is significant with both "good" and "bad" men. In *Ride the High Country*, Steve relies on Heck's word that he will return his gun after the shooting, and Gil's violation of his word to Steve is the act of betrayal Steve is hurt by; in *Major Dundee*, Dundee taunts and tests Tyreen's honor by forcing Tyreen to live up to his word in serving Dundee's command; and Pike defends Deke's position in that Deke "gave his word." But Dutch provides the wrinkle, pointing out that Thornton gave his word to a railroad; Pike insists that, nonetheless, "it's his word," while Dutch demands, "That ain't what counts—it's who you give it *to*!" Pike cannot respond further, caught in the contradiction of their own idea of loyalty applied outside their personal frame of reference.

But again, the Bunch are not "smart" men. William Holden's face may look insightful, but his expression is really a question mark, as Pike wrestles with the resolution of his life. He hints at a key understanding when talking about the railroad's pursuit of them, personified by Harrigan, and indirectly about himself, with Dutch. "A hell of a lot of people just can't stand to be wrong." Dutch answers that this comes from pride.

Pike continues: "And they can't forget it—that pride—being wrong; or *learn* by it." This is a matter of Pike's own conscience, for we see in the immediately preceding flashback that it was Pike's pride in being right that resulted in Deke's capture. In the flashback, Deke is concerned about their safety, but Pike tells him not to worry. Deke asks, "How can you be so damn sure?" to which Pike responds, "Damn sure is my business." As Pike's line echoes, Deke is caught and Pike escapes. But, continuing their conversation, Dutch asks, referring to the Starbuck ambush, "How about us, Pike; d'you reckon we learned, being wrong, today?" Pike doesn't know himself well enough for that: "I sure hope to God we did."

In fact, Pike hasn't learned, and his being wrong precipitates their problems all along. As his being wrong got Deke into trouble, he is wrong about Starbuck, walking into the ambush; he is wrong about letting Angel take some guns, thinking it won't be discovered; he is wrong thinking they have gotten rid of Deke's pursuit on the trail. Pike has not been able to reconcile himself to his mistakes, even as he tells Angel, anguished over his woman's going to Mapache, "Either you learn to live with it or we leave you here." Angel doesn't learn to live with it, and neither does Pike until the very end. In a sense, Pike is constantly running away from a confrontation with Deke, who has become a symbol of Pike's conscience and fallibility. This in part also leads to Pike's final resignation.

What is finally the only thing to take pride in is the group's honor in "playing their string right out to the end," accepting the consequences of whatever actions they take. They respect Angel for doing so; Tector and Lyle respond to it, in loyalty to this idea as well as to the notion that they owe it to Angel. Indeed, Lyle's response of "Why not?" to Pike's last "Let's go" is less a matter of understanding that there is nothing else than it is a reaction to an idea of what's right. Lyle's response is to Pike's leadership; he is accidentally right on the larger issue. Dutch likewise knows that they have to go to Angel, if only to "play their string out," whatever the end; only Pike realizes intuitively that, in fact, this *is* the end. It is perhaps this pride that is all they ever had: Pike and Dutch acknowledge that the "last job" won't be easy, but Pike asserts, "I wouldn't have it any other way," and Dutch agrees. It takes

The final "Let's go."

A contrast in serenity: The farewell at Angel's village.

toughness to play your string out (especially when you're wrong), and there is the feeling in *The Wild Bunch* that, at least, this *is* something. Peckinpah similarly makes films *his* way, which may not be the easiest way, but he "plays his string out"; he, too, "wouldn't have it any other way."

The limitations and quality of the men and their relationships set up the opportunities for consideration of "larger issues" that the film involves, primarily that of the question of violence. For the members of the Wild Bunch, who have lived by their guns, violence is a fact of life. It is precisely this that dictates that the violence of the film be so ugly. The onus of the violence is critical, for the problem Peckinpah poses is that, despite the blood they spill, they are still men (and please, nothing so simplistic as the "macho" connotation that they are manly *because* of the blood they spill, but that even as they are criminals they are human beings). If we sympathize with Pike and the Bunch at all, which the film tempts us to do by seeing things from their side, we set ourselves up for the debacle of the final slaughter: we cheer Pike and Dutch in the end, and then find ourselves ashamed of it. It is Peckinpah's thesis that, as violence is a part of all of us, such capacity lies within all humans and we must recognize and be made conscious of the face of violence; it is important for human beings to "understand" violence if we are to know ourselves. If you reject the violence and the film entirely, you may also be quick to judge others as well; for Peckinpah, such rejection is a lie, albeit a common one, which flies in the face of his idea of an aspect of human nature common to all. Witness the vituperation and almost *physical* violence Peckinpah was subjected to over the film's bloodbath by some critics! Those who worry about the effects of such (screen) violence on *others* might be better off examining the effects it has on themselves.

But when one does acknowledge the violence, and is caught cheering the Wild Bunch, one finds an idea similar to one found later in Stanley Kubrick's *A Clockwork Orange* (1971), wherein the end of the film is a slap of recognition to the viewer who has sympathized with the "villain," Alex. Peckinpah says likewise in *The Wild Bunch* that people must wake up to this aspect of themselves—and the idea becomes central in *Straw Dogs*, where the resulting confusion in the film's reception grows out of similar circumstances. "Liking" screen violence in this sense doesn't make one a "bad person," but it does point out that certain circumstances can lead to an idea of justifiable cause, based on the realization of the capacity for violence in all of us. Abhorring violence is not enough; we must recognize that the enemy is within, and understand how that capacity for violence works and shows itself. Eventually, it lays bare the real threat of war as a practical inevitability of human nature.

At the same time, the violence in the Wild Bunch is intended as a cathartic, not simply as a purge but also to facilitate the realization of the foregoing idea about human nature through emotional impact. This intention necessitates an overwhelming depiction of violence, especially since this is a film: the audience is automatically distanced from the events. As Roger Ebert, writing for the *Chicago Sun-Times*, points out, "Realism is not the same thing as reality."[3] It is precisely to the point that the viewer is not spared the bloodiness of "realistic" death. And, while the increased blood is of "realistic" import, the members of the Wild Bunch do not kill people, they kill a *crowd*. Any possibility of sympathy for the victims of the bloodbath is consistently undermined throughout the film, from Mapache to his anonymous soldiers. By contrast, the opening massacre in Starbuck is inflicted mainly by the forces of "law and order," with the idea that "power corrupts just as much as lawlessness":[4] the civilian victims are in the same position as the Bunch. The opening is the introduction to the ugly chaos of violence; the ending is the exploration of the infliction of that violence. As viewers, we are placed first *under*, then *behind*, the gun. Finally, Peckinpah's technique is applied in order to engage the viewer as much as possible. "I hate an audience that just sits there," he has said.[5]

Audience response is also set up by the fact that the film is predicated on a traditional sympathy for the Western outlaw. Though we are told and reminded of the Bunch's criminal record, its members are seen in the film primarily as bank or train robbers—and when did a railroad or a bank ever get our sympathy as a victim? The Bunch does not rob *people*, and the tradition, in line with Jesse James and any other Robin Hood notion of outlawry, invites our tendency to romanticize and side with the outlaw. *The Wild Bunch*, however, realistically defies that tradition, even as it plays upon it.

It is important to acknowledge, in this film as in other Peck-inpah films, the differences in the released version and the "director's cut." The film was cut at several different points, resulting in its being reviewed at various running times. The original-release running time of 148 minutes was cut eventually to 135 minutes, and while the 148-minute version involved some cuts from *longer* versions that Peckinpah would sooner have left in, it is for all practical purposes, definitive. This discussion is keyed to this version. The differences between the 148-minute version and the widely released 135-minute version are critical, however, and they include: 1) the flashback of Deke's capture (the technique of which was also compromised by Warner Brothers), which explains Pike's relationship to Thornton, coming during the campfire conversation between Pike and Dutch, as well as the lines previously referred to about the pride of "being right"; 2) a sequence on the trail between Pike and Freddy, where it is revealed that Crazy Lee was Freddy's grandson, a further jolt to Pike's conscience as Crazy Lee was left behind in Starbuck, and some discussion with regard to Deke, about the nature of loyalty and how things used to be; 3) part of the fiesta at Angel's village where the outlaws are seen enjoying themselves, including Freddy cutting in on Dutch dancing; 4) a flashback scene as they ride to rob the train, where Pike explains how he got the scar on his thigh, when he was with a woman he might have married and they were interrupted by her husband, who shot her and wounded Pike, and got away; 5) a scene where Mapache is attacked by Villa, at a village railroad station—this scene is important for it is the only instance of some redemptive quality in Mapache, in that Mapache responds to the admiration of a little messenger boy and, in the boy's eyes, acts the part of the courageous leader, walking calmly in retreat while his men are panicking around him (the significance of the messenger boy's admiration is increased later, as it is another boy who might as well be the messenger's little twin brother who shoots Pike—the fatal blow—in the end); and 6) a short cut where Mapache acknowledges his losses in men, either because of their lack of good weapons or because of their enemies' possession of good rifles—it is not entirely clear which. If the latter, it may be an initial tip-off to Mapache that some of the guns intended for him have been stolen; in any case, the scene occurs before any of the guns are received from the Bunch. As usual with scenes cut from "Peckinpah's version," the film suffers without them and the potential character insight most of them provide.

A great deal of the film's power is achieved by the evidence of the dedication involved in its production. As Warren Oates says: "Commitment, that's what made *Wild Bunch*. People who were able to commit themselves to what they were doing because they were proud of their craft."[6] This is echoed by others involved in the film, and applies especially to Peckinpah. *The Wild Bunch* is complete evidence of Peckinpah's strength as a "total filmmaker" and underscores his need for associates similarly inclined.

Clearly visible in *The Wild Bunch* is Peckinpah's involvement in every aspect of production, and while he depends on the expertise and suggestions of his employees, his is the supervisory umbrella which encompasses the whole. The elements which contribute to *The Wild Bunch* come from a variety of sources: Lucien Ballard's photography, the stalwart assistance of editor Lou Lombardo, the music of Jerry Fielding (points of which Fielding had to argue over heatedly with Peckinpah), and the inestimable efforts of the cast and many others of the crew.

Yet Peckinpah's openness to "outside" influence and inspiration is illustrated by an episode during preproduction with Emilio Fernandez. Fernandez, an award-winning Mexican film director himself, who had helped Peckinpah with the Mexican production unit on *Major Dundee*, was already cast as General Mapache when Peckinpah visited him to discuss the script and further Mexican casting for the film. As Peckinpah relates the story, they were talking about the film when Don Emilio said, "You know, the Wild Bunch, when they go into that town like that, are like when I was a child and we would take a scorpion and drop it on an anthill ... the ants would attack the scorpion. . . ." Peckinpah reacted to the idea with excitement, rewriting immediately to incorporate the idea, such that he stood up his dinner-date (by some accounts his fiancée) later that evening.[7] The idea provided a striking visual metaphor which surrounds the opening ambush in Starbuck.

This is but one example of Peckinpah's characteristic attention to detail, the hundreds of small things that complete the
frame: the "ring" to the dialogue, the contrasts of terrain and
location with respect to the characters (e.g., the verdure of the
respite in Angel's village), the pain in Pike's leg as he falls
with a broken stirrup, Mapache's automobile, the Gorch
brothers' romp in the wine cellar, the look of anticipation in
T.C.'s eyes before the Starbuck slaughter and the way Coffer
kisses his rifle muzzle, Thornton's helpless disgust with the
green army recruits and his bounty hunters, and the shot of the
Mexican woman with a bandolier across her chest as she
breast-feeds her baby. All of these items testify to the back-
breaking commitment made to the film by its makers and en-
rich the film in countless subtle ways, until the "rightness" of
one element blends into the "rightness" of another, producing
a whole experience greater than the sum of its parts.

A few other things will also bear witness here, as they relate
particularly to Peckinpah's other films. One is found in the
structure of the film, a plot which physically develops linearly
but which emotionally develops in a symmetrical, circular
fashion. Briefly, this involves—as previously mentioned—being under the gun in the beginning (the Bunch and
the audience) and being behind the gun at the end. For the
Bunch, this is important because it underlines the ending as a
matter of choice, a choice which was taken away from the
Bunch in the beginning. The fact that the consequences in
both the beginning and the end are objectively disastrous is
not the point, for violence is the outlaws' way of life. The significance for the bunch is that the members make the decision
to take the stand at the end, committing themselves to "playing out their string" in a way which gives their last play some
meaning *for them*. This is further illustrated by another
change Peckinpah made in production. Originally, the shoot-
out was to have begun with the deaths of Angel and Mapache
and continue until the Bunch was killed. But Peckinpah altered the shoot-out to contain a pause after Pike kills Mapache.
As the members of the Bunch regard each other and the soldiers in that tense "freeze," Pike and Dutch (with the Gorches
to a slightly lesser extent) realize that *they've done it*, that matters are in their hands, and this has become a fitting place to

die. It is a moment of vindicated "professionalism." It is this moment of taking the offensive and making their own choice which causes Dutch to giggle with glee as Pike pivots and chooses the German officer as his first target. They know they're out-numbered and that they probably won't get out, but this is not suicide; instead, they have made their play and if it comes to that, well, "by doggies," they'll have picked the spot. This is why there is a sense of loss at their deaths; in the moral confusion of the set-up, they have yet performed "heroically" in playing their string out, to the end. As Pike chooses for the others to make the walk back for Angel, it is his realization that this is indeed the only thing left, even as he stares at the "whore" in an exchange of might-have-beens. He does learn something, just before it is too late, accepting everything in making the choice. Deke Thornton understands this; he takes as his souvenir of his friend the token object that symbolizes Pike's choice, his gun. He lived by it, and died by it. The circular emotional structure of this idea may seem minor here, but it is an aspect which recurs in other Peckinpah films, wherein an individual is initially confronted with a problem that is resolved at the end. (It is also plainly an aspect of good storytelling.)

Another common aspect of Peckinpah's film structure seen in *The Wild Bunch* is the conflict between appearance and reality. In the opening of the film, the Bunch appears as a group of soldiers, helping a lady with her packages, but by the end of the credits they are revealed as robbers. Remembering the Indian stagecoach "attack" in *The Deadly Companions*, and the tranquil scene of the Knudsen farm before the Hammonds are revealed there in *Ride the High Country*, (as well as looking forward to the opening shots of *The Getaway*), other examples of this visual conflict can be found in Peckinpah's work, the result of which is that, indeed, things are not always what they seem; one must be wary of quick judgments.

Comedy, which plays an important part in Peckinpah's films, figures significantly in *The Wild Bunch*. Comic moments are developed to be consistent with the nature of the situation and charcters, however; the comedy found in *Major Dundee*, in the humorously under-rated Lt. Graham, for instance, is different from the shared fraternal comedy of *The Wild Bunch*. Laughter within the bunch lends a humanizing, warming effect to the characters, especially in the by-play at Lyle's expense, which is endearing though appropriately crude in context.

This sympathy of humor extends through the idea expressed by the old Mexican, Don Jose, in Angel's village. As Lyle and Tector play like children, Pike laughs and says that he finds their behavior hard to believe. But Don Jose observes that it's not hard to believe: "We all dream of being a child again; even the worst of us—perhaps, the worst most of all." This is a bridge to an idea with larger implications. In childhood lies innocence for Peckinpah; children are the omnipresent innocent observers in his films of an often chaotic, insensitive adult world. This innocence is not equated with goodness, though; children are also cruel, as the treatment of the scorpion and the ants illustrates. But their cruelty (again, the capacity for violence we are born with) is not accompanied by morality. Peckinpah states: "I believe in the complete innocence of children. They have no idea of good and evil. It's an acquired taste."[8] In acquiring that taste, they observe everything neutrally, allowing them to make rather incongruous comments in their mimicking of adult behavior, such as imitating the shooting after the Starbuck massacre, with no remorse for the victims (which the law-and-order perpetrators likewise do not show), and playing on the gallows in *Pat Garrett and Billy the Kid*, things which are incongruous to *adult* eyes. That children do acquire adult tastes is also seen: one can recall the taunting of Kit Tildon's outcast son in *The Deadly Companions*, an ostracism acquired from the children's parents, and another example in "Noon Wine" where Thompson's sons reject their father as his neighbors and wife do. And again in all innocence, Henry Niles, as an adult child in *Straw Dogs*, is helpless to understand what he has done in his accidental murder of Janice Hedden. Children, in Peckinpah's films, are constantly on the perimeter, watching. It is finally to them that we must explain the world; and we must know ourselves, if the children are to grow up any the wiser from that explanation. It is a child imitating adults who kills Pike.

I would mention one other minor reference to an earlier film here, in that it succinctly illustrates Peckinpah's concern with realism in context. As the bounty hunters move out with

the bodies of the Bunch, Coffer acknowledges that they'd better get moving as the corpses will soon "go ripe" on them.
With that, Peckinpah corrects the nagging flaw of seven years
earlier in *The Deadly Companions*, which had a corpse that
didn't "go ripe."

Something of Peckinpah's camera technique in *The Wild
Bunch* is especially worth noting, for rarely can a filmmaker
use a combination of telephoto and "zoom" shots which call as
little attention to themselves as they do here. Their significant
use without interrupting the film testifies to Peckinpah's talent (and Ballard's) in employing the devices successfully.
One particular example: when Thornton tells the bounty hunters that Freddy may be up in the rocks pointing a rifle at
them, the camera jumps as they do, zooming into the rocks,
frenetically searching for the unseen Freddy, and zooming out
again. The camera device is so well tied to the bounty hunters'
fear that it is hardly noticed as such.

But the supreme achievement of Peckinpah's technique in
The Wild Bunch is found in the editing, in a complete mastery
of the effects of flash-cuts, slow-motion, integrated progres-
sion of simultaneous detail, and visual pace. It is said that, at
least at the time it was made, *The Wild Bunch* had more
"edits" than any other film in studio history. Whatever the record is, each "edit" in the film was done with a purpose. The
opening credit sequence alone is an excellent example of how
to build a scene in the cutting, establishing for recognition
every element of the shoot-out about to take place, and recapitulating those elements in shorter cuts as the scene builds,
just before the chaos erupts. (It is also characteristic of Peckinpah in his choice of title-card placement, especially the location and visual accompaniment for the director's credit title;
his own credit titles, if traced throughout his films, are consistent with each film while functioning as somewhat oblique
personal symbols.) The editing of the train-robbery sequence
is an equally integrated, detailed example of narrative, a long
scene with no "dialogue" at all until Thornton (!) says, "Let's
go."

Throughout the film, Peckinpah's "editing style" is evident
in the pacing of the film keyed to emotions rather than to physical events. In this sense, Peckinpah is closer stylistically to
someone such as Hitchcock as opposed to "physically keyed"

directors like Howard Hawks or Raoul Walsh. There is a lot of brooding in *The Wild Bunch*, and the longer moments, such as Pike riding away from the group after the fall down the sand dune, are carried out through longer "cuts." By the same token, moments of tension are achieved by short takes, exemplified both in the prelude to the Starbuck shooting and in the train robbery—especially in the moment where Pike backs the train up so Angel can uncouple the cars.

What has seemed to many to be a cliché device is really only a cliché in the hands of others. Peckinpah's use of slow-motion is of several types, but primarily it is used in conjunction with "real time" or normal speed shots to achieve the impression of simultaneity of actions. For example, in the Starbuck shootout, the shooting of the outlaw who goes through the store window in slow-motion is broken up into six fragments intercut with nine *other* shots from the beginning of the action until the end of the fall. This temporal extension of the single action allows for the viewer's following of other action happening at the same time. This tends to put the viewer in the middle of the action, and affords the temporal disjunction found in moments of chaos. A secondary effect of this editing, which allows the viewer to separate his attention visually through alternate camera speeds, is that it also allows for *aesthetic* concentration that would not otherwise be perceived without the loss of simultaneity. The viewer, thus engaged in concentrating on "simultaneous" information, sees *more* than he would if the actions were not broken up. The illusion attained of more visual information, coupled with the physical demands of changing speeds, heightens the impact of the scene emotionally. There is actually more blood in several scenes in *Major Dundee* (although a lot of violence was cut from it), but the impact of the violence in this opening shootout of *The Wild Bunch* is far more severe. And this impact is achieved, as elsewhere, through the editing. Peckinpah also uses slow-motion by itself, but its use is again dictated by its function to the needs of the scene, if the scene emotionally allows for the "stoppage" or distortion of time. Peckinpah "never" uses slow-motion *solely* as an aesthetic device. Nor is slow-motion necessarily unrealistic; it can be observed that some tense seconds in real life seem longer than others.

Peckinpah's editing style draws directly from his experience in the hands of Frank Santillo on *Ride the High Country*, in the lessons learned about montage (the "third" shot created by the juxtaposition of two shots) and flash-cuts less than a second in duration. That Lou Lombardo shared this expertise is also apparent in *The Wild Bunch*. It is a technique of editing that will carry through brilliantly in Peckinpah's later films, and an important fact of his filmmaking methods to remember with all of his work, especially in those films which he does not have "final cut" with. Peckinpah's shooting ratio (film shot to film used) is very high, sometimes as much as 20:1 or more. While this tends to lengthen shooting schedules and put films "over budget," it is his method to finally "make" the film with the editing. As a result, if someone not in agreement with Peckinpah's conception supervises the editing, a lot of balance and emphasis can be thrown off, damaging the work, as can be seen to some extent in *Cross of Iron* and *Convoy* and disastrously in *Pat Garrett and Billy the Kid*. (This is another reason why reedited television versions, especially of Peckinpah's films, are mainly worthless.) The partial saving grace on Peckinpah's films is that, because of the attention he gives to the shooting, almost everything printed is of good quality. Consequently, even in the hands of others, Peckinpah's films can be damaged but not totally destroyed. Witness *Major Dundee*, for example.

The last step in Peckinpah's filmmaking process has to do with sound. Peckinpah went so far on *The Wild Bunch* that after a major preview he redubbed the sound-effects track from scratch.[9] But credit must also be given here to the efforts of Jerry Fielding in constructing a music score completely in line with and enriching the film totally. It is the sort of element which bears little explanation in place of the hearing of it, but the quality of which, keyed as it is to the edited emotional pace of the film, is finally essential to the film's experience. It is, after all, one of the elements which makes *The Wild Bunch* a *movie*. Films don't have to have music, but music can help set an emotional tone of approach, and where music *is* used, it has to be in keeping with the spirit of the work, as the score for *The Wild Bunch* certainly is. In particular, the music accompanying the Bunch's walk to the final shoot-out is a curious blend of contrast between the Mexican song and the march drum-roll underneath, lending a romantic air of

The walk to the plaza: "playing their string out to the end."

spiritual conviction to the "rightness" of the group's decision to make the walk.

This consideration of *The Wild Bunch* is perhaps only the tip of the iceberg. Individual assessments of the film rely ultimately on one's view of human nature; we have seen something of Peckinpah's view. The film is a masterful work; even allowing for skepticism, it is at the very least a landmark Western, and that is hardly a small achievement for an American film. *The Wild Bunch* is in that sense a complete confrontation between form and audience. Peckinpah has stated that "the Western is a universal frame within which it is possible to comment on today."[10] The film does rely on the Western frame for identification (recognition), but the "comment on today" may also be a function of the viewer. Some have seen relevance to the Vietnam situation in the film, but I suspect this is a result of the film's coming out when it did and the topic's being of such immediate concern to its audience. In retrospect, *Major Dundee* seems to have more potential relevance to Vietnam, as a mission that backfired which we were lucky to get out of when we did. Pike's choice of the German as a target may be taken to have some political significance, but finally the German is only Pike's first target in the Bunch's final self-assertion. Scenes which might have attempted to show the fallibility of *both* sides of the revolution are not in the film. Peckinpah is not interested in direct political comment, in any event. His idea in *The Wild Bunch* is finally one about human nature. It is not cynical, either; it's just that we ought to wake up to certain facts.

6

The Ballad of Cable Hogue (1970)

"IT'S CABLE HOGUE talkin' . . . Hogue . . . me . . . Cable Hogue . . . Hogue . . . me . . . me . . . I did it . . . Cable Hogue . . . I found it . . . me. . . ."

The Ballad of Cable Hogue is the film Peckinpah should be remembered for personally. Without arguing whether one film of Peckinpah's has more "depth" than another, *The Ballad of Cable Hogue* comes closest to being a full, personal statement. If the relatively open-ended conclusion of the film seems at first superficially vague, consider that it is the eloquence of its inconclusion which gives the film such poignance. "He wasn't really a good man; he wasn't a bad man," says the Rev. Joshua Sloane in his funeral sermon for Cable. "But Lord, he was a *man!*" Cable Hogue is the indomitable spirit of the human being.

Cable is the potential in all people, the assertiveness of the species, which won't "lay down," and sometimes gets into trouble for that stubbornness. He exhibits a range of emotions—love, hate, tenderness, shame, jealousy, pride, humor at life's ironies—not because he is unique, but because he is a complete human being, a character drawn with the depth of humanity.

Outwardly, though, he is a loser, and at the beginning of the film is reduced further, until he is absolutely alone in a barren desert. The situation is between Cable and God. As his pride and spirit wear thin in his wanderings in the desert, Cable at first "jokes" about receiving help, calling for it tentatively: "Gettin' a little thirsty . . . just thought I'd mention it. Amen." Finding the simple request insufficient, Cable next tries sincerely to make a deal with the Lord: "Send me a drop or two . . . and I won't do it no more . . . whatever it is I done." But the

101

Jason Robards as Cable Hogue.

Lord doesn't make deals, and Cable next *argues* with the Lord, telling Him he has suffered enough, that the Lord "ought to try going dry for a spell." Cable, near total exhaustion, yet has the spirit to *remind* the Lord that if he doesn't get water soon, he won't have the *chance* to repent. In his last defiance, he *warns* the Lord that he is about to get *angry*, but finally submits, giving himself over wholly to God: "Lord—you call it; I'm just plain done in. Amen." And in that moment of surrender, God gives Cable another chance. God will forgive human pride, up to certain limits. But Cable, egocentric human being that he is, is not about to share credit for the discovery of water, and the human spirit reasserts itself. Cable proclaims his identity, the one thing he has "alive again," and says that he alone found the water. "He found it where it wasn't" becomes Cable's pride, his motto, and finally his epitaph. An outwardly apparent loser, Cable finds and asserts life, in the desert and in himself, apparently where it wasn't.

But God will only forgive pride within certain limits. "Revenge is mine, sayeth the Lord," and as Cable in his pride pursues his own revenge, God extracts the payment for that pride with Cable's life. He gives Cable an opportunity, though, in the love and promise of Hildy, to reject his revenge and leave the desert with her. As Hogue stays to take his revenge, and doesn't leave when he has the chance, so he is denied a second chance when Hildy returns; for in insisting on his revenge, he delays too long. There is a particular irony in Joshua's funeral oration when he says that Cable "built his empire" (asserted himself in the desert) but was "man enough to give it up for love when the time came." He was about to do that, when he was run over by the car; it looked like the right time to leave. But the time to choose had already passed, and Cable then was not "man enough to give it up." The problem for humans is in properly recognizing the time for choice.

Part of the brilliance of this film is in the seamless integration of this aspect of religious allegory into the film. *The Ballad of Cable Hogue* is dressed as a simple, personal story of one man's ability to survive, but Peckinpah through Hogue is describing nothing less than the basic potential for redemption in all people, as well as the characteristic of the species which permits its survival. Cable Hogue "defiantly" maintains that a man is worth something, as a man. Joshua suggests that the Lord take Cable, but having known Cable, suggests that the Lord shouldn't "take him lightly."

The quotation marks around "defiantly" are there because Cable is finally insecure as well. When he asks for a loan from the bank, after having been thrown out by the stage line, the bank manager asks for collateral. Cable has only his land, bought for $2.50, and himself. He asks for a confirmation of his faith which he doesn't expect to receive: "I'm worth somethin', ain't I?" And because he doesn't *expect* to receive it, he gets the loan, more than he'd asked for. He is immediately filled with sincere gratitude and ashamed that he had thought the worst of the bank manager. It is an authentically touching moment, a moment related to those in the opening where Cable is naked, alone as a human being.

Peckinpah tells Hogue's story without pretense or sanctimony, as Joshua's funeral speech tries to present Hogue honestly, without exaggeration. For Hogue, like all people, has flaws. He is stingy, mistrustful, an occasional cheat (though Joshua also points out that he cheated without favoritism), and vengeful. Whenever he is about to become too lovable, Peckinpah pulls him back to reveal his flaws, as he does in his meanness to Hildy when he says that the reason he doesn't charge her for food is because she never charged him. This statement precipitates Hildy's leaving; we feel sorry for Hogue, but cannot blame her, either. We are glad to see Hogue in his initial revenge; as Taggart and Bowen do come along, they deserve what they get. There is satisfaction as we witness their fear as Cable throws snakes into the pit; Cable's decision to send them wandering in the desert as they had forced him to do has an eye-for-an-eye ring of justice to it. But Cable's revenge is a trap for him and the viewer. Taggart resists and forces Cable to kill him. It is not Cable's fault for killing Taggart in self-defense, but it *is* Cable's fault for *waiting* for them to show up, and not going with Hildy earlier. "Revenge always turns sour," Hildy warns Cable, but Cable maintains that there are "some things a man can't forget," and he has two of them, Taggart and Bowen. This insistence, a matter of pride in revenge, is Hogue's fatal flaw. Cable kills a stranger in self-defense, but that is a matter of survival.

Ironically, right from the start, Hogue's revenge is a motiva-

tion for survival. Rescued by finding water, Hogue's reasser-
tion of self is embodied in his reacquired strength to fulfill his
vow to live to spit on his former partners' graves. After he proclaims himself alive, his first words are that he *told* them he'd
live, and now all he has to do is *wait*. Cable doesn't realize
that he is in fact reneging on the offer he made to the Lord to
repent, nor does he recognize that his desert survival is a second chance, which he does not fulfill by rejecting Hildy's offer
to leave. In his own eyes, Cable's oasis is of his own making,
but it is difficult to distinguish whether Cable finds or is given
the tools he needs to build that oasis. In any event, "Cable
Springs" rises from the desert as "miraculously" as Cable
does. Cable gets his grubstake, but seems to receive most of
his support from the "barren" land itself: he finds lumber and
reclaims trash, the waterhole gives him an income, and the
desert supplies the meat for his table. Cable thinks of it all as
being of his doing, his ability to "find it where it wasn't." He
even identifies his find out of himself, spelling it "W-A-T-L-
E." Whether or not this is finally a religious question is left to
the viewer; Peckinpah pointedly leaves the door open, for it is
the viewer's judgment that will finally give Hogue's life
meaning or not. Peckinpah suggests that we not judge the
man, indeed, "lightly."

Hogue is not anticivilization. But being mistrustful of
others, he maintains his independence, choosing a niche on
the fringes of civilization. As a member of the fringe, his is a
more difficult matter of survival, but it is primarily a matter of
identity that he makes his stand as he does. As Hogue stands
on the road, he realizes his potential "fortune," in that this is a
road used by "people goin' somewhere . . . wagons and
buckboards . . . with kids and mommas," i.e., civilization, and
he is *on* this road. He makes his claim, stakes out his identity,
and he is truly proud of his "acceptance" by society when he
receives that token, the flag. "Me, me, Cable Hogue." Organized society and organized religion, more susceptible to
hypocrisy in their relative security, get Hogue's suspicion (he
is tickled to find the banker agrees with him on religion), but
Hogue deals with society rather than reject it outright.

The Ballad of Cable Hogue might be a "tougher" film as a
story of one man's survival and revenge, but it is important to
recognize that the film is also a love story. This is critical to
Peckinpah's outlook, for in offering Cable the promise of

Hildy, Peckinpah allows that there is a capacity for redemption in love. Practically all of Peckinpah's main characters need love and the comfort it can provide, and live their lives affected by their lack or possession of it. Cable Hogue is one of the most complete expressions of this in Peckinpah's work, and as such can serve as a comparative example in approaching other character relationships in Peckinpah's films.

Peckinpah's female characters have suffered at the hands of critics who seem disposed to an interest in labels which conform to a personal image of the director. Inspection reveals that Peckinpah's women are found to be "good," "bad," and, more often than not, combinations of both: they begin as people. It does not make Peckinpah less "valuable" that his films are primarily centered on male characters, for the lessons he makes available about human behavior are applicable to both sexes. Women begin with the same opportunities as *moral* human beings as men. If bias is perceived, it is only a matter of predilection: Peckinpah is not antifemale, he is simply, as a man, more familiar with male experience and points of view. There is nothing in his work to suggest that Peckinpah is categorically deprecating to women *per se*, or that men are superior morally to women. If the number of women as whores in his films (and there are many more who aren't) are taken as a sign of such deprecation, this is a response of the *viewer*. Peckinpah does not condemn a woman because she is a whore. But again, due to the nature of the material, the women the male characters are often most likely to deal with are prostitutes. Cable Hogue is not apt to turn to the town schoolmarm for "affection." In Peckinpah's male-dominated settings, women are mainly seen as they relate to the men, but simultaneously as a matter of circumstance, not as a diminutive. They are not seen strictly in terms of sexual relations either, but this is certainly a circumstantially primary fact of contact between men and women. In addition, historically, women have had the use of physical sexuality to "define" themselves superficially more than men, whether they were forced to by societal models or not. This means that a woman can be seen as a sex object by a male character, but Peckinpah does not necessarily *side* with that male character in that view. Amy Sumner in *Straw Dogs* is no more definitive with regard to Peckinpah than is Hildy; they are both women, but they are different people.

Symmetry: Cable and Hildy tend each other.

Hildy is a prostitute by profession. It is a way to make a living for her, and she holds no illusions, or at least seems to recognize the illusory potential of some of her dreams; she is fair and honest, and is accepted as a person by Cable. Even as she is introduced to Cable as a whore, she is not an object as such but more a person who provides a service. And as Hildy grows in Cable's affection, she is also realized as a character of some depth for the viewer. Cable, however, is the central character; we do not follow Hildy to San Francisco, but stay with Hogue in the desert, and consequently our main information about her comes from her relationship to Cable. She is worthy of our respect, and she receives Cable's; indeed, as Cable describes her, she is a "lady," regardless of her "profession." We delight in the warmth and humor they share as their mutual love grows; as she accepts Cable, we accept her as Cable's opportunity for redemption, through the promise of contentment his love for her offers. Cable rationalizes that it is not up to him: "Hildy doesn't belong to anybody." But he does become jealous of Joshua's passes at her. In rejecting her offer of "peace," in not forgiving his partners by that rejection, Cable makes his choice and has to accept the consequences, being forbidden to have both when he dies upon Hildy's return.

In a sense, *The Ballad of Cable Hogue* is partially a thematic reworking of *The Deadly Companions* to Peckinpah's satisfaction. The two films both take place near "Gila City." On the trail, after Turk goes after Billy, Yellowleg rides off to pursue Turk, the object of his revenge, but stops himself and returns to help Kit, rejecting revenge and choosing the woman (love's redemption). Even though he gets another chance to fulfill his revenge, Kit again stops him, and they indeed "ride off into the sunset." But Peckinpah, being more interested in "sinners" (i.e., people) as opposed to "saints" (ideals, and therefore illusions), has Cable Hogue stick to his revenge. He finds that he can't fulfill it anyway; he is probably not able to shoot Bowen when Bowen refuses to go out into the desert and begs forgiveness. But he has already killed Taggart, and Cable's sin is in setting up that confrontation in the first place. I say Hogue "probably" can't shoot Bowen because Peckinpah interrupts this resolution with the appearance of the stagecoach. Following with the appearance of the car (and Hildy), it is clear that Hogue's life in the desert, his purpose and function there, is over. Hogue gives it up, but it is "too late." This is, of course, a highly moralistic interpretation of the film; Peckinpah purposefully resists being conclusive in the film, in order to leave the "judgment" to the viewer. Yet if one denies the moral implications, and denies Peckinpah's ideas, then the film's end becomes *merely* a contrivance; even as an unexplained "twist of Fate," it is linked with the other events of the film, but beyond that notion the film is just a "story." We are drawn to the moral question; an atheist would have a much different experience. It is to this extent that the film is brilliantly constructed, in that the judgment is *not* made, but is left to the viewer's discretion. If Peckinpah has moved you to accept the moral question, you will accede to the depth of the film. But even if one rejects the film as a narrative contrivance, the set-up of the film is worth considering (i.e., spending the time in viewing) because of the way it forces the viewer to question his own values. Peckinpah's "lesson" as such is not that the judgment (of Hogue) *must* be made, but that the judgment is *difficult* to make, and must be reviewed carefully, not making it "lightly." Dogmatic, knee-jerk conclusions are to be resisted; the "Truth" is not easily seen. There does come a point when values are chosen, as Mike chooses to finally reject a corrupt world in *The Killer Elite*. We must each finally find our own way in the world. But before we get too confident in the "righteousness" of our chosen attitudes, Cable Hogue, with all his sides, is the Lord's "dim reflection," as Joshua describes. We need to accept the built-in ambiguity of the limits of our perceptions.

Cable's acceptance of death is in keeping with his character. He does not "give up," but honestly appraises his injuries and realizes their severity. That we are not witnesses to his pain in this stoic acceptance is another measure of his pride, for Cable, scruffy grifter that he appears to be, retains his individual dignity in death. He admits that he has been scared of life, but estimates the only fear of death as being the uncertainty of the judgment; he wants to know what's going to be said about him. Joshua obliges Cable's request for an honest appraisal. "Don't make me out no saint, but don't put me down too deep." The telescoping of time in this sequence focuses attention on Joshua's sermon. Our concern is Cable's last; Joshua makes suggestions, but what is to be made of the man is finally up to us, and God.

Setting the film in the West around 1908-1909 makes *Cable Hogue* another "last Western," but, as indicated, this is a "last Western" about *people*, part "good" and part "bad." The period setting makes possible the revenge situation outside of law-and-order concerns. At the same time, it affords the drawing of characters as human individuals somewhat apart from society, by contrast uncorrupted by civilization. There is the idea that individuals must adapt in a changing world to survive, as progress and its main symbol, the automobile, make Cable's livelihood in the desert unnecessary. Hildy, the survivor, makes the "adaptation" to society, but she is never really interested in living apart from it anyway. Cable's way-station in the desert is not for her; that she stays as long as she does is a measure of her love for Hogue. Certainly there is irony in the mechanics of Cable's death, at the "hands" of civilization which he does not represent as a "full member" by his independence, but Cable *is* ready to accept progress's making an anachronism of him in his turnover of the station to

Credit: The Museum of Modern Art/Film Stills Archive.

Mortally wounded by "Progress": Hogue doesn't leave the desert in time.

Bowen. Progress takes victims, and there is danger in resisting or not adapting to change—the Wild Bunch ran out of room and Steve Judd is outmoded as a frontier marshal—but the greater irony of Hogue's death goes back to the revenge theme: Cable is run over by the car as he pushes Bowen out of the way, trying to protect one of the men he's waited three years to get even with. It is the maintaining of his revenge as a keystone of his identity that prevents Hogue from leaving the desert. And, in his mastery over his "desert empire," it is altogether "fitting" that he should die from something alien to that kingdom. After Hogue's burial, the mourners leave in different directions by different means, a visualization of the variations in lives brought to one spot, touched by one man. There is sadness from these mourners, perhaps also a twinge of regret from Peckinpah and us, at the loss of such a man of spirit. Civilization will not really miss Hogue, but civilization too often doesn't know what it's missing.

The lyrical quality arising from the love story and the gentle aspect of the warm character humor shown in the film are further enhanced by Peckinpah's use of montage construction to bridge the development of Hildy and Cable's relationship. Also, the montages of the construction of Cable Springs, Cable's routine, and of Cable's desert wanderings in the title sequence achieve a feeling for Hogue and his environment while economizing on the time spent depicting those scenes. These are details which fill out the picture, presented with care that the technique tends to hide. The film's lyricism is a testament to the talents of cast and crew, as it belies the grueling rigors of production which Peckinpah and company were subjected to.[1]

Though Peckinpah's capacity for lyricism comes as a shock to some, it is hardly surprising to find it here, for as the title suggests, *The Ballad of Cable Hogue* is a song, a story-song about a man. The ballad form suggests a short story, usually about some person and / or events, which usually involves some kind of illustration for others, though not necessarily a clear "moral." But Peckinpah goes beyond the title notion, using direct vocalization as an emotional narrative device as well. Vocalization, like narration was for *Major Dundee*, is another risky proposition cinematically, for song lyrics over visuals have a distinctly "unreal" quality about them which can remove a viewer from a scene more than the viewer wants to be. It is essential that if songs are used as a narrative device in an otherwise "realistic" film, that they be in fine tune emotionally with the moods of the scenes involved. It follows that the talent involved in making such scenes work is enormous. Peckinpah's incorporation of Richard Gillis's songs, particularly "Butterfly Mornin's," depends on the sincerity of their presentation, which I believe is completely successful. It is important to acknowledge that we recognizably hear Hogue and Hildy sing "Butterfly Mornin's," for as the use of the song takes the viewer "out" of the scene, the characters' singing of the song brings the viewer back in. That this also takes place over a visual montage relieves some of the potential strain on a "realistic" level, for it is simultaneously acceptable that the characters *do* sing. (People sing in almost all of Peckinpah's films.) The "orchestration" behind the song finally functions as "normal" musical background would, save that it also accompanies the song. To say that this scene is unnecessary is meaningless; it may be viewed as being quite sentimental, but even as such, Cable and Hildy sing together as genuinely as they fall in love. And because of that "genuine" quality surrounding the use of the music, it works.

A device that perhaps doesn't work as well is the use of fast-motion photography in two scenes, where Joshua is interrupted in "consoling" a woman by her husband, and where Hildy's bath is interrupted by the arrival of the stage. In both scenes, the effect of the fast-motion is comic, but comedy is arguably well-established enough by character rather than camera mechanisms, such as Cable's boisterous exit from Deaddog, where he knocks down the religious meeting tent and falls off his horse. As a "camera device," the fast-motion is distracting, and consequently "costs" a little more than the laugh is worth; its usage mars the film, though certainly not by much. On the other hand, the winking Indian currency is so totally unanticipated, so disarming, and so slyly underplayed that it is worth the laugh it gets, and works.

More human comedy is found in another Peckinpah-drawn friendship, Cable's relationship with the Rev. Joshua Duncan Sloane. Joshua is a con-man, but Cable doesn't mind that as long as Joshua doesn't try to con him. Their friendship is one of occasional symbiosis, as Cable provides Josh with the physical support of "room and board" while Josh gives Cable the "moral" support of companionship and the sometime guidance of an inconstant conscience. More simply, they accept each other, both living on the edges of civilization.

Once again, the appearance of Joshua as a man of the cloth is in contrast to his true lecherous occupation, but here the conflict is one of "harmless" comic underpinning. Peckinpah seems skeptical of dogmatic, church-going piety, and in addition to the agreement between Hogue and the banker about trusting preachers, takes another swipe at such Christian hypocrisy with the two stage passengers early in the film, well-to-do gospel-spreaders who want nothing to do with the bedraggled Hogue. The stage driver administers justice by untying the baggage strap; Cable gets a new "outfit" as the stage pulls away. Also, the tent meeting collapse comically reveals the nature of the people beneath it. Hearing that meeting going on, Cable remembers that he has left Joshua at his claim; fearing that Joshua might be selling him out, skepticism of one religious item has reminded him not to trust another. But the sentence that Cable hears from the meeting has an ironic foreshadowing that is all but missed: "[They will] destroy you with machines," is the speaker's warning.

The array of characters in *Cable Hogue* is substantial, and most are neither all good nor all bad. Indeed, Cable's name suggests this itself, as a combination of "Cain" and "Abel." There is a feeling of respect for all humanity engendered in the telling of Cable's story, and Peckinpah shows his "sympathy" for all of his characters. *The Ballad of Cable Hogue* is to all considerations a gentle, original, loving film, with a broad affection for the human spirit. It is significant to an understanding of both films that *The Wild Bunch* and *Cable Hogue* were made by the same man. But *Cable Hogue* is perhaps the more revealing as a more personal, "smaller" work. As a personal masterpiece, *The Ballad of Cable Hogue* is a simple moral tale with a lesson in human frailty. Peckinpah does not demand that God take Cable Hogue; but there is the hope in the end that He does. And in that hope for God's forgiveness of Cable Hogue lies the hope for all of us.

7

Straw Dogs (1971)

HENRY NILES: "I don't know my way home." David: "It's okay; I don't either." – so go the final lines in *Straw Dogs*. To accept David Sumner in *Straw Dogs* is to accept Robert Ardrey's thesis in his books *African Genesis* (1961) and *The Territorial Imperative* (1966).[1] This thesis involves more than the idea of man's innate, inherited capacity for violence; it specifies the investigation of man's heritage with direct regard for the total consequences of his animal ancestry. This includes man's innate behavioral aspects, but goes further to suggest the primacy of one trait inherited from animals, that of territoriality.

Although one should be warned that a brief description is probably misleading, the Territorial Imperative is the idea that the possession of territory, the spatial concept, is the key root to an understanding of man's behavior. As the prime underlying mechanism in animal behavior, it follows that as man's behavior evolves from animals, so does the idea of territoriality reside in man. Ardrey develops this idea as the generative quality of *all* behavior, arriving at possibly the three "primordial psychological necessities of life itself," which territoriality is a response to: identity, stimulation, and security. Ardrey clarifies them by their opposites, which we try to avoid: anonymity, boredom, and anxiety.[2] It is tempting to apply this idea to each of Peckinpah's films, as well as *anything* observable; Ardrey is very difficult to argue with. He presents his evidence with such precision that it is staggering to contemplate his even being *basically* correct, for following the logic of his arguments one arrives at certain unalterable conclusions about the nature of man as a being less unique than we have traditionally wished to think. Strother Martin gave

115

Peckinpah a copy of *African Genesis* after the filming of *The Wild Bunch*.[3] Whether one accepts Ardrey or not (and Ardrey is hard *not* to accept), it is clear that Peckinpah does: "Ardrey's the only prophet alive today."[4] It is also clear in his films, particularly in *Straw Dogs*.

David Sumner does not understand something that Major Dundee realizes, that "men can understand fighting . . . truth is, it's easy," and which the Wild Bunch emulate, living by their guns. David does not realize that despite his power of reason he yet contains the primordial inheritance of a capacity for violence. It is an essential gap in his self-knowledge, without which his self-image is not complete enough to deal with situations which call for even limited aggression. But David's problem is that he yet regards himself as a complete human being, a totally functioning man whose ego takes pride in his capabilities. But without the *knowledge* of aggression, David feels anxiety in the insufficiency of his *incomplete* responses and is forced to prove himself and confront the contradiction in his nonviolent self-image.

David's wife, Amy, has been described too often solely as a type, rather than as the individual she is. Peckinpah's blunt comment about two kinds of women—"There are women and then there's pussy"—was a simplification to make a point, about the existence of a kind of woman who is immature and "ignorant as to what is of value in life,"[5] of whom Amy is an example. The sexual connotation of the description is an identification of this kind of woman, who accepts at least superficially the chauvinist male view of woman as sexual object. It is certainly not to say that women do not exist in the same variety that men do (perhaps if he'd also said, "There are men and then there's apes"), and is not a characterization of women as such. Peckinpah also said in the same interview that "Amy . . . wasn't an attempt to make a statement about women in general, for Christ's sake."[6] Amy is a physically oriented woman, drawn to ego games of pride which fulfill her image of herself as well as her image of David. She is constantly searching for that missing aggressive response from David, although *not* consciously, testing him for those qualities she wants in her man. She does not wholly accept David without that aggressive response, which she does not fully comprehend the significance of, either. She does not know what it is, but she prods David for that something that is missing in him for her. She enjoys being physically "dominated." To some extent, Amy's acceptance of male dominance is traditionally engendered in some "classes" of English people; certainly one reason the other men disrespect David is that he cannot "handle" his woman.

At the same time, David's egoism resides in an intellectual superiority over Amy and others, which is frustrated by situations where intellectual reason is not enough or, worse, irrelevant. Amy as well is proud of David's intellect and strives to achieve recognition herself from David for that quality she admires in him. But the missing link is the capacity for aggression, which David finds in himself during the siege. It is shown to be an innate mechanism for survival; David would die without it. But this is not simply a machismo attitude that "manhood" is achieved through violence. David always was a "man," but with a capacity for aggression denied, David is incomplete as a human being. Nor does this mean that human beings are fulfilled by doing violence. David's case is severe; the important thing is to *realize* that the capacity for aggression is always there. *Knowing* that is is there, one isn't compelled to have to prove, as David is, that it *might* be there.

Straw Dogs is a carefully orchestrated work, built to pursue the theme of David's final realization in three distinct "acts." Act One is the definition of the characters and identification of the situation which sets up Act Two, the definition of the specific character problem, escalating to a demand for the resolution provided in the particular crisis of Act Three. Differences between the film and the novel it is based on, *The Siege of Trencher's Farm*, are enormous, the two works really having only the siege itself in common. The author of the book, Gordon Williams, disclaims the film primarily over the sexual content, as the book is also violent.[7] For most practical purposes, the film is an original conception.

The film's title comes from a quotation attributed by Peckinpah to Chinese philosopher Lao Tse: "Heaven and earth are ruthless and treat the myriad creatures as straw dogs; the sage is ruthless and treats the people as straw dogs."[8] The quotation is embodied in the film by David, who *thinks* himself to be the sage, but finds out that to be the sage involves realizing the second half of the statement. At first, David and Amy seem to be the "straw dogs" (artificial victims used in sacrificial rites), but David becomes the sage and makes the siege gang the victims.

"Act One" begins with children playing in the church graveyard, teasing a dog, metaphorically reminiscent of the scorpion and the ants of *The Wild Bunch*. The church itself, as in other Peckinpah films, is an empty symbol, and will prove to be of no real help to anyone. We meet David and Amy in front of the pub amidst many other observers, including the children. Peckinpah brings the characters on stage from different directions; there is a sense of convergence implied in the camera choices. The children are reminders that we, too, are in the same position, as observers.

Because of its use during the siege, the man-trap has to be accounted for earlier as it is an out-of-the-ordinary device. But in introducing it right at the beginning, Peckinpah gives it an additional significance. Its presence is explained as a "birthday present," but its nature is darkly foreboding, and it is a prop to Amy's introduction: our first view of her is of her chest, and with the rest of her characterization in this first section, we realize that Amy is indeed a sexual animal—not a sex object *per se*, but a woman whose personality is informed by her physical attributes; she is proud to "look good." Her introduction is underscored by her carrying the man-trap.

David, we find, is an academic, and is proud of himself in that respect. It is his domain, and David cuts short Amy's attempt to explain his work to Charlie Venner. This begins the definition of David and Amy's relationship; they are found to be competitive, but the competition is mainly a matter of how David succeeds as "boss" between the two. Both David and Amy are shown to have an incomplete image of the other, each acting to interpret the other's behavior in terms of his or her idea of the spouse. David regards Amy as something of a child, which works as far as Amy responds to that. Amy tries to elicit David's domination by testing his authority; but David's dominance is incomplete as it lacks the physical authority required to back it up in Amy's estimation. When they can't find the cat the first time, David says the cat doesn't answer his call; Amy asks, "Do I?" to which David replies, "You'd better," then threatens to "kill that cat." The analogous implication seems to be that Amy indeed would like to be treated like the cat (David throws fruit at the cat later, an act of casual ruthlessness), and in many ways is analogously feline in her behavior. Amy consistently tries to goad David into putting his money where his mouth is in action, and is frustrated by David's refusal to that response.

David has effectively cut himself off from that type of response, and the reasons behind their coming to England are hinted at variously, the result being that David and Amy both may be guilty of moral cowardice. Amy can excuse that in herself, looking to David for protection, but she cannot forgive it in David. This is a complex adversary relationship, as Amy tries to get David to conform to her needs of him, and as David uses her as his opportunity to assert himself on *his* terms, which he noticeably cannot do outside their relationship, except in intellectual areas: his delight in intellectually defeating Reverend Hood makes his pleasure in that sort of dominance apparent, especially in his comment afterwards that he indeed *likes* the Reverend (someone he can feel superior to). David's problem is that outside his home he is in an environment where intellectual superiority is worthless and, in fact, subjects him to outright hostility.

David is the outsider, a fact made painfully clear to him—and the viewer. In his first encounter in the pub, David is taken aback by the sudden violence demonstrated by Tom Hedden breaking his glass. But Hedden and the others cannot understand a man who wears sneakers, either. For them, David is a foreigner, automatically contemptible for that, and worse, a person of "higher" rank who doesn't know his place, who maintains an idea of superiority and yet tries to be accepted as an equal. David does not understand the natural resentment he receives from the men; his joke about only seeing people killed between commercials is lost on Cawsey and Scutt, who take it as something of a put-down. Tom Hedden insults David by buying his cigarettes; David pays for them, but too late, only making a fool of himself in their eyes, compounding the insult later by *leaving* money to buy them all a drink.

Likewise, as David watches John Niles slap his brother Henry's face for causing trouble, David is repelled by the vio-

Challenging David: attraction and repulsion.

lence inflicted upon the half-wit, not understanding that level
of life in the village. (Yet David will duplicate that *same* violence upon Henry later.)

David enjoys playing lord of the manor, but it is his study
that is his principal domain. When Amy violates its sanctity,
David is completely frustrated by her lack of implicit understanding of his authority there. Amy is challenging him by
changing the minus sign to a plus sign, and by defiantly sticking her gum wad to the blackboard; it is a part of her game. But
David cannot understand the game as it applies in the study,
refuses to play, and is hurt that Amy does not appreciate this.
In "Act Two," a physics toy on David's desk sums up their
relationship: two magnets in a constant imbalance of attraction
and repulsion, an underscoring of the tension within their relationship. David ponders the world outside his study, won-
dering how to deal with Amy's challenge of standing up to the
hired men he watches from his study window.

As their relationship is indicated with tension, David and
Amy are similarly revealed in their "happier" moments. Their
preparations for bed are marked by David's ordered rituals on

the one hand and Amy's desire for more spontaneity on the other. David will play, but only on his terms. At the same time we see Amy's desire to be seen by David as being intellectually capable: David's joke about doing his exercises by binary numbers leads to Amy's studying them for a later bed scene, winning David's approval with his superior comment, "You're *not* so dumb." Peckinpah also takes care to show that David is not sexually inadequate (and Janice Hedden watches voyeuristically)—that his later violence is not an assumption of virility. But there is a deft foreshadow-undercut to David's sexuality, as the scene shifts abruptly from Amy pulling David to her to the men in the pub playing with Amy's stolen panties.

The first "Act" of the film lays the background, carefully introducing the characters with enough information to provide the keys to understanding the motivations for later actions. Peckinpah is economical with these clues, using the camera to illustrate the script ideas visually, placing people and objects in the frame precisely to indicate the subtext of underlying tensions and irony beyond the dialogue, offering complete psychological characterizations in the combination of sight and sound. There is not room here to catalogue completely these instances, but one is hard pressed to find a wasted frame. By the same token, viewer inattention in the first part of the film leads to serious misinterpretation of later developments.

The "second Act" of the film "begins" with the discovery of the cat, hanged in the closet. It is an act of ferocious simplicity which incapacitates David; his response is to lock the windows and doors, to isolate them—perhaps as he has attempted to isolate them from the political unrest in America at the time, by coming to England. Amy understands the act, recognizing it as an insult and threat to *David*, "to prove they could get into your bedroom," which David refuses to believe.

This becomes the particular test of David's self-assertion. Amy is too impatient to allow anything but a fairly direct confrontational response; lacking that from David, the wedge between them grows, as does Amy's contempt for David. David does not know how to deal with the killing of the cat, but insists on the opportunity to deal with it his way, an intellectualized mechanism of "catching them off guard." Amy, rejecting what appears to her to be a useless attempt as David invites the men in, takes it out of his hands, and includes a saucer of milk with the tray of beers. David, thrown by Amy's interference (and her rejection of his ability to deal with the situation), loses whatever initiative he had, and, in trying to recapture his position, agrees to go hunting with the men. David's position is underlined visually as he gradually isolates himself in the *corner* of the room in this scene. Amy emphasizes David's defeat by writing on the "sacred" blackboard, "DID I CATCH YOU OFF GUARD?" and leaving the saucer of milk in front of it.

David is still trying to maintain his self-image of capability despite increasing odds. But in denying himself an aggressive response, his efforts in that maintenance are increasingly futile, until he is symbolically made completely helpless by the rape of Amy. It is important to recognize that David is never made aware of the rape, though during the climax of the siege he may by then suspect something in Amy's betrayal and responsiveness to Charlie. But the rape's occurrence demonstrates devastatingly for the viewer how helpless David is in his limited capacity to deal with the situation at hand and how ruthless the men are. The rape itself, figuratively the "end" of Act Two, is David's symbolic total humiliation. During the siege, it is important to note that he is not defending his sexual honor.

Amy, in being raped, is a victim of David's lack of assertion and a victim of herself, in underestimating the desires of Charlie Venner and Norman Scutt, and in overestimating her own ability to deal with the consequences of her behavior (e.g., showing herself half-naked at the window was both a taunt to the men and a taunt to David). Charlie Venner, out of old lust and new contempt from Amy, has had enough of her taunts and takes Amy, to her shocked horror.

Amy, contrary to some interpretations of this scene, does not like it or the idea of it to begin with. But Charlie Venner attacks her, returning her slap to her surprise; to avoid physical pain, Amy submits to Charlie physically, although pleading with him not to (not to hurt her, primarily). It must also be remembered that Charlie and Amy once had some kind of relationship—where Charlie didn't "take care" of Amy, an indication of what she wants from David—and because of that, Charlie as a rapist is not necessarily so bad to Amy. With this in the background, Amy does accept Charlie (she has been forced initially), responding on a purely physical level in which the degree of pleasure is a matter of interpretation. It is, however, within the logical bounds of Amy's character that she would respond finally to the aspect of physical domination inherent in the rape. Because of her previous relationship to Charlie, it is not the violation that Norman's attack is.

Amy's "real" rape comes from Norman Scutt, who has been seen to be the most malevolently lustful of the group of men. Norman forces Charlie to move away from Amy at gunpoint; Charlie cannot stop Norman because he is technically guilty of the same thing, and Norman could cause Charlie trouble among his "peers" in the village, apart from this *isolated* couple in whom they see no threat at all. Amy's screams at this point are from this second, true violation. Many critics took Norman's rape to be sodomy, a potentially more brutal attack than rear-entry. But since the film does not clearly indicate what happens, Norman's attack is not necessarily sodomistic. The important point is not the *method* of violation, but Amy's psychological reaction to the second attack. If one *assumes* sodomy, then one has misread the point of Amy's horror. (This scene was slightly trimmed for American release, to avoid an X-rating, along with a few other shots. But the trimmed frames do not make the specific nature of Norman's rape inarguable.)

Intercut with Charlie's rape of Amy are shots of David alone on the hill. The hunting party is a set-up, with David completely in the men's hands. His attempt to show himself as their equal is broken early by his simple mistake in gun safety, which Scutt corrects succinctly. The men only wish to make a fool of him, though Charlie and Norman separately develop ideas about Amy. As they leave David, going off in opposite directions, David is trapped alone on the hill, whether he realizes how complete the joke is or not. As they watch from the bushes (along with us), David is seen to be totally inept in his "purpose," trying to prove that he is capable but not having the experience or the desire to actually hit anything. It even seems that the birds know this, too, flying past him safely as David *throws* the shells at the birds in frustration.

As Charlie's taking of Amy begins, his usurpation of David's position is clearly indicated by the juxtaposing of a shot of Charlie removing his shirt with the same shot of David removing his shirt seen earlier, also indicating the transposition from Amy's point of view to further her acceptance of Charlie. Intercutting views of David on the hill with the rape stresses the simultaneity of the scenes, implicating David in the rape to the extent that it is partly his fault that the rape can take place. Furthermore, David is impotent as a hunter, repulsed by the corpse of a bird he does manage to shoot which he puts back into the bushes, trying to avoid the blood on his hands. David's killing of the bird is followed by Norman's rape, which is not intercut with shots of David.

The structure of these scenes is accomplished with the same tactical care as the rest of the film. This sequence intercutting shots of the first rape with others of David on the hill is paced as a sexual encounter, the length of the shots decreasing to a climax of a few frames per shot, followed by longer takes. Peckinpah has been criticized for the "violence" of this scene, but, as in *The Wild Bunch*, the necessarily brutal impact of the scene is achieved in the editing. The end of Act Two has David walking back alone from the "hunt," to a fade-out to black. David has reached the depths of his humiliation, without knowing about the rape of his wife. For him, it is enough that he has been made such a fool of in the hunt; the viewer alone sees just how bad things are.

The situation remains unimproved at the beginning of the last Act, where Amy bitterly puns on David's reference to their having "stuck it to him" on the hill. Her meaning is lost on him, and his firing of the men the following day is ineffective in light of the severity of their actions, of which David is unaware. It is a resolution of sorts, but even David doubts that it is resolution enough.

The church social is an evening of visual ironies for the viewer, as the events of the film are figuratively recapitulated while introducing the development that will lead to the film's climax. David again snubs his constant admirer, Janice Hedden, who turns to Henry Niles for what she believes will be some (safe) sexual excitement. At the same time, Amy's thoughts flash to the memory of the rape, the perpetrators of which lounge in the back of the room with impunity. It is established that the men, now including Tom Hedden, are drinking heavily and continue to do so. (This provides for some of

the escalatory nature of the siege, as well as possibly evening
the odds a bit for David.) Meanwhile, the raucous atmosphere
of the church social builds innocently, but accentuates Amy's
emotional anxiety. The "Church" is irrelevant to what is happening: the Reverend Hood's patter is counterpointed by
Amy's memories; shots of the program's singer are intercut
with others in which the men realize that Janice Hedden is
missing, along with Henry Niles. As Janice invites Henry to
kiss her, the men beat up John Niles, demanding to know
Henry's whereabouts; lines from the church service are combined in irony with shots of Janice and Henry. The religious
service continues, and David continues his puzzled notice
that Amy is distraught, finally offering to take her home. The
cries of the people looking for Janice startle Henry, who accidentally strangles her in trying to "protect" her. There is the
suggestion throughout that Tom Hedden and the others have
brought the calamity on themselves in an "as ye sow, so shall
ye reap" fashion. The stage is finally set as David, driving
home, hits the running Henry Niles in the fog.

The siege is David's test. The situation gradually strips
away his logical defenses, until all that is left in order to survive is the defense of equal violence. Very quickly the pre-
sumable issue of Henry Niles is dispensed with; Tom Hedden
and the others do not know for sure that Janice is not safe. We
have been told earlier by Charlie that they take care of their
own; for both sides it becomes a simple question of who will
dominate and indeed ultimately survive.

The initial demand for Niles is refused by David with logic;
they have no proof of Henry's culpability. But when Charlie
suggests David go for the doctor, David allows that he won't
leave Amy alone with Niles either. Caught in his own self-con-
tradiction, David proclaims that Niles is his "responsibility."
But Norman cannot believe this, saying it never was any of
David's business and asks why David takes such a position
now. David responds out of the Territorial Imperative: "This
is my house." Further on, David explains to Amy, who wants
to release Niles to the other men out of fear for her own safety,
that even as she has revealed her cowardice and doesn't care,
he cares: "This is where I live; this is me; I will not allow
violence against this house." This identification with owner-

ship of a space is an ancient one which David responds to intuitively. He accepts it logically, without yet realizing that he'll
have to back up his assertion with violence.

At first, David rationalizes the men's anger; he says he
knows how they feel about Janice being missing. As they
begin to assault the house, David threatens to press charges,
still trying to pursue a rational course. After more windows are
broken, he allows them "one more chance" to stop, or else
"there'll be real trouble." He holds on to reason where reason
is irrelevant; he still thinks he can handle it. As Amy's cowardice is revealed, David asserts more authority; he will handle
it ("this is my affair") *his* way. Even after the Major is killed
and David and Amy are truly isolated, David still believes he
can keep them out until *somebody else* shows up. He begins
systematically preparing defenses, but he is not yet forced into
action.

Appropriately, Amy initiates David's action. Showing her
implicit lack of faith in him, she is willing to betray him by
opening the door for Charlie, who calls to her, saying that *he*
will protect her, as David has not. David stops her at the door;
he can't believe her betrayal. But when she threatens to leave
unless he gives up Niles, he calls her bluff and in so doing
commits himself. Stopping her again, David grabs Amy by the
hair and slaps her hard: this is David's first act of violence,
performed only when no other course is left to him. To stress
its effect on Amy, it is seen in the same slow-motion as Charlie's earlier matching slap beginning the rape. Amy responds
to the threat of physical pain. David *explains*, however, that
they will be killed if the men get in now; he is now using
reason *and* force to assert himself. It will escalate until he is
only using force, in hand-to-hand fighting. David develops
pride in his clever defenses, outwitting the attackers, until he
finds himself not using his wits at all, but beating down physically both Riddaway and Cawsey. David is sickened at what
he finds himself capable of in bludgeoning Cawsey after he is
down. He has become as brutal as his attackers.

When Charlie enters the room with the gun, David, in
exhaustion, says that the gun is empty. David believes it is the
gun which he tried to use on Riddaway, which didn't fire for
him. This is significant, for if the viewer misses David's revulsion over his hand-to-hand fight with Riddaway and Cawsey

(whom he beats with a poker), then the idea of Charlie's being told the gun is empty may be seen as a bluff on David's part. But if this is indeed thought to be a bluff, then the viewer has already gone *past* any revulsion at David's violence; one cannot be *against* David's action and yet *interpret* the gun comment as a bluff from the start, which, in effect, is a way of cheering David on. David's revulsion is clearly indicated, if one is *looking* for such revulsion. From this point on, David is no longer in charge of his defense. It is only a scrambling for survival based on *instinct*. David is lucky that Charlie kills Norman, and lucky that he survives the bout with Charlie. The final (anticipated) use of the man-trap shows that David as a human animal will use *anything* ultimately; the vicious brutality of the man-trap underscores this. After Charlie's death, David assesses his "victory"; he is disgusted and triumphant over Amy, who has been screaming for Charlie more than for him, and it is he, David, who has survived. He is right in thinking he "got 'em all"; he has dealt with each man physically and been the victor with each, skipping over the fact that his trapping of Norman in the window was only temporary. This is a moment of pride in capability outside of the nature of what he has done; at this point his violence has been justified to himself as a necessary means for survival. But he has also subdued one other only temporarily; the sudden attack by Riddaway makes clear that it is not David's prowess that is at issue in the film, only that he admit to himself that he is capable of responding violently and *allowing* that response. It is also with something beyond conscious thought that Amy finally shoots Riddaway; David has been overpowered and would be killed without Amy's help. Pointedly, David has not been able to do it all by himself; the important thing is that he finds he can *attempt* it on those kill-or-be-killed terms.

Henry Niles, the "MacGuffin," has been all but forgotten. Yet during the siege, David dealt with Niles as well, duplicating the treatment he had winced at that John Niles gave his brother. Henry, in panic, breaks out and grabs Amy; David pulls them apart and subdues Henry with one slap and a "no-no" shake of the head, which Henry *understands*. This moment often receives audience laughter, yet it is completely in keeping with both characters: David, using reason and force, subdues the hysterical child.

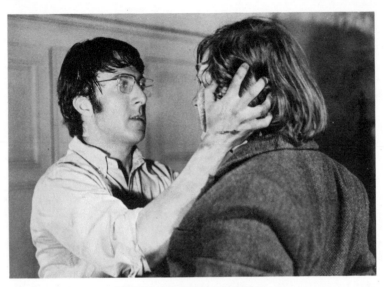

"Subduing the hysterical child."

In the car with Niles, David says that he doesn't know his
way home either, and smiles. This smile has caused a lot of
interpretive trouble with critics, but it is clear from the rest of
the film that life indeed will not be the same for David and
Amy; he cannot "go back home" in that sense, nor does he
know what "home" is with the new knowledge of himself.
David is not proud of the violence he has committed; but he
knows now that he is not the coward he was afraid he was or
that Amy accused him of being. He has made his stand, de-
fended his person and his house, and found in himself the
ability to commit the violence necessary to make that stand; he
has proved himself, most significantly, *to* himself. His for-
merly hollow threat that there would be "real trouble" if they
didn't stop, now has the evidence of David's ability to back it
up. He can still intellectualize his experience; his final smile
is at the realized irony of his reassurance to Henry.

In a sense, David engineers the situation as a test, though
not consciously. David has been, however, afraid that he *won't*
be able to deal with the defense of his "territory"; his insistence that he *can* handle such a situation forces him into the

corner where he *must* handle it, or die. If David had been sure of the extent of his response, he and Amy might never have come to England at all, let alone allow the situation with the village men to develop as it did. As Peckinpah has described it, "David Sumner gets the blinkers pulled off."[9] To his horror, he finds himself capable of brutal murder. To his credit, he realizes he can live with that potential inside himself. "The sage is ruthless . . ." Now, all he has to do is channel that potential constructively. As we all have to.

In fact, the original ending of the script was even less ambiguous than the end of the film. In the script, the children of the village, led by Bobby Hedden, were to show up, survey the carnage and likewise attack David and Amy, the last line of the script reading, "Just like the rest of us . . . sooner or later."[10] *Straw Dogs* does not *recommend* violence, nor does it *excuse* violence *per se* as a means. What Peckinpah is saying, in an echo of Robert Ardrey, is that we are all *capable* of such violence and we must find ways to deal with that primitive inheritance. It is an innate survival mechanism, and it will backfire if we deny its existence. When David Sumner denies it, he backs into a situation where it explodes—out of necessity.

If this idea is to come across in the film, the violence must be of sufficiently shocking dramatic impact to validate the idea that we are capable of such abhorrent behavior. Once again, the key to Peckinpah's impact is found in the editing, right down to the structurally efficient total surprise of Riddaway's final attack. Yet the depiction is not a gratuitous one for shock value; were it so, we would expect to see a shot of Cawsey's bloodied head at least. Yet even that would not necessarily be gratuitous. The idea here, as in *The Wild Bunch*, is that the violence be perceived as being sickeningly, realistically grim in order to produce a catharsis and, at the same time, not allow a *denial* of its grimness. There is unwitting support for Peckinpah's idea in some of the film's criticism which identifies the cooking oil David boils as *acid*, which would be (or at least would *seem* to be) more severely violent.

Straw Dogs is a brilliantly executed film, with much to be revealed in terms of its cinematic organization in a frame-by-frame analysis. The continuity is exceptional, complete to the sound of the still-revolving record player as David leaves the house with Niles. Jerry Fielding's score for the film is a masterpiece of growing tension and foreboding, married exactly to the moods of the film. Fielding fortunately knew how to interpret Peckinpah's demand for "irony" in the music.[11] John Coquillon's photography captures and supports the bleak atmosphere of the film; the stones of the house are visibly cold.

As Peckinpah's first contemporary or "modern" film, *Straw Dogs* demonstrates his concerns outside of genre settings, with a vitality and urgency heretofore seen only in, and perhaps limited by, Western conventions. The controversial reception of the film is evidence enough of its successful impact. Peckinpah refuses to lead his audience by the hand, but equally refuses to let it off the hook. As in previous works, the "truth" in the film may be variously accepted or rejected; and, as with other great works, the film demands a reaction: you can't walk away from it easily. But there is a path to be found through the film which provides consistency, which I hope I have indicated in this discussion. Peckinpah's achievement in *Straw Dogs* does not reside in the formation of an original idea, but in the unflagging professionalism and originality with which he and his company unerringly depict that idea. It is an achievement of complete cinematic conception. With *Straw Dogs*, Sam Peckinpah deservedly got his name above the title.

8

Junior Bonner (1972)

" . . . AS GENUINE as a sunrise," Curly Bonner's appraisal of his lone cowboy brother Junior is a good description of the whole film. *Junior Bonner* is a sincere, honest, "little" film with no "profound" messages, no extraordinary gut-wrenching, just some careful, gently understated observations of people against a background of the contemporary "New West." It has the warmth for humanity in all its varied frailty that informs all of Peckinpah's films; that warmth as featured in *Junior Bonner* makes the film seem completely out of place if one approaches Peckinpah from his "blood-and-guts" reputation, but it is entirely natural when one accepts the primacy of that feeling in Peckinpah. It should not be a surprise that the director of *The Wild Bunch* also made *Junior Bonner*.

Junior Bonner is a decent man who knows himself well enough to be true to himself, recalling Steve Judd as another good man. Likewise, Junior is past his prime, and his story in the film is in meeting the unfulfilled challenge of riding the champion bull, Sunshine. There is pride in his determination, for it is a personal challenge which Junior must meet for himself, regardless of whether others can understand it. Junior's persistence, the simple sincerity of his drive, earns our respect as well as the admiration of other peers. It is not an obsession, but just something he has to do.

For, having been thrown by the bull once (in addition to the fact that no one else has successfully ridden him), the quality of the challenge makes it an opportunity for Junior to accept his "eventual" retirement on his own terms. He has been a champion, and has no illusions about approaching the end of those days, but it is better to go out a king than a former king. But even that is not the most important thing. Junior's per-

133

Steve McQueen as Junior Bonner.

sonal dignity rests in part on being the kind of person who can accept defeat, but not for lack of trying. After his time is beaten in the bulldogging event, a spectator says, "Tough luck, cowboy." But Junior's answer makes defeat an everday thing: "Happens all the time, dude." Junior's ambition makes him try to be champion in his chosen field. He understands the reality of Curly's comment, "I'm workin' on my first million, and you're still workin' on eight seconds," but it is lasting those eight seconds, and being the best at it, that Junior has chosen as his goal. Maybe it's not that much of a goal to some, but the value of the prize is measured by what it takes to attain it. When Curly speaks with pride about his parade float's winning second place, Junior allows that "second's better 'n third," but Junior's meaning is clear: whatever the contest is, it's not first. It takes more to be first. Junior, by riding Sunshine, wants to satisfy himself that he still has what it takes to be the champion.

The timing is appropriate to the challenge as well; Prescott being Junior's hometown, it will have more meaning for him to meet the challenge in full view of his friends and family. He would ride Sunshine elsewhere, but it is good to prove yourself to those that know you.

Junior is also a symbol, though certainly not consciously, of the self-reliant individual, the lone cowboy, the traditional Westerner, if you will, who chooses his own way without regrets, and who hardly takes advantage of anyone, including himself. He has genuine personal integrity; although he is slow to repay a loan from his mother, one senses the terms might have made it more of a gift, anyway. While Junior would pay it back if he could, his mother knows that Junior's drifter road is not economically easy, and she also understands that Junior has to follow that road. Junior is a late example of older Western tradition; the progressive, "modern" urbanization of the New West, embodied by Curly's enterprises, acknowledges and uses the historical tradition but has no contemporary place for it. At best, Curly can acknowledge Junior's way, but he cannot understand it. Times *have* changed, and the businessman enlists the pride in tradition as a commercial aid. Curly thinks Junior would make a terrific salesman because of his Westerner image; Junior even rolls his own cigarettes. He sincerely worries about Junior's future, offering Junior a job, but cannot possibly appreciate Junior's way of life. Curly's New West concept of the joys of "total electric living" in model mobile homes does not celebrate the Old West beyond its commercial use. Curly doesn't want to breathe clean air, he wants to sell it. By contrast, Junior's financial views are utilitarian: "Money's nobody's favorite."

What ties Curly and Junior together is, ironically for Curly, another traditional Western value, for family. You"re my brother, and I guess I love you; we're family," Curly acknowledges. Family ties are stronger than economic philosophy; one need not *like* one's family, but one takes care of one's own. This leads to Curly's arrangements for their parents (on his terms); but Junior is disappointed in the way Curly is using them, even if he is willing to "take care" of them, where Junior can't. Junior resents Curly's plan to use their mother as a mobile home demonstrator and curio seller, and Curly's short-changing of Ace by buying the family ranch land cheap. It is sad that the "New West" does not make an allowance for the dignity of its forebears; the respect and affection for the ways of the past has its limits. Curly recognizes that the Prescott "Frontier Days" rodeo is not just another rodeo as his wife describes it; it is a "part of history." But as history it has a limited place; Curly is content to let Ace's dignity reside in the picture of Ace which hangs in the Palace Bar.

Ace, the figurative "top o' the pile" of the family, has in effect lost his position from his lack of economic success; Curly has taken Ace's place in practical terms. But Ace is respected for former glory (he was a rodeo champion in his day) by most; he is colorful, authentic, harmless, and unstoppable. Ace is a dreamer, but his persistence in never giving up on those dreams makes him lovable. Outside his family, he is affectionately tolerated as a symbol of bygone days. Ace has become a legend. In a land that lives off of old legends precisely because it has no new ones of value, living legends are appreciated despite their impracticality. Ace is not about to change from the attitudes that made him the man he *was*. But the rules have changed, and he is hard pressed to maintain that dignity from the past. Admirably, Ace *knows* he has "run out of room" in the new landscape—both he and Junior laugh at the realization that they at least aren't fooling each other when Ace finds that Junior can't help him get to Australia—but

Ace will not admit defeat, and outwardly insists on the viability of his dreams and schemes, whatever the reality. Junior respects this in Ace, his individuality, and tries to make it easier for his father. Ace ponders whimsically, "If this world's all about winners, what's for the losers?" Junior allows that "somebody's got to hold the horses, Ace." Ace truly never was a "winner," outside the rodeo; he continues to come up "just short," missing the "mother lode" by twenty feet. Junior, in relating to Ace, knows that Ace's winning quality was and is one of attitude, but that practical considerations in the New West are not met by pioneering spirit. That's just the way things are, not to be lamented by the individual as such, but a fact that has to be accepted by those who must follow their own road despite the fact that the rest of the world may not reward those who take that road.

Ellie Bonner has the same spirit and maintains the dignity of one who has to accept the changes. It has been hard for her, tied to a dreamer and free-wheeling rascal like Ace, but that indeed is part and parcel of the man she married and still loves in spite of himself (or herself). She cannot follow Ace, for all of the disappointments and broken promises of the dreamer, but she undoubtedly does not regret her life. For survival, she made the adaptation and took the choice off of Ace's hands. "Times have changed," she says with the family assembled in the bar; "I changed them." Junior respects his mother's stoicism all the more because he knows that *she* knows why Ace can't change, even if it forces them apart. And because she understands Ace, she understands Junior. But Junior is rankled by the indignities Ellie must suffer, exemplified by Curly's wife's pained admonition not to smoke cigars while holding her grandchild. Curly's wife is the embodiment of changing attitudes in the New West, apparently linked to the Old West only by marriage, barely tolerant of the holdovers from the old and outmoded West.

Peckinpah is clearly sympathetic to Junior, Ace, and Ellie, for they persist in intangible areas of the human spirit. At the same time, he cannot pointedly condemn the New West, because times *have* changed; but it is clear that something has been or is about to be lost in the transition. There is nothing to blame particularly for the change, but the danger of the facelessness of "modernization" is in its capacity to swallow individuals, making the individual less valuable. It becomes more difficult for individuals to assert their individuality. When one such as Junior does, it is a victory, albeit a bittersweet one for a vanishing breed. As Junior watches (and we see) the ranch being turned into a gravel pit, there is a feeling of resignation and loss. This is keyed visually by the anonymous power of the machines: first, Junior has to back off physically from the shovel of progress (underlining the idea that there is no room for Junior) and second, the ranch house is inexorably torn down several times in several different shots, to emphasize the finality. These shots are finally intercut with flashes of Ace, who is likewise being cut out of the landscape. Progress is the villain by default; there is no attempt to explain why things are this way; yet, like Junior, you squint into the sun, look at the land, and know that something's wrong, something's gone. There is no place for Junior here. But *Junior Bonner* is a partial refutation of any despair in this direction; it is a celebration, not a lament. Change is acknowledged, but it cannot be stopped. One would be foolish to try to stop it; one looks for room where one can. Junior is a "hero" of individual-

Robert Preston and Ida Lupino as Ace and Ellie Bonner.

ity; in his being true to himself, he is heroically looked to as a symbol of individual pride and commitment. But to be sympathetic to Junior and the rest, one has to love humanity first.

Peckinpah's narrative is again contained in the visualization beyond the script. Reactions are more telling than statements; the film is felt more than said. This is apparent everywhere: in the way Junior and the bull Sunshine eyeball each other in the stock pens; in Junior's dealings with the stockman Buck Roan, wherein a tacit understanding is reached as to why Junior needs to ride Sunshine again; in Ellie's acceptance and abiding love of Ace as they ascend the stairs for one more private moment, an incredibly tender scene whose emotion resides in the looks they give each other; in Junior's talk with Ace after they have shared the wild ride out of the parade, where Ace knocks Junior's hat off in frustration and Junior is seen to be equally frustrated by his inability to help his father, the train passing between them underscoring their separation at that moment; and even in Junior's gradual "winning" of the girl, Charmagne, where mutual looks of honest admiration and attraction score the points that will lead to their going off together. All of these scenes reflect Peckinpah's insight and knowledge of human nature; there isn't a false note among them, indicated by dialogue but delivered visually.

Riding Sunshine is not a "big deal" in that there's nothing at stake beyond Junior's pride—he can't "save the farm" by being successful, nor can he keep his family from drifting apart—but we understand why Junior has to do it, anyway. His need is further indicated visually by the subtle tension of the draw; Junior's fingers twiddle with the typewriter carriage in anticipation, and he spins the carriage as the tension is broken and he wins his draw of Sunshine. It is left unclear as to whether Buck has fixed the draw for Junior or not; Buck does not agree to it "up front"—that would go beyond the notion that a person has to take what comes and his chances thereby—and Junior's asking for the "fix" is a practical matter that can't afford to rely on luck because of circumstances (the "hometown" aspect as well as the idea that Junior's time is running out). There is the suggestion that the fix was not made, as Junior would undoubtedly not have enough prize money to pay for the airline tickets at the end, but it is still possible that Buck has yet helped Junior's draw. (From Buck's position it would make for a better show in addition to indicating his respect for Junior.) In any case, it is fitting that we are not privy to exactly what transpires, as it allows for luck without relying on luck's coincidence. Fate and Buck Roan, in some combination, understand that Junior deserves his chance.

Entering Ace and himself in the cow-milking event is a testament to Junior's acceptance and faith in his father as a man; Junior is proud to walk behind Ace in the parade, proud to join him on the horse, and sticks by Ace and Ace's worth as a person in the cow-milking. Though his individual identity is allowed by his being called "J-R", Junior is, as his name which "just stuck" implies, truly Ace's son. Father and son defeat themselves in the event, as much by nature as anything else, with Ace's dog, like Ace himself, spiritedly joining in but only getting in the way. "We could 'a won," Ace complains to Junior. But Junior's answer goes beyond simple winning: "We did, Ace." They won by sticking together, by not rejecting each other over a lack of success, by entering the event in the first place. That Junior calls it a victory despite the ludicrous physical indignity of the event points to the value of their not giving up on each other and their individual pride. Indeed, the nature of the event is a self-parody of sorts for Ace and Junior, a good-natured humiliation by *choice*, and, as such, something which calls for real pride and "size" in a person to undertake. The crowd applauds Ace, "sixty years young" and still hangin' in there; on the sidelines, Charmagne laughs in admiration at Junior's ability to provide laughter at his own "expense."

Peckinpah's accuracy of observation and consummate cinematic ability to deliver that observation are highlighted in three particular areas, the parade, the tavern brawl, and the rodeo itself. The parade is a multiple-camera triumph of continuity, giving an omniscient view of detail, while yet delivering the summary conclusion that the parade, by its nature as a modern attempt to celebrate the past, is something of a cheat on the value of the historical tradition. It may be honest nostalgia on the part of the organizers, but it can't help but finally be somewhat *tacky*, exemplified by Curly's float, a masterpiece of commercialization.

The brawl in the Palace Bar is a harmless and enthusiastic explosion, an exuberance of letting off steam under the influence, in a somewhat typically Western "emotional" outlet. Painful bumps and bruises, yes, but these are people traditionally proud of physical toughness, and, pointedly, nobody gets hurt seriously. Peckinpah, in total control, edits the scene to completely integrate the chaotic action it contains, building pace and excitement by cutting *away* from an action before it is completed. His gift for natural humor consistently undercuts any violence in the brawl ("Watch it, boys, my dog doesn't fight fair"), and before things get too far out of control, the biggest guy decides it is enough and instructs the band to play "something patriotic." Love of country, for whatever it's worth, is another Western tradition; the response of the crowd is genuine and effectively instructive. Here, too, Junior exempts himself from the thick of things, "following his own road" into the phone booth with Charmagne. Junior isn't one to look for trouble, deftly substituting Red Terwiliger for himself before trouble arises in the person of Charmagne's escort. Junior's removal of himself from the brawl points to the fight as not being relevant so much as simply being typical of life in those parts. But because of Junior's removal, the fight becomes an observation, not a recommendation. Junior has already accepted his deserved punch from Curly, and that fight ends there. To be sure, Curly equally "deserved" Junior's punch (on the porch, knocking Curly through the window) for his callous lack of respect for their father; but Junior does not have the right to judge, and so takes Curly's slug.

Peckinpah's handling of the rodeo is equally as deft as his observations in other areas. Two other rodeo-background films were released in 1972 (Cliff Robertson's *J. W. Coop* and Steve Ihnat's *The Honkers*); consequently the territory may have seemed familiar to reviewers, but Peckinpah's cinematic treatment of the rodeo captures its verve, excitement, and color accurately and originally. It is seen as a celebration of the physical stamina required in the contest, underscored by the preponderance of losers over winners. Because of this, there is further instruction to the viewer that the measure of the contestant resides in the trying more than in the actual winning. There is physical grace and beauty (and humor) in the rodeo contest between man and animal: the use of slow-motion here accentuates the movement and, at times, the skill involved in the events, coming back to the idea of depicting "what it takes." A couple of subliminal flashes of hand-held (nonanamorphic!) shots serve to place the viewer in the chaotic "middle," while still being an observer of the totality of the event. It is finally necessary to have an establishing (medium) close-up of Junior on the bucking horse; that the close-up had to be faked on a bucking machine for insurance reasons (which neither McQueen nor Peckinpah liked) makes the shot a flaw in context, but only by a few frames that allow it to be noticed as such at all. To his credit, McQueen did as many of his own stunts as he was allowed to do, and other shots prove this rewardingly for the film.

Peckinpah builds the climax of Junior's ride of Sunshine expertly, exacting the measure of anticipated tension in close-ups of slow-motion and "real" time. We are completely with Junior in that ride because of Peckinpah's careful direction of *us*, so much so that one hardly notices during the ride that the "eight seconds" actually takes almost thirty seconds on the screen. We share fully the honest triumph of Junior's accomplishment, and with great, affectionate pleasure watch him accept his "reward." There *is* satisfaction in the vindication of the individual and, however transitory or relative that achievement may be, there is pride that it has been done this time, at least.

Junior still has "gotta go down my own road," as he puts it to Curly, and finally, with no lies or other expectations, to Charmagne. Junior accepts life ultimately as "just one of those things you grin at and pray," a sideline observation of Buck's we are allowed to hear and consider the meaning of. But when it counted, Junior proved that he could "stand up" to the challenge of sticking to "his road," and be the best at what he *chose* to be the best at. We needn't worry about Junior's future; there is a suggestion, in a glimpse of Buck Roan's passing truck, that Junior might eventually accept Buck's offer of a job, if and when he decides it is the right thing to do. But for the moment, Junior has satisfied himself in his hometown, doing what he can and remaining true to himself. His gesture of the First-Class airline tickets for Ace and his dog is an invitation to Ace *not* to change, to continue to be proud and pursue his own way, however impractical. It is a heartfelt debt of gratitude and respect, a measure of love which is all he can give to Ace. "Tell him Junior sent ya," just as Ace might tell his son. "We could 'a won." "We did, Ace." And so have we, through Junior.

Junior Bonner is a modest film of warmth, a work which does not trumpet itself in any demands, but in whose quiet engagement lies great value for its genuine affection for people. As ever, Peckinpah resists judging his characters, allowing them their faults to consider them as whole people rather than as objects to be manipulated for moral lessons. The "lessons" are more basic than any one ideology could provide, with the one underlying principle being that the book on humanity is not closed. The unprepossessing nature of the film must not be allowed to hide the talents involved in its execution; everyone involved in the film can look to their contributions with real pride under Peckinpah's directorial guidance, and one must not underestimate an achievement of such apparent simplicity. It is as difficult, if not more so, to sustain such grace here as it is to orchestrate the thunder and lightning of more "dramatic" stories.

If *Junior Bonner* is to be seen as being sentimental, it must not be confused with the false sentimentality of idolization; the film is not a "gloss" in its treatment of people or situations. You may not buy it, but you sure are missing something if you don't. In ending the film, Peckinpah does something for each of his characters who could use it most, doing cinematically what he cannot do for them in reality: saying goodbye, he freezes them in time and space, as we wish they could be.

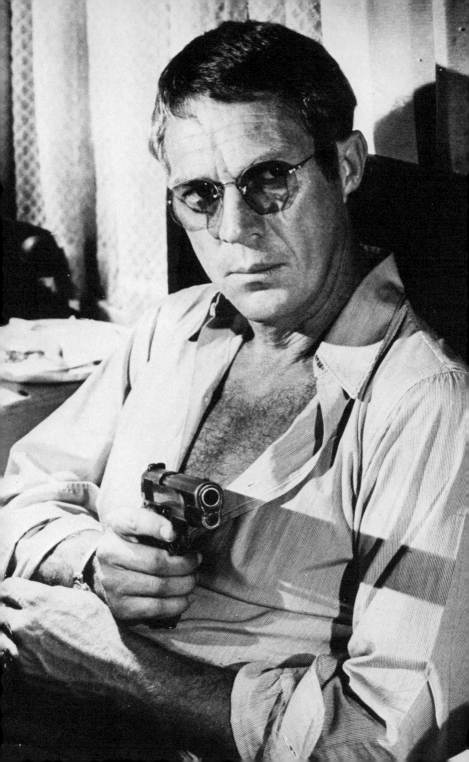

9

The Getaway (1972)

DOC: "What'd I tell ya?–[This] isn't a game."
CAROL: "It's *all* a game."

"THE GETAWAY was my first attempt at satire, badly done."[1]
Peckinpah's description of this film helps to explain a lot, but
with such a tip-off to his approach, it is hardly a bad job. *The
Getaway* is a strange film until one steps back from potential
expectations and takes a closer look at the goings-on.

At first glance, it does seem to be the tough action film that
Peckinpah and McQueen's "reputations" called for, which
they both purposely avoided in *Junior Bonner*. But there is
something hollow and curiously unsatisfying about Doc and
Carol McCoy's final success if one pursues the action from the
idea that the pair, as our "heroes," are forced to deal variously
with less scrupulous forces and are competent in meeting
their challenges. This is the picture of them which is carefully
set up as an image for them to portray. The problem is, they
don't live up to that image–their final success is less a matter
of their competence than it is a victory *in spite* of themselves.
Peckinpah has the last laugh here: practically everyone
bought the violent surface as being the aspect of the film to
"get behind" for enjoyment. Several critics who missed the
boat with *The Wild Bunch* liked *The Getaway* as a good action
film; others were distressed that it seemed empty and cynical,
fearful that Peckinpah had become merely mechanical in his
execution of the film. A few came closer in recognizing that
Peckinpah is a filmmaker of commitment who doesn't undertake projects lightly, and thus that perhaps there *was* something underlying the film.

But the public bought the film overwhelmingly, and even if

145

McQueen as Doc McCoy: the image of the professional.

it was due simply to McQueen's box-office pull in an action film, they bought the violence Peckinpah had been making the comment on in *The Wild Bunch* and *Straw Dogs*, further demonstrating his point and making money on it as well. At the very least, the success of *The Getaway* is a vindication of a very basic idea of Peckinpah's, having to do with the nature of our relationship to violence. Peckinpah is not cynical in *The Getaway*, but there is a sardonic smile behind the camera. The satire is not on the characters, but on the audience's expectations.

Consequently, it had to be played with a very straight face. It is so straight, in fact, that at times the satirical quality matches expectations such that the irony of an action is lost unless the total context of the film is kept in mind. This "confusion" felt from the duality of approach makes the put-on nature difficult to accept for some, in that those skeptical of Peckinpah might see calling the film "satire" as a lame excuse for a flawed work. But unless it is approached as satire, the film leaves nagging dissatisfactions that vanish when it is so accepted. Ultimately the film does become less significant the farther one removes it from Peckinpah and his other work, and approaching Peckinpah initially through it would be a deceptively elusive undertaking. The subject may not have quite the "depth" of his other works (a subjective, relative idea, however), but not taking the film "seriously" doesn't mean that it should be lightly dismissed or that it is not worth one's time. It may be an expensive "joke," but *The Getaway* is a finely crafted, integrated piece of cinema from a serious (read "committed") film artist who indeed has tried something new for himself here, which behooves us to consider what he's up to — for our own benefit. The fact that the film did make money should absolve Peckinpah of any accusations of "irresponsibility" from financial backers.

The duality of approach in *The Getaway* between the "straight" film—the action movie the audience expects—and the "satire" of that expectation can perhaps be better followed if one thinks in terms of the "interior" and "exterior" films being played simultaneously. Briefly, the "interior" film is the world created within the frame perceived by the characters in the film; the "exterior" film is the additional level of meaning or interpretation available to the audience (not necessarily satirical). Doc and Carol McCoy take themselves seriously, at the interior level of the film. But the audience can step back to the exterior film and say, "this is nonsense—these romanticized outlaw types are just playing genre games."

From the beginning to the end of *The Getaway*, we are reminded that "what's going on" on the screen as well as what's happening to the characters from their own point of view is a game. Practically the first thing said after the last credit in the prison prologue is, "Oh, man, it's just a game," when Doc loses his temper over a chessboard. Likewise, in the garbage dump, when Doc complains to Carol that she's not taking things seriously enough ("It isn't a game"), she asserts that "it's all a game," telling him, in effect, to wake up. It is a constant contest on a multiplicity of levels, called "life," called "pulling off a robbery," called "interpersonal relationships," called "fighting for control of the loot," called "surviving prison," etc. Each level can be regarded as a board-game set-up, with its own rules, rewards, set-backs, and dice-rolls. It is also a game called "action movie," the set-up being Steve McQueen's familiar image from *Nevada Smith* to *The Thomas Crown Affair* against a plot that presents him in the unfamiliar role of a ham-strung underdog.

Doc McCoy is a professional who is never in control despite his professionalism. It is his resourcefulness in *attempting* to behave professionally that pulls their chestnuts out of the fire, but never completely enough to ensure a smooth escape. The problems he and his wife encounter are either the result of initiative being "forcibly" taken away from him (a distinct handicap for a self-reliant professional) or the consequences of errors in his own judgment. As a successful bank robber, Doc is somewhat inept as a result of accepted conditions, hard pressed to maintain control in trying to assert his professionalism.

Even his name implies professionalism, and as such seems to be something of a misnomer. One wonders how he got caught and wound up in prison in the first place; if we give him the benefit of the doubt that it wasn't his fault, we are accepting the image of his *assumed* capability. The credits sequence is extremely important to an understanding of what will develop later. Cleverly, a lot of information is delivered between credit titles, which audiences tend to ignore. Peckinpah establishes the initial set-up of Doc and the film before the film "starts" for many in the audience. Right from the first frame, however, the appearance-versus-reality conflict is introduced by the tranquil shot of deer followed by the camera's pulling back to reveal them in front of a prison, and there is·the intimation that there may be more to this film than at first meets the eye. A slender suggestion, yes, but a suggestion whose subtlety is in keeping with the nature of the rest of the film.

For the end of the credits (the "beginning" of the film) shows Doc *losing* his "cool"; prison is getting to him, and he misses his wife: he wants out. Breaking the model bridge he has made, the self-reliant professional is cracking under the lonely, rigid monotony of prison. He is willing to compromise himself in order to get out, a "mistake" which he will pay for through the rest of the film. Using Carol as his messenger, he fails to realize what her getting that message across might involve. He wants her to tell Benyon that he is for sale in exchange for his release, not thinking that presenting the offer will involve any other salesmanship.

The nature of his compromise forces Doc to accept conditions for the robbery that are against his better judgment, which in effect doom the "success" of the job. He has to make extra allowances for probable double-crosses, which he can only make to a limited degree. The uncertainty introduced by having to accept Rudy and Frank, who are introduced as being of questionable ability, as well as Benyon's dictate that he, not Doc, runs the show, is a severe handicap for Doc, and a measure of how desperately Doc wanted "out" of prison. Yet Doc does try to be the professional, living up to his end of the bargain by accepting the job even with its restrictions.

The robbery itself, for all the careful preparation shown, is a case of Murphy's Law (everything that can go wrong, will go wrong), as is the rest of the film. Doc has given key responsibilities to Carol—indeed, she is the only person he can remotely trust at that point—but this reliance on Carol is at best of questionable judgment. Carol is nervous from the outset, narrowly missing a collision with a kid as they drive in to town, and worse, is trying not to show her anxiety and justify Doc's reliance on her. One wonders if she "helped" Doc on the earlier job which landed him in prison; this is doubtful,

but in any case Doc "has" to use her, and her neophyte ineptitude causes problems. Stalling the van is only one mistake.

By the time Frank panics and shoots the bank guard, the
timing of the "operation" is off enough that Doc narrowly misses having the door slammed in their faces by one of his own
diversionary bombs. Recovering from that, Doc crashes
through the porch of a house; his single curse commentary
sums up everything.

With Frank dead and Doc already suspicious of Rudy, the
farmhouse rendezvous seems to be one thing Doc is ready for,
beating Rudy to the draw. But Doc does not "finish the job"
properly, as the result of a combination of several possibilities,
including Carol's implied criticism of the brutality of the
shooting, inefficient haste to get on their way, and perhaps
most significantly, the idea that Doc is not a cold-blooded killer. Shooting in self-defense is one thing, but inspecting the
body is another. Whatever his reason, not attending to Rudy
thoroughly is hardly professional. Rudy's survival is further
indicative of Doc's inefficiency, because what saves Rudy is
the bullet-proof vest which Doc had recommended earlier and
that Rudy had then ironically scorned. The basement scene of
their final checking of plans is another example of the "game"
aspect of the film. Rudy and Doc seem to be engaged in an ego
face-off over the question of who is the tougher professional.
The way things go, it seems that Rudy well might be.

The "pay-off" at Benyon's also goes "wrong," with Doc
completely unsuspecting of the set-up. It is one of the few
things which Carol does "right," and at that, it is something of
a close shave because of her nervousness over pulling the
trigger. But because of Carol's anxiety, doubt rises in Doc's
mind and *ours* as to Carol's complete loyalty. She repeatedly
asserts her innocence in Benyon's double-cross, but it takes
almost the rest of the film for her to convince Doc (and us) that
she did choose Doc after all. This is complicated by her sexual
"infidelity" with Benyon, the price she had to pay for Benyon's
cooperation, which causes Doc more anguish finally than his
not being aware of the potential ambush at the payoff. Once
again, Doc is not in control.

Carol's most disastrous mistake comes at the railroad station
where she is duped in another "game," "the oldest con-game
in the world," according to Doc, where the key to the locker

with the loot is switched. Doc gives chase and proves himself
capable here, but only up to a point, for he is again not ruthless
enough to kill the con-man. (Even if he does try to do so, it is at
least inept, as the con-man survives.) The failure to kill the
con-man (and the more serious failure to search his pockets)
leads to the positive police identification which has them truly
on the run.

Carol buys a car without a functioning radio, critically de-
priving them of the information that the police know who
they're looking for. Stopping to buy a radio, Doc is recognized,
surrounded by his image on the many television sets in the
store. This particular shot serves to highlight literally the nature of Doc and Carol's being constantly boxed in. Even the
technology is working against them. Doc again manages a rescue from the situation; but Carol hits the accelerator too fast
and knocks Doc into the street. Taking advantage of an approaching bus, they escape again by an increasingly narrower
margin. For all of the "errors," Doc *is* capable enough to get
them out of tight spots, but they are mostly situations which he
might have avoided in the first place. Here also, Doc inflicts
violence on a car, not a person, *this* time thoroughly enough to
remove *its* threat. (This scene, an idea of McQueen's, also becomes in Peckinpah's hands a release from building tension
for the audience; nobody ever felt guilty destroying a car, and
a police car at that.)

They are trapped again at the drive-in restaurant; the car has
been identified, possibly by the lady reading the newspaper
next to Doc as Carol bought the car. (The efficient professional
probably would have had that newspaper.) Doc almost doesn't
recognize their trap in time, and perhaps could have avoided it
by being more watchful. Luckily, the trap is sprung ineffi-
ciently, and it becomes a free-for-all game of catch-as-catch-
can. Doc lets out a "whoop" of release in the middle of it,
chaotic as it is; pointedly, no one is hurt, including the cops.
This is lucky and coincidental, but accounted for as we see the
cops ducking. The game is emphasized beyond that by playing the scene for action-comedy, with two parked neckers interrupted by a ramming police car.

Doc and Carol do escape, but their narrow escape here
lands them in the trash truck, joining the figurative and literal
ideas of their hitting bottom, reduced to hiding in the refuse to

make their getaway. They spend the rest of the night as more garbage in a pile of garbage. This is the peak of the put-on, for the scene is at once perfectly ridiculous and yet perfectly logical as they succeed in eluding the police. After being dumped in the morning, it is their last chance for a reconciliation, as Carol, who has previously stuck by Doc despite his antipathy toward her, has reached her limit. "It's *all* a game," she insists, putting it to Doc finally that he be tough enough to get over her infidelity, whether it was required or not. She echoes Pike Bishop's line to Angel: "You either learn to live with it" or she will leave him there.

Even though they thereafter function as a better team, Doc relaxes in the Laughlin Hotel too soon, not being aware of the presence of Rudy (subject of an earlier mistake) and not realizing that Benyon's men are so close. Doc and Carol make it out of the hotel, but only after resorting to the furious defense of the shoot-out, and then by the aid of the cowboy whose truck reads "Specialist—Our Business Is Pickin' Up." They even allow the cowboy to *bargain* with them for the truck. No, Doc and Carol McCoy are not ruthless professionals.

Doc and Carol, and the object of the "game."

They are, however, in love. Doc and Carol need each other, finding out finally that their sticking together is the only thing that will give their successful escape meaning. This is the "other half" of the film, in that Peckinpah is straight with his characters even if the "genre" conventions are skewed to make the overall film a "satire." Taken literally as a serious drama, *The Getaway* is a romance, with an underpinning that personal loyalty between a man and woman as well as between friends is something worth holding on to.

It is because Doc needs Carol that he needs to get out of prison. But they have been separated for four years, and Doc's "coming out" reunification is tentative, tenderly so, based on their mutual need. Waiting for Carol outside the prison, Doc stands by the flagpole, a beautiful long-shot which expresses Doc's isolation in the midst of his freedom, with the national and state flags at the top of the frame, and Doc at the bottom.

They stop at a park, where Doc absorbs the realization of freedom, watching the people and children play. "Even the worst of us . . .", is easily recalled from *The Wild Bunch*. In a marvelously romantic piece of editing (too romantic if you're only looking for action), Peckinpah has Doc watch the children and simultaneously (by intercutting slow-motion shots) imagine himself and Carol doing likewise. When they get home, we see that they indeed have done as Doc imagined, but a voyeuristic element has been removed by not showing us their swim *as* it happens. The privacy of their initial encounter is preserved. The following love scene is gentle and tender, not a matter of Doc's regaining his manhood, but of Doc's becoming a human being again. They eat a hearty breakfast, and are happy.

Carol needs Doc, and further needs him to need her. Doc wants to be able to rely on Carol, using her as a full partner in his (their) work. He is patient with her anxiety during the robbery, and regrets having to "kill" Rudy in front of her. The scene at Benyon's, as previously mentioned, is disastrous for Doc because he then questions Carol's loyalty. They stand in silence, their separation in that moment after Benyon's killing symbolized by their pointing guns at each other in shock and confusion. Doc is frustrated by the surprise and slaps Carol for that (not warning him); but the thing that sticks in his craw, which he brings up repeatedly as the sorest point, is Carol's sexual infidelity. Their problems escaping are her fault as well as his, and she takes Doc's insults, though not easily, giving back to him the allusions to her infidelity. But ultimately, at bottom, in the dump, Doc realizes the strength of his need for her and that their love is all they have of real value. In their reconciliation, they promise to bury the past and to leave it where it belongs. And again, the ludicrousness of the scene is underscored by the romance in the trash pit, but the scene also works logically on a literal, personal level between the characters. Peckinpah describes their mutual need visually in various ways, tying Doc and Carol together even when they seem apart: at Benyon's, they face each other after the killing in a corner of the frame; in the railroad station after Doc returns from the con-man chase, they are alone together at the edge of the frame, the room otherwise empty as they argue; and during the con-man chase, Doc asks for "two" to the "end of the line," as Peckinpah cuts to a shot of Carol alone in the waiting room. The ultimate value of their relationship is comically reiterated by Slim Pickens's cowboy, who is glad to find out that Doc and Carol are married, complaining that the trouble with the world is that there "ain't no morals." There is at least one for Doc and Carol, that of staying together. Carol says that Doc will eventually have to trust someone; Doc asserts that he trusts in God, as per the words on the back of every dollar. But Doc finds that the only important trust is that which they have in each other.

Contrasted to Doc and Carol are Rudy and Fran. Rudy is a false threat for the audience: Doc thinks he's dead (a mistake), and though surprised and consternated by Rudy's reappearance, Doc quickly gets rid of Rudy a second time. But not being a cold-blooded killer, let alone ruthless enough to be efficient, Doc still makes the "error" of not killing Rudy, so that he has to deal with Rudy one *more* time, finally killing him in *self-defense* on the fire-escape. Doc is also lucky that Rudy's aim is off, but it adds to the satirical quality that Doc just can't keep Rudy *down*. Since the audience does know that Rudy is alive and preparing to ambush Doc, more sympathy is generated for Doc and Carol as underdogs unaware of Rudy's threat. It is for (satirical) contrast as well as for sympathy for Doc and Carol that Rudy and Fran are so gross. Their intercut presence is a constant mockery of Doc and Carol's relationship, the black humor of Rudy and Fran's crude behavior increasing that contrast. (Steve McQueen's minor recutting of the film involved removing some business with Rudy and Fran, to increase his own screen time.) If there is any doubt to Rudy's nature, it is concretely dispelled as Rudy goes to a clearly labeled "Animal" doctor for help.

Rudy is ruthless where Doc is not, but Rudy is also stupid. Aside from underestimating Doc (and we have seen how stupid that has to be), Rudy is too eager for his revenge, leaving his back to a door which he has overlooked checking to see if it connects to Doc's room. Because of that, he loses his chance.

Fran, a primitive sister to Amy Sumner, doesn't like blood and certainly can't take any pain or torture. She is a match for Rudy, an empty-headed animal living in a musical head-set who seems satisfied in merely avoiding pain. That she is such a match even surprises Rudy, looking to Harold (her husband) in disbelief as she plays with Rudy's gun and pretends to shoot Harold, laughing hysterically. After Harold's suicide, we learn that the kitty has been named "Poor Little Harold"; when Laughlin takes them to their room, the humor in the similarity to Fran is not lost as he asks if it's all right to "put the pussy on the bed." Hopefully it is unnecessary to say so, but Fran is no more a comment on women in general than Rudy is a "typical" man. Harold is simply an innocent bystander in Rudy's path, obviously ill-equipped to absorb the situation, but under the circumstances one is hard-pressed to recommend an alternative to him. Here, too, Harold's suicide is logical for the character, yet its extremity, coupled with Rudy's non-plussed reaction which quickly turns to "ho-hum," adds to the overblown, satirical "half" of the film. As Rudy discovers Harold's body, the radio blares out with a preacher saying, "Receive the Lord! Receive the Lord!" This should get a laugh, but audience expectations of serious action-drama work against it.

Peckinpah has other, less dark humor in the film. A particular example is the ironic comedy of the kid with the squirt gun on the train, "shooting" our "ruthless" robber hero with devilish impunity. Peckinpah goes one step further with his "observer child," and the kid helps to identify Doc to the police. Another tossed-off piece of ironic humor is the scene with Carol and the soldier in the railroad station bar: "You wouldn't happen to be a Mormon, would ya?" the soldier asks, looking for a good time. And one other bit has Benyon's henchmen hesitantly concerned about whether they should give Benyon a "proper" burial; they dump the body down a dry well.

Peckinpah's uncompromising cinematic eye has the viewer gripped by powerfully edited action scenes, but his carefully composed frame also includes the double level of parody and "straight" character development. The Jim Thompson novel is much more brutal, with Doc McCoy a truly ruthless character, ending in a kind of "Twilight Zone" nightmare wherein crime does not pay after all. Walter Hill's original script, set circa 1949, takes the story some steps closer to the film, employing a combination of elements from *High Sierra* (1941) and *White Heat* (1949), and was dedicated to their director, Raoul Walsh.[2] Peckinpah played with Hill's ideas, but it was his own idea to update the story to 1972, and it is his conception which guides the finished film and the fine work contributed by its participants. Criticisms of Ali MacGraw in particular, who creates a character as Carol, with a *credible* lack of *apparent* emotional range, are unwarranted. The only significant change from Peckinpah's "cut" is the replacement of Jerry Fielding's score with one by Quincy Jones. Fielding's score has been described as more of a counterpoint to the film's action,[3] but the Jones score ironically *follows* the *expected* action level and thereby contributes to the duality of the "straight" film as a simultaneous parody.

Taking the film "too seriously," one finds that the good action is undercut by frustration with the characters, while the character relationships are clouded by some very tough, bizarre action. This makes for a critical flop at that level, but the visibility of the action allows for a commercial success. A lot falls into place however, when the film is viewed as satire, with the tough action "pro" getting out by the skin of his teeth in the "exterior" film. If the "interior" film seems to lack conviction, it is because Doc and Carol are stripped of any convictions beyond the notion of sticking together. ("If you can't do that, you're like some animal . . ."—another *Wild Bunch* echo.)

Doc and Carol's getaway is a snarled foul-up; the final hotel shoot-out is the anticipated explosion releasing tensions that have been built up by frustration with the characters' previous escapes and by action / genre expectations. Peckinpah delivers, and has it both ways, as put-on and straight action. Finally, Doc and Carol are allowed success; they haven't killed anybody who didn't "deserve it," and the bank directors had already embezzled the bank. "Vaya con Dios"; they take the money and run. In a way, so does Peckinpah, without having cheated on himself. If we take the "image" (Peckinpah's *and* the film's) too seriously, we only cheat ourselves.

10

Pat Garrett and Billy the Kid (1973)

BILLY: "You're in poor company, Pat."
PAT: "Yeah, I'm alive, though."
BILLY: "So 'm I."

LIKE *Major Dundee*, the theatrical-release version of Peckinpah's *Pat Garrett and Billy the Kid* is a distortion of a masterpiece that might have been. The studio cut approximately seventeen minutes from Peckinpah's version, severely distorting the director's work in such a way that the remainder only suggests what Peckinpah was after. The body of Peckinpah's interest is still there, but the balance of emphasis is off. What is most frustrating is that what remains is so good, with stunning individual scenes of harsh elegance, but the whole is clearly abridged. We have seen how Peckinpah gives meaning to individual scenes in his editing, but this is also true of his whole films. Visually exquisite moments are carefully edited together to achieve pace, emotional tone, and full character portraits. Removing whole scenes, as well as chopping off pieces of others, interrupts pace, staggers emotional tone, and distorts characters significantly. But because of Peckinpah's care with each scene, what is left is yet engaging, enough so to increase the frustration over the interference with the film as he intended it. Scenes of characters which would have been counterpointed by others are now only clues to these characters. If you view *Pat Garrett and Billy the Kid* "cold," you must hold in abeyance many "final" interpretive ideas. The "rewarding track" is present and can be followed through the film, but holding on to that track means making a lot of allowances for the shortcomings of the theatrical version.

The film originated with a script written by Rudolph Wur-

159

The cost of Garrett's compromise.

litzer at the direction of the producer, Gordon Carroll. The myth of Billy the Kid has endured a host of film treatments, and there is something to learn from comparisons among different generations' handlings of the oft-told tale; but that's another problem. How the legend is recounted is as revealing as the legend itself; and the significance of a particular recounting is our concern here.

Wurlitzer's script recognizes the romantic appeal of Billy the Kid and his symbolic evocation of the freedom the West allowed an individual, but Wurlitzer also became concerned with the figure of Pat Garrett, the friend and eventual killer of the Kid, who is treated here as one who will compromise for survival. Garrett's choice "to live rather than die, to abandon obsolete descriptions of courage and freedom for a more complicated if more corrupt sense of order"[1] became the question of contemporary relevance. Whereas Garrett in earlier renditions may have been seen more as the representative of civilized law and order, which finally dooms the life of the outlaw, Wurlitzer made him the focus for a consideration of what it means to an individual to "sell out," to become someone else's tool for the sake of security.

But Wurlitzer conceived of the two figures as being separate and, consequently, treated their final meeting as existentially destined, with Billy's death being the inevitable confrontation of the two alternatives of changing with the times or not changing. Peckinpah retained the interest in Garrett, but gave the fatalistic quality of the ending added meaning by stressing that the two men had been close friends. With Pat and Billy's earlier comradeship firmly established, the significance of Garrett's choice is foregrounded by the idea of what he loses by selling out. The question which the film sets up and leaves for the viewer to answer is whether either man is to blame; or, putting aside judgments, whether Garrett or any individual can indeed survive the choice of "living" in view of the knowledge of what this choice has cost him. Contemplating the cost of compromise, what kind of meaning does life have if one foresakes one's ideals and values? Garrett's decision to become, literally, a tool of the (corrupt) establishment is of central importance to Peckinpah himself, trying to work in a business that demands constant compromise. From *Pat Garrett and Billy the Kid*, we may perceive dramatically how debilitating compromise can be for a committed individual like Peckinpah—and, ironically, how devastating MGM's treatment of this film must have been to him.

Perhaps the clearest indication of Peckinpah's dilemma is the most striking of MGM's alterations—the removal of the intended frame around the film of an account of Garrett's death in 1908 at the hands of the same interests he had served in killing Billy. This prologue and epilogue would make the entire film a flashback from Garrett's point of view; removing it necessitates other cuts as well, redrafting the film to appear more balanced between Garrett and the Kid. But Peckinpah wanted us to be more concerned with Garrett's problem, for Garrett's choiçe contains the potential lesson for all of us, and further indicates why Billy's independence is seen as being (romantically) "heroic." Billy, in not compromising, represents what we and Garrett cannot do so easily. Few of us can live without compromises, and we must find ways to accept the ones we have to make, or know where to draw the line to retain our self-respect. With this film, Peckinpah asks us to consider how we, and Garrett, can expect to "enter our house justified" in the face of compromises. His interest in and sympathy (or pity?) for Garrett is the realization that we are all probably less than heroic; we are guilty of compromise, even as we try to understand the importance of the values we may *unwittingly* compromise. We search for values to hold on to.

The recognition of this problem without a satisfactory, clear answer and the apparent contradictory behavior it can lead to are indicated in the sequence with Sheriff Cullen Baker. Garrett, on his round-about trackdown of the Kid, is an observer in this scene almost as much as we are. He is scorned and prodded by Baker about the nature of his sell-out, but Baker, too, has compromised himself in avoiding his responsibilities as a sheriff. He is looking forward to escaping from those duties with his boat, to float away down the river. But Garrett's request for his help is an unstated demand to his dignity that he cannot avoid. His wife recognizes this as well, and they both go with Garrett because they know they have to, little as they like it. Baker is mortally wounded in the following gun-battle, even as Garrett kills another former "friend," Black Harris; Harris's death at Garrett's hands is another consequence of Garrett's decision to compromise and survive, and Garrett is diminished by it. But Baker, realizing his time has arrived, has perhaps vindicated himself, with his death as a direct result of his meeting the challenge of his responsibility. Peckinpah gives his death a lamented dignity, made poignant by the notion that Baker did what he had to do and did not opt for the safe, secure way, as Garrett ostensibly has. (During his trackdown of Billy, we never feel that *Garrett's* life is in jeopardy, as he is appreciated as a man of ability; also, we *know* how Garrett will die: if not from the legend, we would have known from the deleted prologue / epilogue.) Garrett watches Baker die and feels the loss as we do, in addition to having to face the fact that he is indirectly responsible for Baker's death. Repeatedly throughout the film, Garrett must face the bitter consequences of his choice. He is never assured of his justification, and his observations only deepen his frustration.

Though MGM cut other scenes significant to Garrett's situation, the film as Peckinpah designed it is apparent if one "reads" the film with the primary concern being Garrett. Without the clarity of approach indicated by the prologue / epilogue of Garrett's death, the film as released begins with the establishment of the friendship of Pat and Billy to stress the enormity of Garrett's principal betrayal, that of friendship. Moreover, it establishes the idea that Garrett has betrayed himself; we are told here that Garrett has been an "outlaw" like Billy, and it is gradually pointed out through the rest of the film that Pat and Billy are perhaps two sides of the same man, such that Garrett's compromise necessitates his eventual killing of part of himself. The film's outcome is fated from this beginning: though he may give Billy as much time as he can to avoid that outcome, Garrett is forced to play out the string he started with his compromise to the political interests of the territory.

Billy's outlawry is defined less as a matter of crime than as an estimation of who is in power. A basic aspect of the frontier West was that the absence of strict, "civilized" law and order made "order" a proposition dictated by whoever had the power to enforce it, and justice another matter altogether. The morality or immorality of "criminals" is thus a shifting proposition. Billy's crimes in the film are primarily committed in self-defense. He steals cattle from Chisum, but doubt is raised as to whether this is bad, as Chisum is drawn as a self-styled power unto himself. Cut from the theatrical version but present in the TV version of the film is a line indicating that Chisum owed Billy back wages, a disputed claim which makes Billy's rustling potentially justifiable. The most serious thing Billy does is kill the deputies, Bell and Ollinger; but Billy does not want to shoot Bell, who has an opportunity to avoid Billy's gun, and Ollinger has already been seen to be murderous himself. The set-up of these two killings increases our ambivalence about Billy as an outlaw "hero," for they are both reprehensible acts which have a sense of slim justification. If one agrees that Billy is unfairly in jail (he has been "tried" and convicted on an old, trumped-up charge for expedience), there is sympathy for his escape. Bell is unfortunate, but by his own actions leaves Billy little "choice." Ironically, Bell relies on a moral code which prohibits shooting in the back, but by turning his back in effect makes his play anyway, "forcing" Billy to shoot him to achieve his escape. Billy fulfilled an idea of fairness by allowing Bell the chance to back down. Ollinger's death is cruel, but fitting to the way Ollinger hungrily looked to Billy's death. "Keep the change, Bob," is an atrocious pun after we see Billy unload the shotgun's charge of dimes into Ollinger, but in keeping with Billy's grim sense of whimsy (death is a matter of fact) and a vicious rejoinder to Ollinger's cruelty. At worst, it is only a minor lapse, but that too, has to be judged finally in context, and there it fits.

Billy the Kid, as seen in this film, is hardly an unregenerate killer. Peckinpah allows the situations with Billy to develop in such a way that we see how the legends may have come about. With an ambiguous concept of who exactly are the "good guys and bad guys," Billy is the romantic individual who will not knuckle under to enforced changes. The rest of his "gang" are erstwhile cowboys whose only handle is Billy's example. They look to Billy for leadership, much as the wild, Lost Boys of *Peter Pan* look up to their hero. When Billy breaks out of jail, people are stunned, but nobody moves to stop him; on the contrary, they know or have heard of the Kid, by then a legend in his own time, and even help him, out of a curious combination of fear and respect. Billy is aware of his legend, and functions within it; as long as he resolutely goes his own way, he will fulfill that legend. "Alias," the printer's devil observer, is drawn to Billy on the same level as we are, fascinated by a man who continues to defy the power structure so blatantly, and who assumes legendary proportions by continuing that defiance.

"Times have changed," Pat asserts in the beginning, but those times have changed mainly because the propertied political interests *want* them changed. Billy, as an individual who will not give ground, is a threat to those interests. "The electorate," Pat explains, meaning Chisum and associates, "wants you gone." But Billy will not be run out of the country. When he heads for Mexico to briefly alleviate some of the pressure to have him gone, he comes upon a group of Chisum's men pillaging his friend Paco, who has left to avoid such trouble. They have for no apparent reason other than "trespass" slaughtered Paco's sheep, flayed Paco, and are raping his wife; Billy kills the men and heads back to Fort Sumner, refusing to give in to the forces that would so indiscriminately rule the territory. But as Paco dies, he suggests that Billy will not save himself because he is "afraid" to change, and perhaps Peckinpah suggests to us that it takes more "courage" to change with the times and find a way to live in spite of the changes, as Garrett has proposed to do. But it is important that we see Billy and what he represents mainly as being victimized by those corrupt forces "in charge," which Garrett has chosen to work for. Billy's "crime" is that he will not change. As we have seen in other Peckinpah films, a consequence of not changing is death.

As stated, Billy's determinedness provides a severe contrast to Garrett's sell-out. Garrett, as the survivor, is the figure of ultimate concern. His weakness lies in the knowledge that in his betrayal of Billy he has betrayed himself, and he must somehow come to terms with his action. For Billy, as a person similar to Garrett initially, is a constant reminder of Garrett's alternative and a refutation of the sheriff's compromise. At Fort Sumner in the beginning, Billy reminds Pat of the times they had, suggesting that it must be "pretty hard to turn your back on all that." "Sold out to the Santa Fe ring—how does it feel?" Billy asks without condemnation. Pat's response that the times have changed is met by Billy's resolution in contrast to Garrett's: "Times, maybe—not me." When Pat captures Billy at the line shack, Billy offers how Pat's in poor company.

Garrett defends his choice, saying that he is alive, but is met with the, for the moment, irrefutable fact that Billy has not compromised and is alive, too, retaining his pride. Standing with arms outstretched in an evocation of Christlike martyrdom, the image is for Garrett to complete as an evocation of Pilate. Garrett is serving to contain the individual, at the expense of personal freedom in the name of questionable civilized growth.

At every other turn, Garrett is confronted with the guilt of his sell-out, having to justify himself: at the Governor's, where he barely salvages his pride by telling the representatives of economic and political power pointedly what to do with their bounty money; at Sheriff Baker's, where he explains that there comes a time in a man's life "when he don't want to spend time figuring what comes next"; in the killing of Black Harris; in his bitterly telling the deputy, Poe, to keep his mouth shut about the Kid; at Lemuel's saloon/trading post, where Holly is killed after he warily expresses his disgust with Garrett, and where Lemuel festers on like an ugly sore about how Garrett used to be "like a daddy to the Kid" and now is just full of himself and the law; at the saloon/hotel in Roswell, where he has to slap around the whore before she'll give him information (*she* "owed" the Kid that much); and at the end of the film, when there is no more backing away, Garrett shoots the Kid but cannot accept it still, and shoots his own image in the mirror, killing himself figuratively as he has just done so "literally" by killing the Kid.

The scene on the trail with Poe has some key dialogue, leading into an important scene cut from the theatrical version. Poe says directly that the "country's gotta make a choice," clearly siding with Chisum (whom he's employed by) and contemptuous of the Kid. Garrett cuts him off, indicating the depth of his problem to us, by saying to Poe: "This country's gettin' old, and I'm to get old with it. The Kid don't want it that way; might be a better man for it, I ain't judgin'. But I don't want you explaining nothin' to me, and I don't want you sayin' nothin' 'bout the Kid. . . ." This touchiness on Garrett's part is underscored by the scene which should have followed, where Garrett and Poe ride in to Chisum's ranch and speak briefly with him. We find out here that Garrett took a loan from Chisum to buy some land; it is the same land he dies on almost thirty years later. We also see that Chisum is hardly the kind of person who tolerates things not going his way.

One other cut scene is significant to the overall picture of Garrett, where he stops at home briefly to see his wife after Billy's escape from the Lincoln jail. Garrett's Mexican wife resents his not being home; she complains that her people will not talk to her, that he is too much of a gringo making deals since he became Sheriff. She also accuses him of being "dead inside"; Garrett yells at her that they'll deal with things when the business with the Kid is over, to which she replies that she hopes the Kid will get away. Garrett asserts that the Kid won't, that there's "too much play in him" to make good his escape from the country. His wife adds, "And not enough in you," referring to Garrett's sell-out commitment to chase down the Kid. Without this scene, the contrast is lost to Billy's romantic affair with the Mexican girl, Maria, as well as the depth of Garrett's problem being lessened for us.

For the record, the other deleted material is not as drastically missed as the three already mentioned scenes—the prologue/epilogue of Garrett's death, the scene with Chisum, and the scene with Garrett's wife—but it is missed nonetheless, for knowing about its removal nags at the question of precisely what effect the deleted footage had on the overall balance and pace of the film. There are several clipped moments from other scenes, shots of Billy and Pat individually on the trail; a sequence where Billy tries to romance Maria innocently while several young boys tag along and tease Billy, and Billy winds up playing with them; a scene where Poe finds out from two miners played by Dub Taylor and Elisha Cook, Jr., that Billy is at Fort Sumner; and a few more lines to the scene toward the end with Garrett and Will, the carpenter, played by Peckinpah himself. (All of these scenes except the prologue/epilogue and the scene with the miners can be found in the TV release print, but that version is also chopped up to the extent that it, too, is by no means definitive.)

Peckinpah had long been interested in doing a film based on the story of Garrett and the Kid; his script for what became *One-eyed Jacks* included research on the "true" history of the Kid, as had the book upon which that script was based. Rudolph Wurlitzer also researched the Kid's life for his script, and Peckinpah directed the film with a keen eye for character based on a foundation of historically accurate events and locations. Because of the damaged nature of the released film, I recommend to the reader's attention the real Pat Garrett's own book, *The Authentic Life of Billy the Kid*, which provides the "facts" for the setting of the film. With that book as background, gaps in the damaged film about the Kid's and Garrett's relation to Chisum et al. can be filled, and there is indication by contrast of what Peckinpah did with the story. Understanding the historical aspect makes Peckinpah's film more of a fictionalized narrative of what "actually" happened, rather than simply a personalized retelling of the legend. Curiously, by sticking more to the physical facts in a story famed for the license taken with it, Peckinpah achieves a picture of "realistic" legendary quality, where events are rooted in particular motivational contexts of time and place which can be read as "real" or legendary. Accepting the interpretation as realistic yet allows the perception of what would become legendary. Or, merely regarded as legend, the story carries its contemporary lesson no less strongly. The logistics of Billy's escape from the Lincoln jail and of his death at Pete Maxwell's house are mainly accurate; but the details and interpretive motivational contexts are Peckinpah's (out of Wurlitzer).

With an understanding of Peckinpah's approach to the story, the remarkable power and haunting beauty of his images come across with a sense of purpose, and the film which may have seemed "attractive" visually can be appreciated as a whole work consistent to a thematic conception. Never before has a Peckinpah film seemed so magnificently *fated,* the foregone conclusion of Billy's death a relentless shadow over Garrett and the entire atmosphere of the film. This feeling would have been further increased and, more significantly, would have been *balanced* by the framing aspect of Garrett's death. Peckinpah's characters from previous films may have seemed resolute in pursuing their certain destinies, and with their conditions set, a certain amount of inexorability to their fates is achieved; but previously this has meant building to a peak of resolution, whereas *Pat Garrett and Billy the Kid* strives to *avoid* this peak. Garrett is committed to Billy's death by his own choice as well as by Billy's opposite choice, but the killing of Billy is an inglorious act of finality for Garrett. As the wheel set in motion by Garrett and the Kid in opposing directions at the outset of the released film comes full circle, Billy has returned to his original position, while Garrett finally realizes that, no matter where he turns, he must wind up on Billy's doorstep. Because of who Billy is and who Garrett has become, Garrett must complete the circle by killing Billy. At Pete Maxwell's, Garrett sits on the porch before entering the house for one last moment to consider any other way out, but he has already accepted the inevitability of the doing, and must take the deep breath of that acceptance. We have already seen this sort of last-minute hope for a way out, when Billy faces off with Alamosa Bill. Neither of them can think of anything else to satisfy the demands of the situation; "Let's get to it" is the only answer short of running away from it. Even the director of the film has to nudge Garrett into his final acceptance: as Garrett approaches the house, after having walked there as *indirectly* as possible, Will, the carpenter (who is building a coffin), recognizes Garrett and the situation in an unobtrusive moment of omniscience. "Finally figured it out, huh?" the director says. "Go on, get it over with."

Garrett goes, and, in the moment of Billy's death, it is too much for him to face himself with the realization of what he has done; with the killing of Billy, he has killed the part of himself that he began choking off with his compromise as sheriff, and he shoots himself in the mirror, completing the analogy. When Poe moves to cut off Billy's trigger finger, Garrett erupts with the power of his own guilt, kicking Poe savagely. (It is the same sort of eruption release that will be seen later in *The Killer Elite*, as Mike Locken slams into his assistant Miller after Miller kills Locken's former buddy, Hansen—whom Locken would have had to kill.)

MGM's mutilation of the film is especially reprehensible because *Pat Garrett and Billy the Kid* is a decidedly mature work, visually and thematically, more complex than the epic *Major Dundee*. The tragedy of *Pat Garrett* is all the more serious than *Major Dundee*, as the nature of its careful, cinematic subtlety is all the more fragile. This is substantiated by the degree of atmosphere the film retains even after its mutilation, with its losses of richness that much harder to pinpoint. Peckinpah has always composed his frame with a concern for a visual and audial totality consistent with the thematic development of his characters. Looking over the films discussed thus far, it is easily recognized that Peckinpah's work is only partially represented in the scripts; the richness and power of his films is a cinematic accomplishment as opposed to a literary one. This is indeed the key factor of Peckinpah's value for us, for we may have had the questions posed and have heard the moral arguments before, but we have never had them demonstrated in such original ways. It is therefore a tragedy when the evidence is tampered with; the film-that-might-have-been is frustrated by the film-that-is. This deepens with a work such as *Pat Garrett and Billy the Kid*, where the film-that-is points securely to the film-that-almost-was.

Analogous comparisons to other art forms can be misleading, but Peckinpah's visual sense in *Pat Garrett*, as a direct consequence of the interior mood of the film, is painterly. If realism is accepted as a subjective idea, it follows that a painting may appear "realistic" and yet be pointedly subjective. While this is true of the body of Peckinpah's work, it is perhaps more blatantly so in *Pat Garrett*. For *Pat Garrett* is a brooding film of interior character (mainly Garrett's—the film was, again, conceived as a flashback from Garrett's point of view), and Peckinpah's lighting choices follow this thematic idea. Despite the many scenes of full sunlight, the dominant lighting of the film is of dusk. Indeed, scenes of full light are often significant by thematic contrast, or, to use an idea heavily favored by Peckinpah's view, by irony. Likewise, Peckinpah's compositions in *Pat Garrett* are used to achieve period realism, breathing life into our historical perception of old daguerreotypes, such as the scene in the Lincoln jail where Ollinger steps in and out of such old photographs. This is a point of clever and curious subtlety, where Peckinpah uses our historical visual memory to aid our recognition of his settings. (He had thought about doing *The Wild Bunch* in black-and-white, and also giving it a scratched, newsreel quality).[2] Also, it must not be forgotten that *Pat Garrett and Billy the Kid* concerns legendary characters, and that aspect results in their being used in ways that wholly original characters would not afford the same meaning or "presence." *Pat Garrett* is a blend of historical realism and legendary "larger than life" mythology, into which Peckinpah places real human beings and their personal conflicts. The pictorial quality of *Pat Garrett* might bear fruitful witness to Peckinpah's artistry in com-

Billy the Kid

parative analysis of Peckinpah's films photographed by John Coquillon versus those filmed by Lucien Ballard; each photographer serves the individual film and Peckinpah brilliantly, but the visual mood achieved by Coquillon in *Straw Dogs, Pat Garrett,* and *Cross of Iron* is variously different from the moods established by Ballard in *Ride the High Country, The Wild Bunch, Cable Hogue, Junior Bonner,* and *The Getaway.* Each film is a different challenge, but the three films with Coquillon would seem to be keyed by greater "interior" darkness.

Peckinpah might have preferred a bit less music in *Pat Garrett,* but Bob Dylan's "score" for the film is effective. For all the fuss made about it, the music bridges the legendary aspect of the story and setting with a slightly contemporary counterpoint. The theme, while repetitious out of context, is used as an understated background, and further serves to underline the relentless quality of the characters' hopeless attempts to avoid the outcome. Like the film, the music is an acknowledgment of a predetermined legend.

Similarly, for all the fuss made about Dylan's "acting" de-

. . . vs. Pat Garrett.

but, Peckinpah succeeds in using Dylan as an "actor" as well
as a presence, for Dylan as "Alias" is indeed the observer of
Billy's legend and of the effect of Garrett on the legend of the
Kid. There was a real-life Alias, a friend of the Kid's; it is
pointless to question further whether Dylan is "acting" or not
as far as the film is concerned, for whether or not Dylan's
mannerisms are genuine or created, he does "create" a character. He is an integrated presence as much as the other professional actors in the film. An even more "artificial" character,
yet one who also works, is Beaver, played by Donnie Fritts. A
member of Kristofferson's band, Fritts's *only* dialogue in the
film is to repeat what others have just said!

If Peckinpah is consistent in any area, he is particularly able
in getting excellent performances from his actors. *Pat Garrett
and Billy the Kid* is no less an example, with a variety of veteran professionals and newcomers. Of special interest is the
performance of James Coburn, once again playing a Peckinpah professional, but this time with the important interior regard for his character's problem. Coburn succeeds; he *is* Garrett. The face is a determined mask, but the eyes betray his

Bob Dylan as "Alias." (Gordon Dawson at left).

doubt, and his body's weary movements show the weight of Garrett's burden.

Despite the handling it received, the film-that-is is saved by Peckinpah's dedication. As has happened unfortunately too often in his career, his film is damaged, but not destroyed. With things removed, other pieces have to carry more weight, but because of the precision of their conception, they succeed fairly well. Criticisms of the film as released were primarily concerned with overall balance and continuity, not faulting individual moments.

There is an incredible irony in several lines cut from the theatrical version, which Peckinpah says in his scene as Will with Garrett. "You know what I'm gonna do?" he says to Garrett, leaning over the unfinished coffin. "I'm gonna take everything I own, put it in right here, [and] bury it. [Then] I'm gonna leave this territory." But his last line is even more personally ironic, distressingly bitter, considering what happened to *Pat Garrett and Billy the Kid*, and considering his problems caused by conviction and temperament: "When are you gonna realize you can't trust anybody, not even yourself, Garrett?"

That is not a statement of a man who cynically doesn't care; that is a statement of a man who suffers, from the guilt and consequences of his own compromises. A man who bleeds.

11

Bring Me the Head of Alfredo Garcia (1974)

NOBODY LOSES all the time," says Bennie in *Bring Me the Head of Alfredo Garcia*. Bennie's sharp defense at being called a "loser" is the slender thread upon which can hang the hope of even the least of us. The residual need in all human beings for some kind of identity with dignity can be seen directly in the way such a "loser" desperately seizes the opportunity of the mythical Big Chance. The perceived difference between being nothing and being something is so often conceived of by people in terms of money that achieving that goal can become the source of that fulfilled identity. The defense can be used that "money doesn't buy happiness," but the evidence of society to the contrary is overwhelming. The mistake of that goal is proved by the price one may have to pay to achieve it.

Bring Me the Head of Alfredo Garcia is an intense film on a very personal scale, an intimate "little" film of character study. You have to be able to appreciate a "loser" to get behind the film, and the simple fact is that a lot of people cannot do that easily. The underlying principle at work is similar to that of Arthur Miller's *Death of a Salesman*; the argument about that play was whether the "common man" could be considered capable of assuming tragic proportions, but the response to that work seems to have proved that he could, regardless of academic definitions. Bennie's story goes somewhat beyond the notion of the common man as represented by Willy Loman, however, for Bennie is much more the "loser," the man who never had a handle on "what it was all about" and who is not "equipped" to get close enough to find out.

What is central to Bennie's story as a Peckinpah film is the heavy irony that it is precisely Bennie's persistent delusion

175

Isela Vega and Warren Oates as Elita and Bennie.

that he *is* "capable," the delusion which makes his life a series of unsuccessful defensive poses to fulfill that self-image, which makes him finally dangerous and *capable* of pursuing his revenge. Because he *insists* that he is not ultimately a loser, Bennie does not give up in defeat, but turns his insistence into the strength of an obsession. The film suggests that even the "least" of us have the *intuitive* capability of such persistence, the innate assertiveness of the human species, and that we all have the capability of action based on it. This innate assertiveness can be viewed as heroic, just as Bennie, in his obsessive persistence, becomes heroic. The simple man does warrant "being reckoned with." As Cable Hogue suggested the humanity and consequent value of a "loser" individual ("I'm worth somethin'. ain't I?"), Bennie likewise insists upon that idea, intuitively. In the modern world, however, Peckinpah maintains that it is all the more difficult for the "loser" (the individual) to get along, to assert himself as a human being in a society which swallows and denies individuals their basic value and dignity. The true loser, the person who is not capable of much insight as opposed to the loser of circumstances, is trapped by the modern society which says superficially that money and power are the items by which a person is judged. Achieving the Big Score is the path to successful fulfillment for the person who accepts those standards of judgment. Peckinpah says further that the mistake of that acceptance comes when it forces denial of something of greater power and importance, that something being ideals embodied by love and loyal companionship.

Bennie is a true loser. His attempts to appear capable, his tries to maintain an image of "macho cool," are pathetic, easily seen through. He lacks the conscious wherewithal to see beyond part-ownership of a dilapidated tourist bar. The man doesn't "have it" (or does he—just because he is a person?). The "tragic" irony is that, without realizing it (which would make the poses unnecessary), Bennie is right. His belief in his self-image for the wrong reason provides the mechanism for him to use his innate potential. Innate assertion's power rises out of him, fills the previously hollow pose, and becomes an obsession whose actions are expressed through the superficial frame of Bennie's self-image.

That power is also overwhelming. Bennie's evidenced

capability is almost slick in its bravura handling of each violent situation. His power is a righteous one which precludes defeat, until he finally does take the big money and is killed. There are two particular narrative allusions to the strength of Bennie's power. One is the fact that he does smuggle the head onto the plane to take it to El Jefe. There is absolutely no indication of any difficulty with this; no airport scene to bring the matter up at all. What could appear to be a plot inconsistency can be literally explained by the fact that even with increased security today, worse things are smuggled aboard planes. But more significant figuratively, it demonstrates that Bennie's power *makes* that idea not a problem. We are specifically shown that Alfredo's head is rotting (the flies, getting the ice), but Peckinpah ignores the possibility of any airport difficulty with it. And this from a filmmaker who was dissatisfied with his first feature partly because it did not account for the problem of the condition of the corpse! The other allusion to the magnitude of Bennie's power is a deliberately subtle ambiguity of editing. When Bennie kills El Jefe's guards, the speed of the editing montage suggests that the last guard is felled not by a bullet, but by Bennie's screamed "NO!" of outrage. It seems that Bennie's echoed yell is heard in place of a corresponding gunshot; his outrage alone is powerful enough to ensure his survival. Indeed, the fact that he survives a cross-fire at El Jefe's, in addition to outwitting professional killers (Sappensly and the hotel shoot-out), is sufficient direct evidence of his power.

Bennie's personal tragedy lies in his not realizing that his true "ticket" resides in the love of Elita, and not in the money offered for Alfredo's head. This is a crucial, recurrent theme in Peckinpah's work, recalling directly Yellowleg's redemption through Kit in *The Deadly Companions*, Cable Hogue's opportunity for redemption through Hildy, and even Doc McCoy's ultimate commitment to Carol. Bennie's Big Chance is in his acknowledgement that he loves Elita; his moment of most sincere depth comes when he promises to marry her, as she has put it to him directly. It is a moment of honesty he cannot escape; he means it. The presentation of their love is touching and sincere, from their companionate ease in Bennie's room, to their shared simple joy of being together as they ride in the car. It is the sincerity of Bennie's love of Elita, the depth of that love, which animates his obsession and which gives his rage direction. People have been killed over Alfredo's head by the end of the journey, but it is the shattering of Bennie's future with Elita's death that urges him to find out why the head was so important. The loss of Elita is the blow that makes Bennie a resolute figure of vengeance, sparking the innate power of the man. Peckinpah suggests that the purity of "simple" love is something which anyone can respond to, and which can endow even a "loser" like Bennie with awesome power. In the pursuit of his vengeance over his dead future, Bennie is invincible.

If the second half of the film is to make any sense, if it is to appear more than merely bizarre, the profundity of simple love must be acknowledged, and we must see how deeply it affects Bennie if we are to accept his rage. Peckinpah carefully and naturally develops the depiction of their love and mutual need in the first half of the film to support the outcome of the second half. At the same time, the second half supports the ideas of the first half, the importance of the primacy of love and the nature of the Big Chance, with devastating finality.

The film is symmetrically constructed as a journey; for Bennie, it is a journey within himself, literally into and back out of the grave. By succumbing to the idea of the Big Score and insisting on it despite Elita's protests, Bennie is doomed. The closer the pair get to their "objective," the more barren and deprived the landscape becomes, mirroring the deprivation of love and redemption Bennie causes between himself and Elita. Though he may gradually realize the importance of Elita to himself, the significance of her escapes him until it is too late and she is dead. By holding steadfastly onto what he *thought* it was all about (the Big Score) instead of what he gradually realizes matters (Elita), Bennie's fate is sealed. The turning point is at Alfredo's grave, where Bennie rises from the earth, ironically from the "dead," to his profound anguish over his loss. The journey back to the source of revenge is a mirror image of the journey to the grave, but the events of the return are a deathly mockery of the living first half.

The film opens with another Peckinpah example of the conflict between appearance and reality, on a tranquil scene of a young girl tentatively enjoying the miracle of her pregnant body; but a threat interrupts this tranquility as she is summoned to her father. With only a few shots, we see that her father, El Jefe, is a "man who likes to play God,"[1] as Peckinpah has described him. As the supreme ruler, he commands simple but complete obedience; he orders his daughter's arm be broken if necessary to obtain her obedience and the answer to his demand for the name of the man who is responsible for her pregnancy, which has shamed El Jefe's family honor. El Jefe is ruthless and all-powerful in his domain; Peckinpah emphasizes this by cutting from the tortured girl to an outside overview shot of the extensive house between the sounds of the mother's ineffective scream of protest and the girl's arm breaking in a chilling snap.

Learning the identity of the man responsible, El Jefe announces (to himself and us more than anybody else) that Alfredo Garcia was like a son to him—increasing El Jefe's feeling of betrayal by "son" and daughter and filling him with a need for revenge. But the advantages of power allow El Jefe to have others mete out his revenge. Though he, too, will die eventually because of his choice of revenge, El Jefe demands the head of Alfredo Garcia, which he will pay for. This demand is

Obedience at El Jefe's command. (Note: photo slightly retouched).

the film's opening "title," the prologue which will bring us to
the central characters of Bennie and Elita. (Aside from producer, star, and writer credits, there are no "opening titles.")

Up to the arm-breaking, we have no definite indication of
when the story is taking place; it appears to be the Mexican
"Old West" of 1880. But when El Jefe's patrician-looking hench-
man rips the locket from the girl's neck (a gesture that begins as one of assistance and turns out to be one of callous
brutality), his clothes indicate a more modern setting. And
with El Jefe's demand for revenge, the machinery of his authority is fully revealed: expensive cars are quickly followed
by airplanes, and we are now firmly in the modern era. Peckinpah's suggestion by opening the film this way is to inform
us that this kind of classic "revenge of honor" still goes on
today. Further, with the airplane we do not know for sure
where El Jefe rules; the search for Alfredo goes to Mexico, but
it is not until Bennie returns with the head that a title announces El Jefe's domain, and at that it only says "Latin
America." El Jefe's authoritarianism can yet be found anywhere.

El Jefe's henchmen run an efficient, professional machine,
oiled and fueled by money and its power. They are not concerned with anything caught in their wake; they have a job to
do, which they will do thoroughly. Bennie finds out quickly
that they indeed do not "fool around." Sappensly and Quill,
the two henchmen who find Bennie behind his piano, size
him up quickly. Bennie is obviously out of his depth with
these two, but he tries to play it "cool." The money they toss to
him strains that "cool."

A particular allusion of the film comes when Quill leaves
the bar. Bennie asks his name; Quill replies, "Dobbs – Fred C.
Dobbs." It is a straight-faced ironic put-down which Bennie
misses, a joke for Quill and a tip-off to the audience. For like
the Bogart character in *The Treasure of the Sierra Madre*
(1948), Bennie's undoing is his greedy acquiescence to the
lure of the Big Chance. Quill knows Bennie will jump at the
opportunity, but that, like Dobbs, Bennie is a "loser."

Completing the irony of Bennie's position is the fact that the
source of information about Alfredo which allows him to "take
the offer" is the same person whose "offer" Bennie rejects for
the immoral financial score, his mistress, Elita. She is a

woman whom Peckinpah respects and urges us to respect honestly. Her background is barely suggested: when we meet her she appears to be a kind of Mexican geisha-hostess; she may or may not have been a "whore," and the indication is that while she may have been capable of prostitution, she is not now a woman to be dominated against her will. Moreover, she is a romantic, finding simple joy and hope in the honest, companionate love she shares with Bennie—even if Bennie doesn't consciously realize the nature of that relationship yet. She tolerates his pose of macho toughness with her, seeing deeper into him than he does. She is an attractive, mature woman, looking forward to settling down simply with Bennie.

But her romanticism has caused her to spend three days saying goodbye to another previous lover, Alfredo, and Bennie's sexual jealousy deepens the situation's irony for him. It seems right that Alfredo should provide this chance for Bennie; having spent the time with Elita, "Al" owes Bennie. Bennie carries his jealousy of Alfredo with him, as a source of rationalization for what he intends to do. Like Doc McCoy, it is the thing that nags deepest in him consciously; resenting Elita's time with Alfredo as a betrayal, it is one more urge to him to continue his quest, an idea of infidelity he cannot back away from, let alone accept for what it was.

The overall film is symmetrical, beginning and ending at El Jefe's domain. But the interior of the film is also physically as well as emotionally symmetrical. Bennie's drive for the Big Score against the wishes and promise of Elita is changed into obsessive vengeance for the road back. The conclusion is foregone, however, as the choice present in the first half is removed with Elita's death in the second half. After her death, there is nothing left for Bennie, except to see it through to the end, where it began. After Bennie kills El Jefe's guards, he says, "The first time I saw him—he was dead." He is ostensibly speaking of Alfredo, but the implication is clear that, for the audience, the remark applies more vividly to Bennie himself. Figuratively dead as a loser from the start, Bennie is indeed dead after irreversibly committing himself at Alfredo's grave. Rising Lazaruslike from the grave, Bennie is a dead man nonetheless, the righteous purity of his obsession giving him the will to act. As he has caused Elita's death, his existence thereafter is a hollow haunting of what could have been;

finally taking the money away with him anyway from El Jefe's—in a sense to make the whole thing worth it—ensures his physical death, for those are exactly the wages of the sin which rejects life.

Without being rigid about it, the events of Bennie's journey to Alfredo's grave are matched by similarities on the way back. The hotel scene in the beginning, where Bennie accepts the job, is matched by the hotel shoot-out toward the end. The first instance is characterized by Bennie's appearance as a loser, with a pose of toughness that is mocked by the professional henchmen; the latter is the turnabout of this, witnessed by Bennie's supremacy over the others as he overwhelms them with his obsessive power. It should be noted that Bennie's shooting skill is not simply a mystical product of his obsession; we are told that Bennie has had previous small-arms training, in one of the car scenes with Elita, and it *is* possible that he is an able marksman, especially under the extreme circumstances that his rage encounters. In any case, the basic skill is accounted for. The henchmen make the fatal error of underestimating the "loser."

Following the initial hotel scene with Bennie is the beginning of the trip at Bennie's apartment. The room is dingy and meager like Bennie himself, but he and Elita share their simple romance there. This scene is comically intimate, as Bennie discovers a few lice on himself, and playfully spanks Elita to get moving. The counterpart to this is the later scene when Bennie returns to his room, but instead of Elita, his only company is the head of Alfredo Garcia. The memory of the first scene here haunts the second; Bennie loads his gun in Elita's absence, her singing heard in an echo on the soundtrack. In a counterpoint to another scene of the first half where Elita takes a shower and Bennie says "I love you" to her in simple sincerity, Bennie gives the head a shower—the image a bitter reflection of the former one. Elita's shower scene is a rare moment of purity, between her and Bennie; in a combination of figurative and literal nudity, the characters are united in Peckinpah's depiction of the scene.

The other "events" of the journey to the grave further demonstrate the growing definition of their love against the strain of the immoral quest. Bennie and Elita sit under a tree in a moment of tender peace, as Elita puts Bennie on the spot by asking him to be definite for once about their future. Bennie cannot retreat from the moment; he says he will marry her. But their warmth is haunted by the car of the Mexican thugs; following Bennie and Elita, the thugs (representing the quest for the head) threaten the two lovers' peace. Peckinpah continues to use the thugs as an ever-present comment on the status of Bennie and Elita. He cuts from them singing together happily in their car to the two Mexicans singing drunkenly in a parody of the happiness of the former shot. The suggestion of the final result of going for the head is never far from Bennie and Elita.

The two camp together off the road, but their romance is interrupted here by the two bikers. Elita is better equipped emotionally to handle the situation without catastrophe, and goes away from the campsite with Paco. Bennie cannot accept her handling of the situation, however, and moves to assert his own violent solution to the problem. In the meantime, Elita will not be dominated by Paco; though he may rape her, he will not have her. She shames him, breaking his dominant fantasy by not flinching and returning his physical force with an equal slap to his face. Elita takes control of the situation by *going* to Paco; the price for the safety of Bennie and herself is not too high for her, though it will be paid on *her* terms if at all, not in total submission. In a priceless moment of ambiguity, she moves to Paco; she does not want her peace with Bennie shattered by this intrusion. But the price is too high for Bennie, and his action is to save himself as much as it is to save Elita, whom *we* see is not in particular danger. Bennie moves to protect them both, but our view of the situation is altered; Bennie doesn't know that his violence is unnecessary – it remains necessary to him. He cannot stand by, and we may agree with him, but it is undercut by Elita's dominance. Bennie will kill rather than have *his* woman "violated." Screaming "You're *dead!*" Bennie shoots Paco. This violent self-assertion prefigures the manner of Bennie's later self-assertion as well as his later violence and his own death. Spending the night at a hotel, Bennie and Elita both purposefully assert their dignity over the clerk's insinuations. The assertion here is an affirmation of the truth and pride of their relationship.

Approaching Alfredo's village, the strain between Elita and Bennie has become more critical. Elita knows now the full intention of Bennie's quest, and she pleads with him to avoid

the immorality of the act. To her, they do not need the money
at such a price, but Bennie resolutely insists on going for the
Big Chance, equating the success of that mission with his and
their own. Bennie does not see what will be lost between
them if he persists, recalling Cable Hogue's persistence in
choosing to wait for his revenge over leaving with Hildy. (The
immoral acts are different but both situations represent opportunities for redemption.) But Elita cannot convince Bennie of
the seriousness of the desecration of the grave. Critically for
both of them, the degradation and immorality of the act is *intuitively* perceived. Elita's protest on religious grounds is coun-
tered by Bennie's rationalization that his grounds for doing it
supersede the significance of the act. Yet Bennie likewise
feels the guilt of the act, sensing the dirty, despicable, low-
down quality of digging up the grave to steal the head. When
Alfredo's relatives ambush Bennie later on the road, Bennie
pleads with them to understand, that he is only "borrowing"
the head and will return it. He cannot ruthlessly defend his
action; it takes Sappensly and Quill, the remorseless professionals, to retrieve the head from the family.

This showdown, as well as Bennie's killing of the two Mexi-

"Because it feels so God-damn good."

can thugs, takes place in the absence of Elita (and the life affirmation she symbolizes). The acts figure as the structural
balance to Elita's presence in the first half, and are the results
of her negation. After Bennie kills the Mexican thugs, he
shoots one of them again and again, explaining it to himself
and us by saying, "Because it feels so God-damn good." The
force of Bennie's rage in the loss of Elita cannot be satisfied by
the mere killing of the men who killed her; but the ineffectiveness of the repeated shooting indicates that indeed nothing will really be enough to make up for the loss.

The sequence at the point of no return around Alfredo's
grave is oppressively bleak, demonstrating visually what is
going on emotionally with Bennie and Elita. The room they
wait in before going to the grave is depressingly dingy, appropriate to the degradation of the act. When the moment of finality arrives, Elita cannot remain, as if the life force she represents cannot withstand the life-negation of Bennie's act. As
Bennie moves to complete the act with his machete, he is
clubbed by an unseen hand; Bennie is "killed" figuratively by
the force of moral retribution, even as he is "killed" literally
by the instruments of the vengeful evil he is in service to. In
this moment, the screen goes to total darkness.

The allegorical short story might have ended there, with
Bennie dead. But Bennie's rise from the dead, stunningly de-
picted by a camera view from Bennie's position underground,
his hands clawing through the dirt, is the relentless observation of the second half of the film. Allowing Bennie's physical
survival at this point underscores the fact of his psychological
death. The return from the grave is the brutal assertion that
there is nothing left after the denial of life. Instead of Elita,
Bennie's companion on the road is a rotting head, which he
talks to, accepting death's companionship. If he is to *do* anything, it can only be to take the evil back to the man who
started it all. Bennie is at once a human being overcome with
the vengeance of grief, and a symbolic avenging angel of
death. The quality of Peckinpah's conception and work in the
second half is demonstrated by the recognition that despite
the symbolism we never lose sight of the literal individual.
Bennie's story is told with remarkable realistic consistency.
The tale is bizarre, but realistic credibility is never the issue;
on the other hand, the numbing impact of the second half

forces one to ask the question, "What *is* going on here?—
opening the door to the larger moral issues at stake for all of us.
But the credibility of the second half depends on the credible
set-up of the first half; just as the moral implications of the first
half become clear with the relentlessness of the second part.
Consequently, if one does not pay attention to the character
details of the first part (i.e., if one passes over the "love story"
in particular), the second part of the film seems *merely*
bizarre. It is necessary to realize the extensiveness of the conception of the film as a *whole*.

Considering that whole conception outside of the focus on
Bennie, one returns to the revenge evil of El Jefe and his
machinery. The depth of that evil is represented by the remorseless "cool" of the professional henchmen, Sappensly
and Quill, and their leader, Max. The polished implacability of
Max's administration of El Jefe's demand is the true evil, the
evil that does not care. It is a faceless, impersonal machinery
that does not respond to any humane considerations; its only
concern is the object it chooses, regardless of the means used
to achieve that object. The smoothness and apparent civility of
its surface hide the nature of its corruption, the evil that does
not respect life. The resemblance to corporate machinery is a
warning to us that the danger of corporate impersonality is in
its ability to neglect life in any manner of moral responsibility;
it is easy to corporately forget about life (humanity) and be
concerned only with business in a moral vacuum. Peckinpah's
life and work demonstrate a continual distrust of corporate responsibility and things done in service to the business corporation; the apparently inherent ability of "business" to deny
individual as well as general humane values with ease makes
their motives automatically suspect to individuals. This will
be seen more directly in Peckinpah's next film, *The Killer
Elite*. In *Alfredo Garcia*, the link between corporate implacability and individual evil is on a more primitive level; the
"corporation" served is that of one man, El Jefe. But the
machinery which serves El Jefe or a "board of directors" can
be the same.

Sappensly and Quill, as examples of that machinery, are
shown as being most dangerous for the same reason that the
machinery in general is evil: they do not need anyone; they
are self-contained; they do not care about anything other than

their objective. Any personal external needs they might have seem to be provided for by their apparent pair-bonding. The suggestion just below the surface that they are homosexuals is evidence of their lack of any further emotional responsiveness. This is not to necessarily imply that homosexuality of itself is evil, but that because of their homosexuality they do not need anything outside of themselves; they are not vulnerable. The satisfaction of their self-containment means they cannot be "reached." The one time Sappensly demonstrates any emotion is when Quill is killed; in that moment, when Sappensly attends to his "buddy," Bennie moves to protect himself, taking the advantage so that when Sappensly rises to finish him, Bennie is not there and kills Sappensly instead. The "machinery" cannot survive or allow any emotional responsiveness; it is defeated by emotional humanity. The problem is that it is extremely difficult for humane individuals to crack the wall of faceless power the corporation can put forward.

By the same token, it is never enough to destroy the outward manifestations of that power; it must be taken to the source to achieve a true victory. Bennie succeeds in finding the source here, when it is definably one man. But as will be seen in *The Killer Elite*, where the source is indefinable, the only possible final victory is in a rejection of the corporation, where the individual "wins" by absenting himself from the corporate reach. The regrettable fact is that the organization yet lives on; the individual is ultimately powerless against modern corruption, whereas he might have been able to overcome the individual corruption found on the frontier. Steve Judd "defeats" the Hammond brothers; but Billy the Kid cannot survive the organized power of Chisum. The difference between the two implies the "end of the West" and its defensible values; individual evil is replaced by more powerful organization. It is harder for the committed individual (i.e., the ethical individual) to survive in this modern context. This is what we lost with the frontier, the direct potential of individual ethical survival. It is why we respect the man who resolutely goes his own way like Junior Bonner; it is why we sympathize with those who try to get along with the modern power structure, like Pat Garrett and Bennie, even though they "die" as a result of their submission. Peckinpah paints a bleak contemporary

picture; the odds against the individual are staggering. It is all
the more important that the individual recognize the situation
and struggle to live humanely despite the power structure.
Without values to live by, life is meaningless. But, for Peckinpah, this has always been the way of things; victory must be
counted in terms of the individual. If enough of us win our
battles as individuals, we might be able to win the war. In the
meantime, we must accept the ambiguity of the overall struggle while preserving our individuality.

Bring Me The Head of Alfredo Garcia involves the individual struggle against the organization: Bennie persists despite the organization. But the link to a definable source is yet
maintained in El Jefe. In this situation, at least, it is possible
for Bennie to "take it" to the source. El Jefe will ultimately die
for the evil he has instigated, even at arm's length. It is not
enough that his grandson has supplanted his demand for vengeance. Significantly, it is his daughter who directs Bennie to
kill him; the circle is complete. El Jefe forfeits his life as the
responsible party. Bennie has come all this way to find out
"why," and to make El Jefe understand what he has caused to
happen. But El Jefe cannot comprehend Bennie's outrage; it is
enough for Bennie finally that the daughter "understands"
and agrees that El Jefe must pay.

The last question is of Bennie's survival. Perhaps he could
have kept the edge of surprise and made it through the gate if
he hadn't taken the money. In any case, Bennie does take the
money and is killed; the conclusions we draw must include
that. It is clear at least that Bennie could not take the money
and survive; choosing the money as he had before ensures his
final death. But with or without the money at the end, Bennie's "life" ended at Alfredo's grave, and his mission ends
with El Jefe's death.

With *Bring Me The Head of Alfredo Garcia*, the distinction
in Peckinpah's work between the interior and exterior film
grows. In all of Peckinpah's films, the "self-contained" interior film of characters, events with people described by Peckinpah's views of human nature, is seen simultaneously with an
"exterior" level of the film, the film that alludes and relates to
considerations of Peckinpah and the audience beyond the
interior arena of characters. This would seem to be a natural
part of any narrative work, and to an extent it is. But the rich-

ness of Peckinpah's films can be recognized particularly in this regard, for all his works display a surface density (the interior film) *and* a complex commentary on the world outside the characters' concerns (the exterior film). The former is a matter for our observation, entertainment, adventure, and vicarious engagement; the latter is the (moral) question, lesson, or consideration we go home with, the part we can either ignore or try to learn from.

The distinction grows here in the sense that, more than in previous works, the interior and exterior films *depend* on each other; the surface interior story of a pathetic loser-turned-heroic-psychopath is, again, *merely* bizarre unless one considers the exterior implications. Likewise, the exterior density is dramatized by the story of such a grubby, total-loss "hero." That Peckinpah carefully maintains a balance between the two concerns prevents the one from becoming unrealistically exaggerated and the other from becoming pretentious. Peckinpah knows what he wants to say intuitively in his films, resisting direct statements ("messages") in favor of intense characterization. This leads to a high degree of interpretive ambiguity, which finally for Peckinpah is also realistically proper. Consistently, it is up to the audience to discover the "exterior" film; Peckinpah knows that self-discovery is potentially more meaningful than instruction.

Given the opportunity (*Alfredo Garcia* is his first film since *Junior Bonner* and his last to date with which there has been little interference; it was shown in the form he intended, but few saw it; "original" Peckinpah remains hard to see), Peckinpah makes his films with an obvious density of character, but simultaneously plants the signs to the reading of his own attitudes within his stories with generally complex subtlety. Most significantly, Peckinpah resists conscious intellectualization and analysis of his own work, and insists that that task be reserved for the audience. The fact is that he succeeds in delivering films of powerful engagement *without* careful preanalysis; he works intuitively. It follows that he must be a master of his craft as well, whether he is articulately conscious of his mastery or not.

Peckinpah's cinematic intuition puts him in a very special class, one whose work grows in appreciation with each repeated viewing. I haven't even mentioned the use of sunglasses in this film; Bennie uses them as a protective shield, and he is most vulnerable without them, as if they help protect him from being seen through. Peckinpah wears sunglasses with a similar effect sometimes, in that they help hide a sensitivity which is most often seen in a person's eyes. Further analysis of *Alfredo Garcia* would demonstrate the complexity of Peckinpah's intuitive brilliance, for the film, like his others, is one whose premises are never directly stated; instead, they are intuitively protrayed. This makes for a job of greater work for an audience, but the rewards are consequently greater for that effort. Ultimately, one need not agree with the suggested conclusion to acknowledge that the film is a masterpiece of cinematic command. Peckinpah, as an artist, is always in control. *Bring Me The Head of Alfredo Garcia* is a film to be valued *at least* for its rare opportunity of faultless, relentless engagement.

12

The Killer Elite (1975)

"I NEVER HEARD so much nonsense in my whole life," announces Mike, the main character in *The Killer Elite*. This film was initially undertaken just as a job, but Peckinpah put it securely in his hip pocket nevertheless. It offers perhaps the clearest example of the way Peckinpah commits himself to his work, regardless of the origins of a project. The project probably began as the filming of an extracurricular CIA-type tale— like the Robert Rostand novel the script is based on. The novel is a good thriller of its kind, focusing on a duel between professionals and the rather typical cross and double-cross operations of a traitor on the "home" team. But, as critic Tom Milne has suggested, the film version in Peckinpah's hands becomes a clever combination of genre hi-jinks along the lines of *"Enter the Dragon* meets *Three Days of the Condor."*[1] The terrain is decidedly familiar, but Peckinpah simply could not make it "straight" and pushed the film to marvel from within at the comic-book level of its genre expectations. It is similar in execution to *The Getaway*, but this time the main character himself awakens to the nature of the shenanigans.

Because of the nature of the material, Peckinpah's interior and exterior films present a sharp contrast, until the "two films" are bridged by Mike Locken's removal of himself at the end. *The Killer Elite*'s interior is an intense, bleak character drama centered on a favorite Peckinpah theme, that of the betrayal of loyal friendship. George Hansen's betrayal of Mike is the beginning of Mike's awakening to the idea that everything else is a game, and a ridiculous sham at that. After he is termed washed-up as a cripple, Mike's drive to recover is based on two things: his refusal to be so casually dismissed and his urge to find Hansen, the latter not so much a desire for revenge as

193

Mike Locken betrayed.

much as it expresses Mike's need to understand why his "friend" betrayed him.

Simultaneously, the exterior film develops as a case of an individual realizing and rejecting the valueless organization he has served, while similarly rejecting the meaningless heroics of the ultraspy narrative genre. By mocking the genre, Peckinpah implies the tragic corruption of a society that allows this sort of game to be played seriously, in reality. Whether this is limited to a personal analogy for Peckinpah to the film world or whether it expands to include the corrupt power in control of society, the only victory (of survival) for the individual of commitment is to drop out, to refuse to play, to sail off in search of a better world. The lingering question is, sadly, "Sail off to what?" and Peckinpah acknowledges that the end of the film is only wishful thinking. "Let's go bananas," Mike says to Mac at the end. The women, Amy and Josephine, are left behind; the break with society, the "sailing away," has to be total to "succeed." In making the film as he does, Peckinpah at least invites recognition of the problem, which has to be the first step if there is to be any hope for the future. Peckinpah doesn't presume that he knows the answer here either, but the first step has to be taken in any case. As Mike says to Mac when Mac asks where they're going, "Don't know where we're goin'—don't know where we been; but I know where we was, wasn't it."

The interior film of character within the frame (the "serious" drama, if you will) ends with Hansen's death. Mike has maneuvered things to this type of fatal confrontation; but facing it, he cannot complete the killing as he knows he will have to in one way or another. Facing each other, Mike and Hansen are in a stand-off with Mike looking for the answer to George's betrayal. But George's answer is not enough for Mike; there indeed is no answer that will satisfy the depth of betrayal and rejection Mike has felt. The emotional paralysis, the question mark of the moment, is broken by Miller's killing of Hansen; the only way to break through the moment is for it to be taken out of Mike's hands. When Miller comes up after Hansen's death, Mike explodes in frustration, decking Miller. But Mac and Miller both understand Mike's helplessness and know that the punch wasn't personal. The punch is the release of the tension within Mike over the debacle of his destroyed friendship, probably the only thing Mike previously valued or related to in any significant way, apart from a sense of professional pride.

With this value betrayed, Mike questions the value of anything, leading to the close of the exterior film. With Peckinpah and us, Mike must pick up the pieces, realizing the nature of what's going on. The political game played in the martial arts duel at the end of the film is beyond Mike, as he knows that the man he has been protecting hasn't got a hope in hell of accomplishing anything because of the way the game is played in the modern world, regardless of how admirable the man's individual commitment may be. Mike finally agrees with Mac, who has previously retired from the game; they both acknowledge the fact that they're not fighting for anything, that they have only been pawns in a game that no longer has any objectives (if it ever did) other than the temporary wins and losses of power unrelated to the values of individuals. There is no point in trying to destroy the organization when the whole power structure of society is the organization.

There is also no point to killing Cap Collis, the faceless man who never had any convictions. Collis's death would suit no purpose, whereas crippling him is appropriate: it is the only thing which might effectively "reach" Collis, the personal wounding that is essentially his just reward. The cruelty of his being crippled matches Collis's own cruelty of unscrupulousness; the man without principles is not a "humane being," and his crippling will have him suffer as a human for his inhumanity. Weyburn is almost as bad. While he may have believed in something in the past, he has seen too much and played the dirty game too long; he gave up that ghost long ago and world-wearily continues in his position. The difference between him and Collis is that Weyburn is still a team player and does not tolerate betrayal. It is a thin point, for the nature of the game is such that it involves an "unscrupulous" means (using Mike in a set-up) to achieve the supposedly scrupulous end, and the organization cannot tolerate betrayal on grounds of business efficiency regardless of whether a potential matter of principle is involved as well. In any case, Mike rejects Weyburn, the game, and Collis; crippling Collis is a personal

score. Collis tried to kill Mike; Weburn only used Mike, relying on Mike's skill to settle some "office politics," as Mac describes it; using people was always part of the game.

At the same time, Mike rejects (with Peckinpah) the pointless heroics of the game (and the genre). Peckinpah suggests
through Mike's incredulity with the last samurai showdown
that because of power residing in the untouchable organization, the individual is helpless to achieve any meaningful
victory. At best, Yuen Chung can only hope to be a Don Quix-
ote kind of martyr. Political intrigue in the shadows is ultimately fruitless; it won't change anything. Correspondingly,
Yuen Chung's political philosophy sounds archaic and confused, matched with an equally byzantine arrangement of
concerns voiced by the CIA representative, who talks to plants
with more interest than he has in people. Mike finally sees it
all as nonsense; and we should, too. The battle of featureless
Ninja assassins with Mike Locken and company in the naval
graveyard provides Peckinpah with an opportunity for a magnificently staged fight scene, marvelously edited as if it were a
tense heroic battle, but the whole thing skids to an abrupt halt
as Mike declares it is ridiculous to have it continue. The duel
between Yuen Chung and the Ninja leader is undercut by
Mike and Mac's impatience with the fight, wisecracking cynically from the sidelines, "Buy me 7-5, I'll take the little guy."
To further satirize any drama in the situation, Peckinpah originally planned to have Miller rise up after he was gunned
down, surviving his bullet wounds to go off with Mac and
Mike.[2]

If one recognizes the two endings of the film, one can step
back to recognize that both aspects were set up from the beginning. As in *The Getaway*, the viewer can take the characters seriously and finally wake up to the absurdity and empti-
ness of their situation at the end, or one can stand off from
them and feel sorry for the people lost in such a silly situation
from the start, taking them as cartoons in a structure that traditionally doesn't see itself as a cartoon. (This is not the same
thing as the James Bond adventures, where the tongue is obviously in cheek all along.) Peckinpah invites one to take the
interior film of character seriously, the better to realize the
absurdity of the exterior film. But the interior is constructed so
well that one may not realize the exterior at all (as some didn't

with *The Getaway*). To avoid this last, Peckinpah has the main character of the interior himself recognize the exterior. If you don't follow the end of the film from this point of view, chances are you may still be hoping for Locken to act like a "hero."

Peckinpah builds the interior film on the basis of intimate, dimensional friendship relations. Mike and George are buddies, working efficiently together, singing in the car, laughing at the practical joke George plays on Mike (the girl Mike was with had the clap, according to a doctor's report George says he "found" in her bag). The expectation is there that either would "stand up" for the other. Mike's trust of George is so complete that it makes him entirely vulnerable to George's betrayal. The professional knows better than to trust anyone so implicitly other than himself; Mike is crippled in the locker room because he cannot imagine George's treachery. Likewise, their friendship prevents George from killing Mike as, "professionally," he should; the tie is strong enough to subvert the completion of George's betrayal. George acts not to destroy his friend, but only to take him out of the game.

Mike gets no support from his bosses; he wouldn't get any from Collis anyway, and Weyburn is a realist. Rather than accept their verdict, Mike struggles to make himself whole and useful again, in addition to it being necessary if he is ever to find George again. It is an intensely personal struggle to recover, emotionally as well as physically, such that Mike is embarrassed by the simple concern expressed by his friend Mac, shooing Mac away when he shows up with flowers. Mollifying Mike's potential bitterness is his relationship with his nurse, Amy, an unadorned romance of support which Mike needs and accepts. She, at the same time, has no illusions about reaching the inner man; their relationship is of simple direction and honesty, with no strings.

When Mike does get the call to action, he chooses his backup team on the basis of loyal friendship outside of any professional dictates that his friends are not suitable. He has faith in Mac and Miller, choosing to rely more on their loyalty than on the pure measure of their abilities. Miller has been labeled a psychopath, but Mike is yet ready to use him; Miller knows that Mike's offer is a measure of Mike's respect beyond labels and responds to it. Similarly, the disillusioned and officially retired Mac responds to Mike's appeal for his help on the basis of friendship.

Peckinpah designs all of these scenes with acute sensitivity, the understating of each moment subtly revealing the emotions underlying each scene. The camaraderie of Mike and George, Mac's moment in the hospital, and the scenes in the garage where what is really happening is decidedly left out of the dialogue, the scenes of Mike's recovery with the nurse and his martial arts instructor friends, and the scene with Miller overlooking the Golden Gate—all of these are finely keyed moments to establish the bedrock of real emotions in the characters of the interior film.

The human dimension of Mike and his friends is contrasted with the hollow corporate impersonality of Collis, who has no attachments to anything except himself. In the scene in his limousine with Mike, Collis declares his dissatisfaction with the world and that there is no sense fighting for anything. He resents Mike's determination to make a "comeback." But where Weyburn in a similar position might be sadly sympathetic (he has the potential to understand lost ideals), Collis is a shell who never had any ideals. It is nothing to him to orchestrate the betrayal of Mike and of the organization he serves. Cap Collis is indeed a "pod," one of the emotionless horrors from *The Invasion of the Body Snatchers*.

Collis is the running link between the personal interior and the impersonal exterior. For constantly, while the character relationships of the interior film develop, the exterior tale runs about pell-mell, with an excitement that's consistently undercut by the feeling that this is all much ado about nothing. The interior characters are really fighting the exterior level of the film, not the phantoms of the "MacGuffin" political interior which is at best confused and more easily seen to be frustratingly pointless. From the very beginning, the precredit prologue of a typescript interview about the nature of Com-Teg, the elite organization, is rolled against a soundtrack of children playing games. Following that, the opening credits are seen over intricate details of a covert demolition operation, which explodes with the finality of doomsday, only to reveal that it is a diversion to spirit away the defector client, Vorodny. Starting the film with a bang, it is yet clearly out of proportion to the job.

The confusion and resultant comedy in the airport kung-fu battle (intercut with the CIA explanation of what it "means") inhibits any serious implications of the episode. Pointedly, it is difficult to tell who's who; ultimately, it doesn't matter, not to the film or to the genre. The scene is a magnificent parody of extremes, ending with bodies coming up on the baggage ramp. In a final undercut, Peckinpah finishes the scene with a "flasher" joke. This observed absurdity indicates the pointlessness of Mike's (a "real" human being) applying himself to such a job seriously. If we recognize it early, we may enjoy the derring-do while hoping that the characters of interest will also recognize it, which they finally do.

Picking up Yuen Chung and his party is a cinematically romantic bit of heroism undercut by the extreme frenzy of its ineptitude, while remaining securely within the "realistic" confines of the genre. They do not use special gadgets as Our Man Flint would, but escaping from the hole they find themselves in is nevertheless quite a trick. At the outset, Miller saves them by neatly recognizing the contradiction of the false policeman's firearm; Mac recognizes that the garbage truck blocking the street has no garbage to pick up. The scene is sensationally crafted, shooting up the street (and a Chinese laundry!), while somehow getting around the obstacles to further outwit a few Keystone Kops in modern dress.

The final pay-off to the sequence is the scene with the bomb in the taxi. Mac, alerted to the danger by a funny noise or something mysterious in the car's performance, stops the show to deal with the problem. This is a potentially tense moment if it is to be taken seriously, but Peckinpah steers it away from such tension into pure comedy, with another hapless policeman. As the taxi makes good its escape, we hear the bomb go off in the distance; nobody pays any attention to it.

On the boat, Yuen Chung's daughter Tommie (of course she is going to cause trouble later, as George uses her as a shield) approaches Mike with her idea of the whole thing as romantic fantasy, but Mike abruptly dismisses her as if to say, "C'mon, kid, be serious." Mike himself is only one step away from the realization that none of it is "serious."

The only serious matter at stake is the idea that values don't have much of a chance in the modern world. Both Vorodny, the defector client of the beginning, and Yuen Chung are impotent

as committed individuals in a society where power has nothing to do with commitment. They cannot survive through
their own powers; they have to rely on the help of organizations whose help is likewise not provided through commitment, but only from temporary political convenience.

It is possible to construct an analogy from this film to Peckinpah's personal situation, as an added dimension to the nature of the outlook of the film. Peckinpah, too, needs help from
organizations that do not respond primarily from commitment
to a purpose, in order to make films at all. Sadly, there is no
place for him to sail away to, to avoid the compromising nature
of the business; he cannot escape the Weyburns and the Col-
lises, who have no interest in committed ideals. What he can
do, however, is make films that refuse to totally submit to the
forces that would destroy his conceptions. He will accept jobs
of work to survive, but makes them his own in spite of their
nature. What becomes especially apparent in *The Killer Elite*
is that he would like others to recognize his predicament. The
end result is always original; no matter what is done to him or
the films, he still makes films unique from those of anyone
else. His tendency to empathize with all of his characters puts
a little bit of himself into all of them; he is hampered like Yuen
Chung, tired like Weyburn, battle-scarred though still resolute
like Locken.

As with any filmmaker so driven to realize a personal vision,
the private, autobiographical aspect of that vision is always
present. It becomes more apparent in a film like *The Killer
Elite*, where the conception is more closely related to that private analogy.[3] Peckinpah may not deliver the "expected" film,
but he does not lose sight of the particular object at hand. The
result is definably his, but the film will perform in a vacuum of
perceived authorship. Realizing the authorship adds another
level to the effect of the film; familiarity with that authorship
can make that level inescapable, to the obfuscation of the surface concerns.

The Killer Elite is a well-crafted whole, directed to the
complete integration of a bifocal ending of character and
genre. Phil Lathrop's photography supports the hollow ambiguity of the mission with its lack of full sunlight; Peckinpah
may have chosen the location of the mothball fleet intuitively,
and it is a perfect background of lifeless neutrality (pointedly

of impotent war materièl), matching the gray tone of the rest of the film. Similarly, Jerry Fielding's score is a brilliant mimic of a Lalo Schiffrin "Mission Impossible" score, but one can also hear the discordant, "ironic" horns of his music for *Straw Dogs*. Peckinpah, as always, directs his cast unerringly to performances completely "right" for the film's ends, using the individual actor's "baggage" of appearance to inform each character's role; each character is drawn to include the actor, such that the actor can succeed in "creating" the character. Peckinpah's powers of observation include these details, and his casting is consistently "correct" as a result.

Viewed strictly at the surface, *The Killer Elite* is a harmless, well-paced thriller indicative of its genre. Peckinpah delivers the film on his own terms, however, in such a way that his attitude lurks just below that polished surface, tugging at the question of the nature of the genre itself. Sailing away at the end is neither cynical nor nihilistically defeatist; it is a finger thrown up to the establishment that would deny an individual his value, or a filmmaker his vision, and a self-consciously romantic gesture at that. The reality is unfortunately more severe, more so than the genre could possibly indicate. Multi-million-dollar filmmaking patrons are sadly nonexistent. One survives as best one can; you look for another job, or quit the business altogether. Sam Peckinpah cannot quit.

13

Cross of Iron (1977)

DO YOU KNOW how much I hate this uniform, and everything it stands for?" asks Steiner, the German squad leader, in
Cross of Iron.

Though it may at first sound simple-minded to say so, *Cross
of Iron* is a triumph: it is an ugly war film. Its debilitating
grimness is all the more "triumphant" because of the relative
rarity of this quality in films with ostensibly similar themes.
Peckinpah's image of war is brutally clear—war is a most an-
tihuman activity—but his execution of the film sets up a trap
for the audience which at first seems so patently obvious that a
viewer can leap into it believing himself to be sophisticatedly
aware of his ground, only to find himself dismally lost in a
morass of ironic expectation.

The trap is set by the ease of our acceptance that we think
we have been here before. We are quick to identify the characters and situations which seem endemic to films about war
and to equate them facilely with intellectualized ideas which
automatically, properly condemn war. But our intellectual
familiarity with the images of war clouds our potential perception of the realities of war. Subtly fictionalized or several steps
removed (Vietnam footage on TV), we have forgotten the gap
between direct experience and second-hand observation; we
tend to overlook the implications and truth behind the familiar
image. Clichés are dismissed and taken for granted without
recognizing both the limits and the facts underlying those perceptions. We must remind ourselves that no matter how much
we feel we understand war, that understanding is devastatingly limited by the nature of what it is based on. The extremes of war are mainly beyond human comprehension.
Similarly, we must recognize that inability to describe com-

203

James Coburn as Steiner.

pletely the experience of war. No matter how bad or reprehensible you may think it is, it is worse.

But our concern about, fear of, guilt from, and fascination with war urge us to try to describe and understand it nevertheless. In a desire to feel secure, we accept descriptions that assure us that the worst *is* comprehensible. We generalize our images, victimizing ourselves by tackling war from a variety of viewpoints without understanding the narrowness of those viewpoints. We make the mistake of analogizing war to one-to-one conflicts which seem to be comprehensible; we look for heroism, courage, and evil in the assumption that those are rationally definable concepts. We look for justice—and excuses.

War films particularly offer a confusion of images. Intervening decades change the meaning of those images while not altering the images themselves. What appeared to be necessarily heroic in 1943 is especially antiheroic in 1977, but we are too quick to forget the possible "truth" of the 1943 view, considering ourselves to be more enlightened by the revised 1977 view. It is important to consider both views, for only then can one appreciate the idea that both are incomplete, based on fundamentally simplistic assumptions that we "know where we stand" on the issue. The simple poetry of *All Quiet on the Western Front* (1930) did nothing to impede the leap of many into World War II; yet the last image of that film (reaching for the butterfly) would be emphatically reexpressed by one of the most common anti-Vietnam War posters, whose legend read, "War is not healthy for children and other living things." And were we "wrong" to fight in World War II?

Cross of Iron, as Peckinpah's film of modern war, accepts the existence of war and its fundamental incomprehensibility without flinching from its equally fundamental ugliness. Peckinpah tests our assumptions of familiarity by resolutely ignoring such familiarity, begging the reconsideration of an image as if it were being seen for the first time. To underscore the necessity of that reconsideration, he maintains the relentless severity which has more often than not been missing from the image.

At bottom lies the establishment of the inhumanity of war at its most physical. This is accomplished with more than merely graphic violence. John Coquillon's rich photography of the film is obsessively dark, its deep blues and greens contributing to the overall atmosphere of dank, thoroughly oppressive griminess. Peckinpah is after more than the "1,000-mile" look of war-weary troops, a look that has been seen to some extent before in films such as Sam Fuller's *Fixed Bayonets* (1951) and *The Steel Helmet* (1951), and Anthony Mann's *Men in War* (1957). More than that "look," Peckinpah tries to indicate the taste and smell of war, what must be a sickening combination of oil, smoke, sweat, and filth. Rarely has a war film looked so close to being physically rotted. In addition, the film is characterized by what seems to be fairly constant, indiscriminate bombardment; there is hardly any let-up in the shelling at all. Bloody, inglorious death is a constant companion. The carnage and destruction are debilitating because they are not climactic.

The time and place of the film are relevant insofar as those facts are where Peckinpah and the audience begin. The physical conditions of the story are not made to seem unique to the particular historical setting; the fact that it takes place during an especially disastrous German retreat in Russia in mid-1943 serves to clarify the depth of *readily* apparent disillusionment and debilitating weariness of the characters. Victory obscures the issues; defeat emphasizes the horror. In defeat, there is no rationalization of achievement to mollify the combatant's suffering; the only thing to fight for is survival.

How then is the human spirit to survive such a beating? Can we, as nonparticipants, dare presume that we can understand the spiritual suicide war can inflict? It is perhaps all we can do to bear witness to it, observing it empirically. For Peckinpah, war is an extreme test of an individual's ability to hold on to any virtues at all; because of the nature of war, it may be all one can do to preserve any shred of human dignity.

Steiner is an individual of conscience and ability, trapped in the mechanics of war. However he came to be where he is (a fact which few men pretend to understand), the onslaught of the massive effects of the war has removed the possibility of individually coherent action to any "victorious" end. What is left for him is to survive as a human being rather than as an animal; that choice dictates the duty of his responsibility to the lives of the men under his command. Within the platoon, it is apparent that you rely on your "friends" and leader, or you die. The men have only each other to protect themselves from the horror and destruction of the war. That the breakdown of a comrade is serious because camaraderie is a last refuge of humanity is demonstrated repeatedly in the film, but never more dramatically than when Kern threatens to break apart during the party in the platoon's bunker and Kruger snaps him out of it by kissing him forcefully on the mouth. The moment seizes the platoon and the audience; all the men have is each other. Steiner, because of his position of authority and his ability, accepts as his job the "protection" and survival of his platoon.

It is both strange and altogether natural that desertion is precluded; it would not enhance chances of survival, and it would also be clearly dishonorable. This last is an insurmountable question mark of war, the irony of maintaining a sense of honor in a situation which defies rational explanations on ethical grounds. In the immediate confusion of front-line warfare, larger issues are inevitably lost; Steiner accepts the uniform he wears, even as he despises it, and, where individual initiative is possible, he directs himself to issues of survival (which also include obeying orders) within his immediate control.

But this also includes a grim paradox for Steiner and the audience, indicated in the opening of the film. The first scene has Steiner and his patrol ambushing a Russian squad. Their stealth and surprise over the Russians are murderously complete; at the finish, Steiner measures their success, saying, "Good kill." Peckinpah brings us into the film with what appears to be a scene of recognizably "standard" action, "courageous" battle action which is interrupted by a question for the audience of bloodlust with Steiner's line. But shortly we realize that this *offensive* action was part of a greater *defensive* action; the Germans are the "underdogs" (until we indeed realize that at the front, at least, the only victory is survival). The "kill" is a "good kill," a successful maneuver; never is it suggested that the killing itself is good. But war is a unique situation of "justifiable" homicide. Emphasizing Steiner's squad's opening action for its murderous violence underscores this level of irony. It also dramatically and directly grabs the audience at the beginning of the film. In a way, Peckinpah begins the film in the middle, dropping us into the hellish situation without the defenses of knowing exactly where we are. We are lost from the start morally, as are the men of Steiner's platoon. All we have to root for is their survival as men.

Given our position with the platoon, it is easy to despise the self-serving, unethical treachery of a Stransky. Allowing the audience to focus on Stransky's villainy builds the expectation of a final, vindictive confrontation between Steiner and Stransky, which Peckinpah ultimately denies the audience, to a greater purpose. The end of the film is in keeping with Steiner's character. His initial rage after the slaughter of his men has been met by his machine-gunning of Triebig, the man directly responsible for the slaughter. Steiner pauses before killing Triebig, unconsciously judging Triebig's evil and the righteousness of his immediate retribution in killing him. It is a moment for Triebig to realize why Steiner will kill him, that his treachery will not be allowed success, and, indeed, that Triebig will not be allowed to survive.

But Stransky represents a greater evil, a greater inhumanity that is unreachable by simple execution. Stransky, as an officer one step removed from the consequences of his orders, reprehensible for that fact of responsibility removed from punishment, must be made to suffer with the living before there can be any "gain" from his death. Steiner realizes that Stransky has no understanding of what he has done, and because Stransky would not realize what he has violated if Steiner gave him a pause before killing him, Steiner knows that simply executing Stransky would prove nothing. Stransky, at least at that time, is not worth killing.

Steiner knows that Stransky's weakness is the same vulnerability of self-image that drives Stransky to obtain an Iron Cross. We see in their conversations throughout the film that Stransky's inability to dominate Steiner from a position of authority (which Stransky believes in but which Steiner knows is hollow) is what Stransky finds intolerable. Stransky tries everything to enlist Steiner's aid in getting an Iron Cross, including an open confession of his need based on the humiliation he would feel if he didn't go back a "hero." Stransky believes himself to be of the elite, based on his social position, a position which also believes in the "heroic" significance of the Iron Cross. It would be a crushing contradiction of his image of superiority *not* to win the medal. The particular situation which makes Steiner's cooperation necessary to Stransky's Iron Cross dramatizes the irony of Stransky's feared inferiority. For Stransky, "winning" the Iron Cross would be the proof of his position; for Steiner, the Iron Cross has no meaning, but he will not falsify his testimony to allow Stransky to get the medal, thereby denying Stransky the "proof" of his superiority by default. Steiner likewise, however, will not testify *against* Stransky, either, removing himself from the consideration which would give the medal significance by denying it to Stransky. For Steiner, it is a personal matter. Stransky does not understand that, but the effect is the same: Stransky responds to the denial of the symbol, while Steiner refuses to give the symbol significance though denying the bestowing of the symbol on ethical grounds. What is even more frustrating for Stransky is that Steiner *has* an Iron Cross, but does not place any value on it. Stransky is diminished because he cannot "get to" Steiner, and Steiner happens to be the one who stands in the way of Stransky's self-justification.

Realizing Stransky's weakness, Steiner recognizes there is no point in killing Stransky, as it would not teach Stransky the lesson of total humiliation of his position. It would remove Stransky, but the damage has already been done. Steiner's survival of Stransky's plot to have him killed is partial vindication of Steiner's position in terms Stransky might understand, but to kill Stransky would yet have him die in ignorance, which is pointless. Steiner instead chooses to show Stransky the meaning of the "heroism" Stransky believes in but is too cowardly to achieve on his own. Steiner gives Stransky a gun and turns his back to him, daring Stransky to prove himself to be the soldier he declares himself to be. Stransky realizes that shooting Steiner would be the ultimate proof of Steiner's superiority over his own position and accepts Steiner's challenge to "prove" his superiority as a Prussian aristocrat.

Steiner's victory over Stransky is the only possible one of any consequence, that of Stransky's total, obvious humiliation. As Stransky fumbles in fear, we see a Russian boy-soldier shake his head in disbelief at Stransky's ineptitude. Steiner has the last laugh, at Stransky's totally devastated expense. But, as the music rises and Steiner's laugh dies down, Steiner is fully aware of the senselessness of the war and the point he has just proved. His laughter ends with a tired, quietly desperate, "Oh shit." The whole thing is too much for one man. Surviving death is easy compared to surviving the staggering dimension of the incomprehensibility of war. The only survival is in not trying to make sense of it all.

The end of the film from a standard "heroic" action viewpoint is frustrating because it denies the violent retribution we might expect in such a dramatic situation. Peckinpah says with this ending that this kind of (genre) expectation is wrong; if we are looking for a more conclusive resolution of the conflict, we are caught in the same pattern of false belief that Stransky maintains, and we have missed a basic understanding of the dynamics of warfare. Pointedly, nobody wins in a heroic sense; the illusion of values used to justify a war is dangerously false, providing defensive excuses for the parties responsible. One should not be allowed to escape the idea that war is *all* shit. The paradox is that it seems possible to find a situation where fighting *is* necessary. Man will continue to fight at least as long as he perceives an intractable enemy. But if mankind cannot rid itself of war, it must not be allowed to fool itself as to the calamitous nature of war.

To this end, Peckinpah refuses to make a traditional war movie. It amazes me how some people can call a *war* movie *too* violent! Anything less than grim, savage horror would seem to be some kind of lie. The nature of the film's situation (as well as that of the book on which it is based) demands excess, for only in witnessing what *appears* to be excessive can one begin to perceive the horror of the truth. Accepting the limitation of the screen's distance from the audience, Peckinpah "stylizes" some of the violence in recognition of the limitations of our perceptions. In order to convey an approximation of reality, the film has to go beyond simple photographic "reality." (This was one of the criticisms of the 1978 television movie "Holocaust," in which the images were not striking enough to convey the depth of the real horror for some viewers.) Peckinpah further breaks with genre convention in the battle scenes themselves, cutting away from an action before its completion, intercutting and interrupting actions with slow-motion and "real-time" actions until one is *lost* in the action, and only the action itself remains without an idea of what is happening (i.e., what the action represents). It seems *logical* to me (never having been in combat) that in the *midst*

"Grim, savage horror."

The child: the ultimate victim.

of combat one would probably *not* be aware of what was happening or who-was-who in any orderly sense, that the dominant feeling would be one of utter chaos. Correspondingly, Peckinpah constructs the battle scenes to this end, in an onslaught of powerful images connected only slightly by time, and hardly at all by orientation. The result may seem to be an omniscient view, but it is yet a view of chaos. One does not know exactly where the bullets come from. One particular image sums up the violence of war to a great degree: a corpse in the mud, crushed further by a half-track personnel carrier, with the living-to-be-dead rolling over the already dead.

In a sense, it is a mockery that a war film should be given an "R" rating. *Cross of Iron* was variously trimmed by about ten to twelve minutes for American release, with the cutting of the sequence of the Russian women's platoon obviously part of this reediting because of its graphically violent sexual connotations. The impact of the scene of Zoll's castration is weakened by the reediting, in such a way that it lessens the horror of its reason for being there at all. This scene (though it takes place earlier in the novel) is as literally graphic in the novel as it is visually graphic in the film. It bears witness to the devastatingly animal level human beings can be reduced to, chilling in its horrible finality. Zoll gets what he deserves from his animal act of sexual abuse, with a punishment as bestial as that which he gives the woman. Steiner is sickened by Zoll and his condition and leaves him to be torn apart by the Russian women. (They can't take Zoll with them, and it seems "just" to leave him there.) I have not seen the "uncut" version, but cutting the scene is a cheat on the nature of the film; arguing that the scene is sensationally unnecessary is also weak due to the nature of what the film is about.[1]

The film's depiction of the complete oppression of war is consistent, turning what otherwise might appear to be a romantic interlude of genre convention into part of an inescapable nightmare. Steiner is haunted in the hospital by the faces of his men, to the extent that he must rejoin them when the first opportunity arises. The fact of his "interlude" with the nurse achieves nothing of consequence, demonstrating in its ineffectiveness that there *is* no escape from the war and that Steiner cannot desert his friends. At best, the interlude is a momentary respite, significant by what it shows Steiner is denied. Personally sympathetic compassion and the affirmation of romantic intimacy don't have a chance in war. One gets a moment of it, if one is lucky.

For Peckinpah, the child is the most depressing victim of war. If wars are fought to obtain a "better world" for the next generation, what kind of betterment can there be if the war kills those children in the process? And what kind of inheritance is to be passed on to the survivors? Peckinpah figuratively offers us his own son here, as he has almost literally before. Matthew Peckinpah was a child observer of the Starbuck massacre in *The Wild Bunch*, a stagecoach passenger in *Cable Hogue*, a nephew of Junior Bonner, and an observer of Mike Locken's recovery in *The Killer Elite*; he might as well have been Pat Garrett's barber shop messenger boy, and the Russian boy-soldier here, cast in his image. Steiner ponders the situation that places such a child in uniform; he bluntly refuses Stransky's order to kill the boy (Stransky sees only a prisoner, while Steiner sees a child), and lets the boy go. But the killing irony of war has the boy shot by his own "comrades," and Steiner's responding cry is an insensate cry of anguish. There is no coherent verbal response to such cruelty. Peckinpah haunts Steiner and us with the image of the boy, finally "resurrecting" the boy as the one who completes Stransky's humiliation. In a sense, the men of Steiner's platoon are Steiner's children, his charges. He reprimands Dietz for playing a children's shadow game as they move through the woods behind the Russian lines. Considering the presence of the physical child, there is, in addition, the reminder that we are all children.

For me, the still photo montage of the victims of war at the close of the film seemed redundant, but Peckinpah may have felt it necessary to leave no room for doubt as to his "message" in the film, recapitulating it in the photo-montage which joins the victims of all wars, particularly the one of most recent consequences. He has indeed been proved "right" to have underscored this feeling at the end, as many have misread and dismissed the film entirely. The quotation attributed to Bertolt Brecht, following the photographs, is eloquently, unavoidably direct;[2] we have no reason to cheer the end of the film, as the beast of war is yet alive.

Cross of Iron is a brilliantly complex work, its depth of

maturity obscured by Peckinpah's daring in making a war film which the viewer is not supposed to "enjoy" in any traditional sense. The film is frustrating to analyze because of the nature of its production (and release) problems, but like other "damaged" Peckinpah films, the strength of its conception is witnessed by the complete success of individual scenes. Extraordinarily faithful to Willi Heinrich's massive novel on which it is based, the film seems to suffer at times from narrative condensation, but the knowledge of the existence of problems during production militates against laying any fault to Peckinpah's conception; the film as it stands is all of a consistent piece. I would estimate in that sense that Peckinpah would have preferred a longer film. The practical nature of commercial filmmaking suggests that if there is any fault of Peckinpah's here, it is in undertaking the project at all in the first place, but that is a luxury he probably couldn't afford, and considering the practical difficulties, Peckinpah's rise to the challenge is successful.

While the scope of the richness of this film is beyond the space available here,[3] in the main the success of Peckinpah's complex achievement needs to be recognized. *Cross of Iron*, regardless of the "final cut," is a grim, claustrophobic, relentless, debilitating, and frustrating film—as it *should* be. Peckinpah's depiction of war forms the question of earlier films, that of the nature of individual ideas of the meaning and definition of heroism, courage, loyalty, and honor, as borne by human beings who (at times ignorantly) carry the seed of their own destruction. Modern war particularly precludes the rational application of these virtues; heroism, if it exists at all, is strictly relative. Moreover, war crushes the individual; the sooner we stop looking for war heroes, the closer we may come to avoiding war altogether. It is important to Peckinpah that the observer find nothing to cheer about at the end of the film, except perhaps the indomitable "survivorship" of Steiner, the individual.

Cross of Iron is a film that is *not* to be "liked" in the heroic tradition of many other war films. Furthermore, we have perhaps gone too far to be allowed the hope at the conclusion of Jean Renoir's *Grand Illusion* (1937); Peckinpah denies any romanticism in war, in a manner reminiscent of Kon Ichikawa's *Fires on the Plain* (1959) and Andrzej Wajda's *Kanal*

(1956), and related to the suggestion at the end of Don Siegel's *Hell Is for Heroes* (1962). Too often in our view of war have we looked at it primarily with the mind, protecting the gut. The complexity of Peckinpah's cinematic conception in *Cross of Iron* is indicated by the way it goes for the gut, leaving the mind to pick up the pieces of that primary devastation. In defying our expectations, Peckinpah leaves us with something to think about. War is too serious to play games with; the tragedy is that the voices of children singing at the beginning and end of the film are not recognized as our own.

14

Convoy (1978)

"THEY'RE NOT followin' me—I'm just in front," says the Rubber Duck in *Convoy*. As the director of this film, Peckinpah is also "in front," and has been subjected to an inordinate amount of criticism for a film whose release version was decidedly not his responsibility. Few critics seemed prepared to enjoy this film, much less to make allowances for the idea that production problems have a great deal to do with what finally comes to the screen as a "finished" film. Taking the final cut "away" from the person whose conception guided the filming of the work "damages" a film at least in the sense that the film no longer represents a unified conception. It is certainly possible that the work-as-is might be "better" than the work which might-have-been, but the evidence of *Convoy* and of previous films is to the contrary.

Yet *Convoy* is highly enjoyable, and beyond that initial enjoyment lie suggestions of engaging subtlety as to what Peckinpah is up to here. As with *Major Dundee* and *Pat Garrett and Billy the Kid* in particular, Peckinpah's film sense is so strong that even truncated works of his carry such rewards that it becomes all the more frustrating to realize that his vision has been altered. What evidence there is is consistently supportive of Peckinpah's talent; considering our frustration, we can only vaguely appreciate how great his frustration must be.

Viewing *Convoy* as a Peckinpah film, it becomes apparent that something is "off," and that "something" is a question of balance and emphasis which resides in the overall editing of the film. For example, the fight in the diner does not seem to have quite the same pace as previous Peckinpah sequences utilizing slow-motion; the slow-motion cuts seem a few frames too long, and the sequence doesn't quite look polished. Be-

217

The "stars": the Convoy (top), and Kris Kristofferson as the Rubber Duck (bottom).

yond tentative examples such as this, it is difficult to isolate problems "felt" with the film; in any event, it is a great deal more gratifying to acknowledge the indelibly good things about the film as a whole. For however it may be incomplete, *Convoy* is a film of energy, drama, and real humor. Once again it is evidence of Peckinpah's great talent that the film he made can be damaged but not destroyed.

In a manner related to *The Getaway* and *The Killer Elite*, *Convoy* is a "serious" film which should not be taken seriously. As with the previous films, Peckinpah blends the interior film of character involvement which the characters take "seriously" with an exterior film accessible only to the audience, where the actions of individuals are distorted and skewed by a suggestion that individual purposes are rendered meaningless by a society that responds only to mass movements and media events. This is a theme that runs through Peckinpah's work, taking various turns of relative approach, and in *Convoy*, an individual action with one set of meanings to the individuals directly involved is taken over by societal interests which blow the whole thing to severe and ridiculous proportions that have nothing to do with the original "purpose." Moreover, the individual is shown to be ineffective in achieving anything of significance. The "personal" conflict between the Rubber Duck and Lyle Wallace is eclipsed by the massive attention it receives, but Davy Crockett can no longer "go to Washington" as is made clear when the Duck meets with the Governor. The sociopolitical response to the Duck as the "leader" of the truckers is to take the whole thing "into committee," more or less. But the Duck is resolved to pursue direct action of consequence, and goes to rescue Spider Mike rather than be swallowed up by the amorphously confused "social movement" which has sprung up in his wake.

Completing the satirical tone of the exterior film, the Duck survives as an individual by escaping the social issue with his "death," yet providing the "Movement" and the Media with the hero they were trying to make him out to be. With his "death," the Duck becomes a better "hero" than they might have hoped; as a martyr, he cannot be found later to have feet of clay. The irony is with the nature of the joke that he is not dead and the fact that his position of leadership, his suicide run on the bridge, and everything else never had anything to do with any large social issue, but society and the Media interpret it as such anyway, believing in the myth they have created. This is a joke that even Lyle can appreciate, for it was always a personal matter between him and the Duck, even after it was taken over by the Media. Peckinpah's conception of the film in this regard is as a fable designed to honor and preserve the committed individual (all the Duck really wants to do is to "enter his house justified," in a sense), while poking fun at society's penchant for making a fool of itself in not comprehending (and denying) the potential capacity of meaningful individual action. Contemporary individuals have the power to affect themselves by their actions, but their effectiveness is zero when broader issues are involved. It seems no longer possible for the marshal to clean up the town, or for a few good men to make much of a difference. But society still looks for the marshal who *can* clean up the town(!). Peckinpah is not necessarily being cynical here, but he is at least sadly recognizing our state of affairs.

The Rubber Duck is established at the outset of the film as a legendary figure among his peers, one suspects due to a combination of expert professionalism at his job and basic integrity of character. He is a "stand-up guy," the "best front-door in the business," and a natural leader for his capabilities and even temperament. There is a ballad about a legendary truck and driver called the "Phantom 309," who suicidally swerved to avoid hitting a hidden school bus. If there ever was a "Phantom 309," the Duck is that driver to others. (Although some of the other truckers could be; it is Pig Pen who actually avoids the school bus in *Convoy*). The Duck has few, if any, misconceptions about his way of life, while not pretending to any eloquence or special insight achieved. As a "legendary" character, however, we see the Rubber Duck as an individual operating within a mythic context which has been forced upon him ("I'm just in front"). The Duck rescues Spider Mike out of a sense of personal responsibility, not from a commitment to live up to his legend. But by remaining true to his (moral) convictions, the Duck substantiates the mythology built around him. His "greatness" is thrust upon him. The truckers of the convoy, in electing a reluctant noncandidate as their spokesman, set themselves up for an initial disappointment when the

Duck apparently deserts the convoy (and the political /
mythical significance thereof) to rescue Spider Mike. Ironically, in "leaving the legend behind," the Duck adds more
fuel to the legend by his subsequent actions. The truckers who
join him in the rescue are still responding to the mythical ethical hero. The lesson here is somewhat similar to that of *The
Man Who Shot Liberty Valance*, in that there is a danger in
subscribing to myths while forgetting the real individuals and
the reality those myths are based upon.

"Dirty Lyle" Wallace is the principal adversary who provides the basic conflict of the story, a corrupt local cop who on
the surface exists merely as a trucker's harpy. While we have
certainly seen this character in other films enough for it to
have become somewhat stereotyped, the real existence of
such a type is easily accepted, since the speed-trap cop who
pockets a portion of the fines he assesses has become a com-
monplace rooted in our folk-culture. Lyle is initially simply a
fact of the highway, a rule of the game to be reckoned with.
But it is Lyle who initiates the convoy indirectly and continues to precipitate the other events of the film. As things
escalate, the personal matter between Lyle and the Duck gets
lost in the media shuffle, but it is to be remembered as the
underlying cause of things, even as they are forced to carry out
their personal conflict in public.

It is important to recognize that although Lyle's character
exists primarily in relation to the Duck, there is more to him
than the enjoyable but facile cardboard of Jackie Gleason's
sheriff in *Smokey and the Bandit* (1977), just as there is more
to *Convoy* than being another "Smokey vs. the Good Ol'
Boys" road movie. There is evident in Lyle a certain amount of
grudging respect for his adversary: in the initial ticketing
where Lyle allows that he and the Duck have their independence in common (the Duck is definitely *not* a Teamster: he is
independent as a professional and as an individual); in Lyle's
disgust with the incompetence of Federal Agent Hamilton,
who simply doesn't know the "rules"; in Lyle's setting up a
trap for the Duck (with Spider Mike as bait) which depends on
an ethical foundation that the Duck knows it's "between" the
two of them and not the other truckers; in the close-up reaction of Lyle to the explosion / "annihilation" of the Duck, a
mixture of simultaneous victory and sad loss of a worthy ad-

versary as well as human shock; and finally at the "funeral" where Lyle discovers the Duck's survival and reacts with great laughter at the expense of their common enemy, the bullshit politician.

There is also a glimpse of Lyle's character which is at first confusing: arriving in Alvarez, he is disgusted at the sight of Spider Mike's battered face. Mike is a pawn in this game, certainly not an object of Lyle's *personal* hatred. It is an "annoying" surprise to see Lyle concerned about Mike, to see it so plainly stated that he has nothing personal against Mike: Lyle promises to let Mike know if he hears anything about Mike's wife and baby. This is annoying because it sets Lyle clearly apart from a more stereotypically cruel view, but to dismiss this scene as insincere on Lyle's part would be unnecessarily cynical, and not in line with other aspects of Lyle's character. That Lyle is predominantly a "piece of meanness" is not in dispute, but a characteristic of Peckinpah's "villains" is that they have signal ambiguities which indicate that they may not be incorrigibly evil, but perhaps are ultimately more misguided than anything else. It is the businessman / politician with no apparent code of ethics beyond successful expediency who gets the clearest Peckinpah scorn; *Convoy* is no exception in that.

The most easily overlooked part of *Convoy* is in its particular environment of trucks and truckers, the manner in which its peculiarities dictate the style and characters of the film. Peckinpah maintains a consistent tone in the atmosphere which at first seems so familiar that we might assume that we know where we are well enough. But we risk a tendency to be caught in our own preconceptions and biases about the particular environment if we assume that the "colorful" trucker's world does not involve "real" people. Consequently, one can "lose" a lot of this film if one is not ready to involve oneself in considering the trucker's point of view. The irony for the viewer here is that while the overall, exterior film is played for comedy and satire, the interior film *is* taken seriously by the characters of the film. In a sense here, the world outside the immediate world of the characters *is* absurd, while that interior world is likewise absurd and / or at least incomprehensible to the outsiders. Peckinpah offers the viewer a choice to see things from the peculiar interior, or to remain with the exterior. Indeed, *Convoy* becomes another example of Peckin-pah's concern with how an individual with values is to make his way in a world which doesn't seem to respect those values in a situation where the individual must confront this world.

Meanwhile, you don't have to love trucks to enjoy this movie, but you do have to be open to appreciate trucks as being capable of possessing beauty as well as power; you have to be open to an appreciation of the physical artifact, the main presence of the story. For only through a minimum sense of trucks and trucking can one begin to understand the nature of the people involved. Peckinpah hardly agrees with all the at-titudes of the various truckers in the film, but he does grant them at least initial respect as individuals. In addition, Peck-inpah recognizes the unique qualities of the trucker's envi-ronment, allowing that the mannerisms and slang of C.B. jar-gon set that world apart from an outsider. For the outsider (and this includes most of the film's audience), the trucker's world appears to be something of a romantic carnival, obscuring the fact that the C.B. code, for instance, serves a particular pur-pose within the "peculiar" environment. If we cannot take the truckers "seriously" as human beings, we are probably guilty of accepting the simplistic "Good Ol'Boy" romantic myth our-selves, indeed, the same myth that the Rubber Duck finds forced upon him by his "followers." If you approach *Convoy* as a cartoon, the people involved will also appear cartoonish. In a way, the characters' laughter at the end of the film is di-rected as well at that part of the audience which subscribes to the romantic myth. The characters of the interior film (and Peckinpah) escape by subverting the myth, by "sailing off" as Mike Locken does in *The Killer Elite*, while ironically leaving an even greater foundation for the myth-makers and believers to build on. Understanding the full extent of Peckinpah's joke involves recognizing the idea that it is "Martin Penwald" (the Duck's real name as an individual) who survives, and that the "Rubber Duck" is dead. Not only does he survive the situation *within* the film, he also survives the film itself, which swept him up as a romantic hero from the start.

There are numerous "little" indications of this all along the way. Mainly, it involves the Duck's resistance to the constant hoopla surrounding him within the film and his equal reluc-tance as a character to accept the attention the film itself forces upon him. Consistently, the Duck is only trying to go his own way without disturbing anybody; Lyle's pursuit has the Duck merely "running for his life," not trying to make a statement. Likewise, amidst all the confusion over Pig Pen / Love Machine's handle, the Duck simply calls him "Bobby," not needing the C.B. slang (or the image / myth) in a personal context. In another instance, when the Governor moves in and talks about the convoy as a protest movement, the Duck maintains the truth that it has nothing to do with the speed limit. But since everyone else insists that the convoy means something, it is impossible for the Duck alone to convince anybody that they're not following him, that he's "just in front." Try as he might, the Duck cannot destroy the myth; all he can do is play it straight, while he remains committed to his sense of personal integrity and responsibility. In this regard, *Convoy* lampoons the idea that it doesn't matter what the Media pays attention to, for by granting an object its attention, the Media makes its subject automatically important.

Convoy presents its depiction of the environment in a fairly straightforward manner, while yet offering an explanation for the romantic myth that has been built around it even as it plays with that myth. The opening shots establish the connection between the myth and the reality simply and vividly, with the barren landscape of heat and oppression, pierced by an indomitable juggernaut which automatically is perceived as an extension of the driver inside (the idea that it takes a "big man" to drive a "big rig"). Introduced to the world of the long-haul trucker, we have an immediate impression of solitary movement through a physically demanding space. We sense (and will see) that there are rules and rituals unique to this life-style, and we sense the loneliness implied by the isolation; we will come to see how the C.B. radio is a tool used to fight the monotony.

It is acknowledged in the film that some, though not all, truckers define themselves partially through their rigs. The cab is the trucker's real home. How he decorates, maintains, and feels about that home is an expression of the individual. By the same token, the trucker chooses (or is given) his C.B. "handle" in representation of his self-image and / or identity. Truckers' handles are revealing of the individual, for they are often at odds with objective identification, and may represent

Spectacular stunts, but nobody gets hurt. (The top stunt received an award).

more how the individual would like to be seen. The character of Pig Pen is a particular demonstration of this, obvious in his extremity but not wholly incredible. He sees himself as a modern "cowpoke," living out a romantic fantasy wherever possible: he calls himself the "Love Machine," and his sleeper cab is equipped with a waterbed and overhead mirrors. He dresses in an exaggerated Western costume appropriate to the imagination of such a character who hails from Paterson, N.J.; he has bought the fantasy and revels in it. At the same time, completing the irony of appearance versus reality, he hauls a most unromantic cargo, a load of pigs whose nature and smell earn him the handle "Pig Pen." At bottom, however, Pig Pen / Love Machine recognizes the contrast and accepts the joking at his own expense. (The Duck, meanwhile, calling him "Bobby," does not define a person by his handle.)

The adventure / romance of the trucker draws from and is supported by the analogy of the trucker as a modern cowboy. It is a pointedly incomplete analogy, but the aspect of romanticism is similar. The trucker has his rig as the legendary cowboy had his horse; the two life-styles are conducive to loners; they are both essentially nomadic, with physical roots being more a state of mind associated with the general environment rather than an accomplished fact. Indeed, the cowboy legend seems ready-made for the modern trucker. Whether he works for wages or not, on the road he is independent. And, they both move through an often forbidding landscape. There is a passage in Charles Neider's book, *The Authentic Death of Hendry Jones*, which describes this: ". . . the effect of the land on a man. Out in the open country of New Mexico you could sit on your horse and ride and ride and camp alone when night came and ride again and sleep alone and ride again . . . that kind of space, which rolls along like the ocean . . . could beat a man down. . . ."[1] This is not directly the experience of the trucker, but the effect is analogous enough to foster the comparison. The trails are paved now, but the landscape is the same.

More important than physical similarities, though, is the appeal of the spirit of cowboy legend. The rugged individual, the self-contained independent, the chivalrous Westerner drifter hero, even the outlaw, are all aspects of cowboy mythology which invite romanticized sympathy. The legend is adapted to the individual's needs in such a way that a variety of truckers respond to the variety of the Western "hero." Attitudes of "machismo" remain with the individual, not with the legend *per se*. The biggest appeal of cowboy romanticism, however, is the idea that it seems harmless enough as long as one doesn't get carried away with it (a warning for outsiders!), and it does make a relatively *boring* profession a little less so. The colorful adoption and development of C.B. radio slang decreases the boredom and accentuates the brotherhood aspect of shared experience, just as the use of the radio in itself is a way to break monotony and know that you're not alone out there. Finally, some measure of excitement is added by the perceived defense against a common enemy; just as the legendary cowboy dealt with legendary "hostiles," the legendary trucker deals with legendary (and generally faceless) "Smokeys." Throughout *Convoy* there is the sense of romantic legend in practice, though it is also seen as a self-conscious game used to enliven a grueling way of life. It is felt that most of the truckers know they are truckers and not cowboys, although the distinction is blurred at times. The truckers' ownership of the road is akin to the cowboy's claim to the range. That ownership also suggests possible antagonism on the part of many of us toward truckers, for who enjoys being passed by some clown in a big rig at high speed on the highway?

Cast adrift in this unique environment without a proper "handle," Melissa is a well-meaning outsider who doesn't really have any preparation to deal with things as they appear. Consequently, she is by turns amused, befuddled, indignant, frightened, and simply confused. She is naive about this environment though she doesn't realize the full extent of her innocence at first, and in a sense is the child observer of other Peckinpah films. She tries to make sense out of things with the only logic and reason available to her, that of her background. From her vantage point, significantly available to us as well, she gradually comes to learn about the way of things, and although she never achieves a complete understanding (she doesn't become an "insider"), she does come to appreciate the Duck and the values with which he operates. It is not stretching anything to allow for the romance growing between her and the Duck, for apart from the physical attraction, they are both independent spirits; she learns to reciprocate the Duck's open acceptance of her as an individual, something she was not as ready to do in the beginning. There is no fantasy that they will live happily ever after, but one feels that they will share some good time together with a level of respect reminiscent of that shared between Junior Bonner and Charmagne. Respect for the individual is an important quality common to the characters Peckinpah sympathizes with most; the truckers of *Convoy* are uniformly willing to consider people as individuals first, while the outsiders respond with labels and typing by contrast.

The scene of the traveling interview of the convoy on the highway is a crucial confrontation between the "sane" interior and the "insane" exterior films. What is plainly indicated is that both sides think the other is crazy, clearly demonstrating that the Duck as an individual is trapped by the establishment powers that have decided to deal with the truckers for their own purposes. Significantly, the media representative and the governor's man are the same person in this scene, in a tacit observation of the way the two societal forces use each other. As a satirical point, it is not meant as a generalized characterization, and the comedic level of the exterior film permits this kind of "exaggeration." The scene is put forth brilliantly, however, with the trucker interviews establishing the variety of people and concerns behind the wheels, making it obvious that the convoy is not an organized effort but a reflection of the perceived solidarity the media and politicians ascribe to it. The truckers delight in the attention they receive, for as individuals their voices would never be heard, and find in their accidental coalition a degree of recognition which supports the continuation of the convoy, given significance not by themselves but by the media and political concerns. Something is happening; nobody knows what, however. This scene was only vaguely suggested in the script; Peckinpah seizes it as a priceless moment of underscored absurdity, appearing in it himself as if to say, "Hey, will you *look* at these cats(!)"

Convoy is a story of "real" people (individuals) trapped by a popular mythology which forces them to operate in an unreal world, a world which responds more actively to incoherent mass action than it does to individuals. As such, it is indeed a comedy on the outside, not to be taken as literal, "serious" drama. In keeping with this is the fact that the violence of the film is basically harmless, with nobody getting hurt in the violent acts the convoy is responsible for. The fight in the diner is a brawl related to the Palace Bar fight of *Junior Bonner* and the shoot-out drive-in escape of Doc and Carol in *The Getaway*. What begins as a literally dangerous situation with the Duck kicking Lyle's gun away is replaced by the carnival atmosphere of the eternal conflict between Smokey and trucker. Melissa chooses her participatory vantage point by slugging the cop with her bag; Spider Mike removes the other cop's gun by smashing a catsup bottle over the cop's hand. Clearly, this is not a scene of real injury, where catsup replaces blood.

Similarly, vehicular confrontations are played for spectacular comedy; nobody gets hurt as long as the brawl is kept to the "coherent" interior world of Smokey versus trucker. The only real pain is inflicted by Tiny Alvarez on Spider Mike; it is not Lyle who administers the beating, though it remains his responsibility indirectly. The Duck's rescue is a significantly bloodless coup, with the point of the action being individual power, not retributive pain. The confrontation on the bridge has been taken out of Lyle's and the Duck's control; Lyle never wanted to hurt the Duck, really, only to be acknowledged as the "King of the Road." Within the interior the idea resides that the "game" goes too far when somebody actually does get hurt (Spider Mike); Lyle uses his authority to fight dirty in this respect, and the Duck rebukes him for using the Law this way. If Lyle insists on making the Duck an outlaw by using the Law for personal reasons, then the Duck will accept that outlawry. Rejecting Lyle's "Law" is a rejection of the rule-book corruption of moral law.

Viewed strictly at the surface level, *Convoy* might seem to be a Peckinpah self-parody, but what it really reflects is Peckinpah's attitude that the individual hasn't got much of a chance in the modern world. There is certainly a subjective parallel to be drawn to his own situation, where he as an individual is hard pressed to preserve his individual conceptions on someone else's terms. If the material seems to reasonably permit it, Peckinpah will try to have the last laugh, as he does in *The Killer Elite* and *Convoy* in particular. This sensibility makes it increasingly harder for Peckinpah to accept a job merely as a craftsman without becoming conceptually involved in it, for such an ultimate compromise for survival's sake, denying his individuality, bears too high a price. It becomes self-destructive because of the odds against his personal victory, but a victory would be meaningless if he couldn't succeed on his own terms. The challenge for Peckinpah becomes one of finding the way to give the producers enough of what they want while not subverting his own beliefs irretrievably.

At bottom, however, Peckinpah is always a professional, and a particularly original one at that; whatever the project, Peckinpah approaches it with personal commitment, resolved to deliver a film of complete craftsmanship which is yet honest according to his views of the world. His object is to be able to be proud of both aspects; the two reinforce each other's demands. With *Convoy*, Peckinpah takes a script of romantic comedy and adventure and twists it to question the imposition of that romantic adventure. The film satirizes a question of identity, of reality and "myth," for the Duck knows who he is but everybody else is bent on believing him to be something "more." As with the best of his work, *Convoy* offers a surface of rich dramatic and cinematic texture, suggesting "slyly" some ideas the viewer might care to think about. It is a shame that an artist whose prime commitment is to engage his audience beyond "simply" entertaining them should find it so difficult to achieve the practical support necessary to the uninhibited expression of that engagement.

For Peckinpah's dedication to the medium is comparatively rare. The way things are, we should be grateful for his presence and treasure his gifts however we can find them. Whether one winds up in agreement with the thrust of every film of his or not, Peckinpah's work is never a waste of time, for his mastery of the "language" of his medium consistently invokes the questions of art beyond content; one argues about the subjective "truth" or the questions raised by his content, but his artistry is never in doubt. The staggering implication of his work (and there are relatively few others like him in this regard) is the manner in which the form affects the content, involving complex matters of perception that suggest the nature of the communicative power unique to film. This is clearly supported by the idea that Peckinpah's films have to be *seen* to be appreciated; throughout his work there is the suggestion that we do not fully understand what is happening on the screen in a way that is yet comprehensive at a level of verbal understanding. Truly, there is more to the art of storytelling with film than at first meets the conscious mind. Effective storytelling is a wondrous achievement. We would be fools not to look forward to another film by Sam Peckinpah.

15

The Legend of Sam Peckinpah, With an Overview of Themes

"When the legend becomes fact, print the legend."—John Ford's *The Man Who Shot Liberty Valance* (1962)

INTERVIEWER: "What about all the stories—the booze and the broads—are they all true?" "Sure—make up some more if you want to." —ROBERT MITCHUM

The Legend

THE TWO QUOTATIONS ABOVE serve to remind one of an old truth; don't believe everything you read. The popular image of Sam Peckinpah, typified by "Monty Python" and "Laugh-In" sketches wherein everybody gets blown up, the "legend," if you will, is a broad combination of rumor, antagonistic hearsay, misquoting out of context, and simple misinterpretation of his films. The fact that Peckinpah seemingly does little to discourage this view (often quite the contrary) only complicates matters.

Not that he hasn't tried; *Junior Bonner* in many ways, and aspects of *Straw Dogs, The Getaway*, and *The Killer Elite* are particular responses to some of the criticism leveled at him. *Junior Bonner*, a film often described as lyrical, is conveniently ignored by those who categorize Peckinpah as an exploitative "master of violence."

Tracing the mechanics of Peckinpah's career affords one an excellent view of *how* films come about. We may have a better idea now of how the studio system functioned in its heyday, but with the demise of that system there is little understanding of post-1950s commercial filmmaking beyond the notion of the "deal," or the "package," a more recent development. Looking at Peckinpah's career provides examples of what a committed artist must go through to make films—and make no

233

Sam Peckinpah.

mistake, while he might not want to admit it as such, Peckinpah is first and always a committed artist.

He is also one of the first significant film directors who received a great deal of his experience in television. Someday
someone will analyze the extent of impact this has had on
films—what influence this particular training has on a
filmmaker's visual sense, for instance. Indeed, it could be that
the limitations of commercial television help drive an artist
toward the greater freedom of expression available in films. At
the same time, Peckinpah is one of the last of a group of
filmmakers who are not particularly self-conscious of a film
heritage, as compared to a group which emerged in Europe in
the 1960s, and a group of American directors emerging in the
1970s. (Is he apt to be more cinematically original because of
that?)

But in a time which makes the film director a "star" himself,
we often lose sight of the work in focusing on the artist /
personality. Instead of using knowledge of the artist to inform
our perception of his work, we often place the cart before the
horse: the work is expected to conform to our image of the
artist. This is extremely limiting for all. One need only consider the career of Bob Dylan to demonstrate, for when Dylan
did things (such as his shift to rock in 1965) which *altered* his
image, there was great public protest and desertion by many
fans. Dylan could get away with this for the most part, for a
prime facet of his "image" has always been one of mystery;
one learns to expect enigma from the enigmatic, and attention
would quickly turn to where Dylan was *leading*, away from
what he'd left behind.

But Peckinpah cannot get away with it as easily. Beginning
with a narrow focus on violence in his films, based on superficial reactions to some very powerful visuals, added to an "industry reputation" for being difficult to work with, the Peckinpah myth develops into a publicized image of machismo,
blood-and-guts glory in violence for its own sake, tempera-
mental eccentricity bordering on irresponsibility, and two-
fisted, hard-drinking savagery befitting every male stereotype
in pulp fiction. It is simply not true; it is like describing a man
by his footprints.

Reading through published interviews with Peckinpah, it is
possible to pick out the statements others have seized upon to
bolster the Peckinpah myth. But relying on those interviews

(an aspect of celebrity more than information) is a risky proposition. For when one takes Peckinpah's statements and adds
the remarks of friends and even antagonistic associates, placing them in context insofar as possible, a far different picture
from the public myth emerges, one which provides insights
into understanding Peckinpah's work, just as examination of
the work provides insights into the man. It is a much more
complete picture, and at least holds a lot more water. Ultimately, however, we must rely on the work, not on the artist.

Forgive me for underlining what should be obvious, but
Sam Peckinpah is a very complex human being. As his friend
Max Evans writes, Peckinpah is a wheel of contradictory
spokes: "Among the scores of things I've heard Sam Peckinpah called are: insane, pure genius, chickenshit, son of a bitch,
true innovator, bloodsucker of other men's work, hell of a good
ole boy, deceitful, loyal, doublecrosser, gentle man who loves
children, jealousy ridden egomaniac, man out of his time, man
far ahead of his time, and good outdoor cook. . . . He is a little
bit of every cockeyed accusation . . . more of each or less of
each than most of us are."[1] One should note that "son of a
bitch" can also be a term of affection. Attempts at simplification, as Peckinpah demonstrates in the characters in his films,
are misleading.

Impressions of Peckinpah's work methods help reveal part
of the genesis of the myth, as well as insight into the "truth."
William Murray's oft-quoted and misquoted 1972 *Playboy*
interview says in part: "Watching him work can be instructive.
He's rarely in the foreground of whatever's going on, but you
know, without having to be told, who's in charge. There's
something formidable about him. He's usually dressed in
Levis, an open-necked shirt and windbreaker—a lean, tightly
put-together man with the little black eyes of a gunfighter. His
iron-gray mustache, thinning hair and deeply lined features
make him look older than his [age]; he has the face of a man
who has fought a lot of wars—and lost a few of them. When he
talks, even while giving an order, he speaks so softly that he
tends to draw his listeners toward him. Sometimes they regret
it, for what he says, as well as the way he says it, can be in-
timidating. The trick is not to flinch . . ."[2] Murray's choice of
adjective and metaphor may say more about him than Peckinpah.

Biographer Garner Simmons states: "There are conflicts on

every Peckinpah film. When there are none, Peckinpah, himself, will manufacture them. Conflicts keep his creative juices flowing. They also keep everyone connected with a production more alert and sensitive to detail—less prone to stupid mistakes. But because many people tend to avoid confrontation in any form, Sam Peckinpah is not always successful in using conflict as a creative tool."[3] As we have seen in the outline of his career, Peckinpah does not always have to manufacture the conflict, either.

This helps to explain why it is said that he is difficult to work with. For beyond his initial concern for the physical safety of his "employees," Peckinpah is totally dedicated to the film he is working on. He cannot make a film half-heartedly. This is why the statement in the *Playboy* interview, "I'm a whore—I go where I'm kicked,"[4] in reference to his choice of projects, is misleading. He will accept a project partially through simply needing work (he now has three ex-wives and five children), but once accepting that project becomes wholly committed to it in a spirit of dedicated professionalism. He must make the project his own, and consequently winds up fighting those who see it otherwise. In this sense Pauline Kael is right: it is difficult for him to turn in a "routine piece of craftsmanship."[5] It is impossible for him not to care.

This idea of commitment and professionalism in a traditional sense comes up again and again in researching Peckinpah. Simmons states: "There are only two kinds of people who really offend Sam Peckinpah: those who are not professionals yet manage to interfere with the film making process and those whom he considers professionals but who place a price above the value of their word and sell out for money."[6]

The high standards of professionalism Peckinpah demands on a film can be unnerving for those who don't measure up to those standards. This gives rise to the number of dramatic firings that have often occurred on a Peckinpah film. But from those who respond to and survive the "test," Peckinpah commands an equally fierce loyalty which resides in their statements that they'd work again for him "anytime" or "anywhere," regardless of whatever difficulties they might encounter. Actors particularly respond well to Peckinpah. Alternately cajoling and berating them, Peckinpah identifies with all of the characters in his films; actors become equally committed to the task and trust him, and Peckinpah is able to elicit some of their finest work. For example, actress Stella Stevens went through an emotional hell during *The Ballad of Cable Hogue*, but later cherished the experience: "He [Peckinpah] may have driven me quite mad, but maybe he saved my soul . . ."[7] Or, as Burt Young stated during the production of *Convoy*, "Sam's a pain in the ass, but we all want to be part of his gang. He's a genius, the bastard."[8]

It becomes obvious that a committed artist is predestined to a certain amount of frustration working in a medium that has always been first and foremost a business. One can't always easily "blame" the money interests for not being interested in "art," though in arguments between producer and director one cannot but favor the director; bluntly but effectively stated, money shits on creativity. Film is a bastard marriage of art and economics; it is often a head-on collision. As Charlton Heston described Peckinpah, "It remains an open question as to whether he can make commercially successful films faster than he can alienate the men who must supply his financing. He does both with equal facility."[9] Peckinpah is no saint; he has a temper which sometimes asserts itself with or without apparent justification. The man has bled a lot, but one hopes that he will not become a victim of self-destructive bitterness to the extent that it obscures his abilities as an intuitive cinematic genius. Steve McQueen has a line in *The Magnificent Seven* (1960) to the effect that "you either bend with the wind, or you break." Sam Peckinpah does not bend easily.

Testaments of orneriness; examples of gentility and tenderness. Dedication. "When the legend becomes fact, print the legend." The legend is more colorful, simpler by design; the facts are easily obscured, where visible at all. Ultimately, we'll make of it what we *want* to, anyway, perhaps at our own expense. But when one approaches an interesting forest, one must cut through the bramble to get to the trees. And only after looking at the trees can one understand the forest.

Violence

The most controversial issue raised by Peckinpah's work is also the one discussion of which has been characterized by emotion rather than reason. To some extent, the emotional

reactions generated by the impact of Peckinpah's film violence prove his point, but it is nonetheless amazing to consider the ferocity with which many critics refused to face the
issue.

It is a prime concern of Peckinpah's that violence is an inherent characteristic in all of us, and that we must come to
terms with that recognition of our inheritance. It is equally
important that violence be recognized for being as ugly as it is,
and not side-stepped by intellectual rationalization.

But because of the nature of the medium with its automatic
distance factor, and the idea that film "realism" is still not the
same as "reality," Peckinpah stylizes the presentation of a
large amount of violence to achieve the impact reality should
have. This is accomplished primarily through brilliant editing.
It is precisely to the point that one recalls *sequences* of violence from Peckinpah's work as opposed to single violent
shots. For Peckinpah's violent action is decidedly a matter of
action rather than gore. Blood-packs explode, but victims are
not exploited by the camera; there is no lingering over a
corpse for sensationalism, only to demonstrate the physical effect of violence. Generally, corpses are not seen in close-up,
nor are they ever as bloody as the moment of violence would
indicate. Where bodies litter the ground in *The Wild Bunch*,
the effect is of the scope of the destruction, of death as a consequence, not of individual gore for shock value. The "ballet
of death" often referred to is the distance factor of observation
at work, relating to our tendency to find strange grace in manifestations of awesome power. This becomes clearer when related to something like the famous Capa photo of the Spanish
Civil War soldier caught in the moment of his death (which
has been accused of having been staged; it doesn't matter—print the legend). Nightmarish power is fascinating to us,
though it is difficult to explain why. Such power is most
dramatically witnessed in destruction, whether man-made or
natural.

It is beside the main point to argue the degree of exaggeration in some of Peckinpah's violence. Aside from the fact that
relatively few members of the audience *know* what a body
looks like when it is hit by a bullet (and how fast we seem to
forget old news photos of bloody gangland slayings, as well as
how President Kennedy's head *exploded* in the Zapruder

film!), the point of Peckinpah's violence is made if it is perceived as being horrifically repugnant. Perceiving the horror we are capable of, the hope is that we might be a little less apt to resort to it. Violence must be considered always as an *assault*.

Peckinpah does not condone or cheer the violence performed by the Wild Bunch or by David Sumner. The Wild Bunch's march to the plaza is a set-up of genre expectation; we look forward to the action of retribution that the outlaws are on their way to perform, but do not expect the slaughter it turns into. We are fools to have expected less. Likewise, David Sumner's conduct in *Straw Dogs* is reprehensible, even to David in the midst of it. But having backed himself into the corner by not asserting himself earlier, he finds that he has the capability to violently survive. He feels the pride of his assertion, not of the acts themselves, and learns to live with the idea that he is capable of the violence he intellectually abhors. Again, it is not enough to intellectually abhor violence; it must be recognized for what it is, and where it resides.

Obviously, most of Peckinpah's films are not for "children." Unfortunately, they are not for some adults as well, but Peckinpah is not to be blamed for the misinterpretation of his work. He was dismayed to hear that an audience of Nigerian soldiers had their bloodlust aroused by a screening of *The Wild Bunch*.[10] The power of the visual media is such that we will probably never be wholly free of the argument that witnessing violence breeds violence. Apocryphal or not, a friend related to me a story whose irony is unfortunately graphic: a student doing research for a thesis about the influence of screen violence attended a screening of *Bring Me the Head of Alfredo Garcia*. Just as the film began, a man two rows behind him was shot by another man, over a drug-deal double-cross. I'm not sure if the student stayed for the rest of the film. *Ora pro nobis*.

Themes

Nothing is more dangerous in analyzing art than the isolation of a theme from the context it is presented in. If the whole is greater than the sum of its parts, or if a conceptual creation has a "life of its own," we must keep in mind the "part" of a

work we can *never* single out, the part created by the integration of the parts we *think* we can recognizably isolate. We continue to tinker with a work nonetheless, curious about its
power to affect us; there is a quality of mystery in any work of
art, defying definition. In Peckinpah's work, this mystery concerns the depths of human nature.

Reducing Peckinpah's themes to simple, identifiable terms
belies the subtle honesty and sincerity with which they are
presented in the films. His concerns are familiar, ageold
human conflicts that relate directly to Robert Ardrey's primitive inherited needs of identity, stimulation, and security, variations on which are developed according to the suggestions of
the material at hand.

Essential to Peckinpah's outlook is the principle of life's
constant ambiguity. He resists complete judgments of his
characters, even to the extent of having his characters refusing
to judge other characters. This does not mean that he can't
make up his mind, for characters do suffer the consequences of
their actions. What it stresses is the idea of limitation in a
human being's ability to understand his actions or why he
takes an action. People are constantly frustrated by premature
judgments, not realizing that *any* judgment they make has a
built-in prematurity by virtue of their limits as human beings.
Ethical principles are conceived as abstracts, but that act of
conception dares to ignore the ambiguity which arises as those
principles are applied to real, *personal* situations. "Truth"
(and cinematic realism, for that matter) is a function of perception. "Facts" are as potentially misleading as opinions. The
discrepancies between perceived appearances and "reality"
are everywhere.

Accepting ambiguity, Peckinpah regards the world with
irony as a natural consequence. For whatever position a
human being takes, it can be viewed as ironic for its inherent
incompleteness as a human judgment. Our perceptions are
ironic in that we do not understand what we perceive. The
greatest irony for human beings is that even as we can never
be assured of the depth of our understanding, we are forced to
attempt an understanding anyway. Though the "rightness" of
our choices can never be guaranteed, we have to make choices
nevertheless. We do the "best" we can, and finally look to the

hereafter for help. We are the butt of a cosmic joke, tantalized by being able to form the question without ever having a satisfactory answer. Ultimately, the search for an answer may be the key to survival. In the meantime, Peckinpah sympathizes with humanity, inviting us to do the same. He states: "I once directed a Saroyan play in which one of the characters asked another if he would die for what he believed in. The guy answered, 'No, I might be wrong.' That's where I am."[11]

In the hope that recurrent themes have been witnessed in the previous individual film discussions, I will not dwell on them here except in a summary fashion. Peckinpah is a romantic, if only for his belief in the fundamental worth of an individual. He celebrates the independence of an individual, while recognizing that survival is difficult if not impossible in total isolation. Love and friendship are answers to basic needs; loyalty is of consequent importance, as betrayal is devastating. Revenge "always turns sour." Accused of being a nineteenth-century man, Peckinpah inspires our fantasy of the "good ol' days," adhering to "outdated codes like courage, loyalty, friendship, grace under pressure, all the simple virtues that have become clichés."[12] It is not so much that these virtues belonged to the nineteenth century, but that the "modern era" stresses greed over ideas that do not seem properly sophisticated. Over and over again, Peckinpah warns us that modern society has eclipsed the virtues of the individual. Even if we never actually behaved "ideally," we should have learned something by now, but things tend to look worse. There is hope in the survivorship of the individual, but Peckinpah also evokes the dangers of compromise in adaptive survival. Now more than ever, he seems to say, we must respect the virtue of the committed individual who stands for something, whose virtue primarily resides in that aspect of commitment. Commitment is to be respected for the fact that it is indeed a burden. At least in his own case, Peckinpah is committed to making films according to the truth as he sees it; he may not have gone about it the easiest way, but his commitment *is* a burden in terms of career "success." Even if he is a fool to have ever involved himself in commercial filmmaking, he is to be admired for the stubborn commitment he brings to his chosen profession. He can't quit; even if it destroys him, he "wouldn't have it any other way." And, if he were *truly* cynical, he wouldn't make films in the first place, or at least not these.

Cliché or not, Peckinpah subscribes to the ideal of the Boy Scout Law: Steve Judd in *Ride the High Country*, as an ideal character, is trustworthy, loyal, helpful, friendly, courteous, kind, obedient, cheerful, thrifty, brave, clean, and reverent. But Peckinpah is even more concerned with what it takes to maintain any of those virtues, drawn more to those who struggle short of ideals, or who strive to maintain them despite the cost. Professionalism is a direct result of pride in commitment, and a character can retain that pride even without successful achievement; believing in commitment is half the battle. Commitment is necessary to survival: Cable Hogue's commitment is to himself, and David Sumner finds out that he must commit himself or die. Corporal Steiner is committed to his men, while the Rubber Duck's sense of personal commitment forces him to act on it. Bennie recognizes the importance of his commitment to Elita too late; Mike Locken realizes at last that his professional commitment is rendered meaningless by the organization he works for.

While Peckinpah is adept at depicting action, his films begin with people; central to each of his stories is the audience's involvement with the characters and their internal conflicts. How significant the degree of character engagement is becomes less surprising when one is reminded of Peckinpah's theatrical experience prior to films and his continuing respect for the work of Tennessee Williams in particular. Peckinpah does not seem to be a prime directorial choice for *The Glass Menagerie* at first, but he has directed Williams's plays on stage many times.

Taking that interest in internal conflict and adding it to his respect for the independent individual, then coloring it with the irony of the ambiguous experience of appearance versus reality, one arrives at the creation of the Peckinpah "loser," the misfit-loner who struggles to make his own way and doesn't always know why. It is important to recognize that Peckinpah allows his "losers" and loners to succeed, even though the victory may only be achieved in death. The endings of his stories are victories, as much as circumstances will allow. Steve Judd enters his house "justified" and Gil Westrum is redeemed; Major Dundee, a "loser" in a position of authority, succeeds through his indomitability and survives his reckless identity crisis; the Wild Bunch plays its string out to the end; Cable Hogue finds water where it wasn't and proudly accepts death when it arrives; David Sumner finds out who he is and survives; Junior Bonner follows his own road and rides Sunshine; Carol and Doc McCoy *do* get away; Billy the Kid plays his string out; Bennie avenges Elita's death (though this is a particularly bitter victory, coming as it does too late for Bennie but not for us); Mike and Mac sail away; Steiner survives and "defeats" Stransky with his humiliation (a marginal personal victory only, due to larger circumstances which dictate no victory overall, though hope is allowed by letting Kiesel, an officer of conscience, escape); and the Rubber Duck "swims" away. *The Deadly Companions*'s ending was predetermined and, accepting the conditions of the story, so was the grim ending of "Noon Wine." The one film of predominantly bleak resolution (apart from *Cross of Iron*'s general nature), *Pat Garrett and Billy the Kid*, is also the story primarily concerned with the character who compromised, who "sold out." Garrett winds up as the real "loser." Celebrating the capacity for individual action in the midst of a society that works against the individual touches a responsive chord; as the system shows itself to be inadequate or unsatisfactory, we cheer those individuals who, with integrity, seem to subvert the system and accomplish things as individuals—the way Sam Peckinpah has.

Notes and References

Chapter One

1. The bulk of the information on Peckinpah's family background is obtained from the first two chapters of Louis Garner Simmons's doctoral thesis, *The Cinema of Sam Peckinpah and the American Western: A Study of the Interrelationship between an Auteur / Director and the Genre in Which He Works* (Northwestern, 1975). While some of the information is available elsewhere, Simmons's work is the most comprehensive source for documentation in this area. Rather than follow this note with fifty "ibid." citations, I resume my notes where called for beyond this area of the discussion.

2. Quoted in Simmons, p. 37.

3. "Don Siegel and Me," in Stuart M. Kaminsky, *Don Siegel: Director* (New York, 1974), p. 300.

4. (New York, 1974), p. 85.

5. Kaminsky, pp. 94-97.

6. Don Siegel, speaking in Simmons, p. 49.

7. Kaminsky, p. 299.

8. Simmons, p. 50.

9. Ibid., p. 52. Again, Simmons is the principal authority on Peckinpah's television work.

10. Ibid., p. 53.

11. Ibid., p. 54

12. Peckinpah, speaking in Simmons, p. 57.

13. Simmons, p. 57.

14. Don Siegel, as quoted in Kaminsky, p. 147.

15. Simmons, pp. 58-59.

16. As quoted in Simmons, p. 59.

17. One episode called "The Line Camp," written and directed by Tom Gries, was later expanded by Gries into his feature *Will Penny* in 1966.

18. Peckinpah, speaking to Richard Whitehall, "Talking with Peckinpah," *Sight And Sound*, 38:4 (Autumn 1969), 1974.

244

19. Peckinpah, as quoted in Simmons, p. 62.

20. Peckinpah, speaking in Simmons, pp. 63-64.

21. Peckinpah, as quoted in Simmons, p. 77.

22. As quoted in Simmons, p. 103.

23. Simmons, p. 153.

24. Max Evans, *Sam Peckinpah: Master of Violence* (Vermillion, S.D., 1972), p. 61.

25. Peckinpah, quoted in Simmons, p. 218.

26. As quoted in Simmons, p. 350.

27. Ernest Parmentier, ed., *"Cross of Iron," Film Facts*, 20:ix (1977), 203.

28. "Truckin' with the Big Iguana," *Time*, July 4, 1977, p. 73.

Chapter Two

1. As quoted in Simmons, p. 77.

2. The film was made in Pathé-Color (as it was distributed by Pathé), a process with which it is difficult to achieve realistic color. As a consequence, reds tend to be somewhat "warmer" than they should be, and interiors tend to a red-golden quality here. Beyond that, Pathé-Color prints *fade* rapidly, gradually turning completely red. I have not seen the film in color and, where relevant, have relied on others who have and my own experience in appreciating this aspect. It should also be noted that the film was shot in Panavision, an anamorphic process akin to CinemaScope, with an aspect ratio of 2.35:1; but the film is hard to find today in any format. (For a good capsule description of wide-screen processes and aspect ratio differences, see *The Oxford Companion to Film*, ed. by Liz-Anne Bawden (New York: Oxford Univ. Press, 1976).

Chapter Three

1. Lyons, speaking in Simmons, p. 85.

2. Burt Kennedy, speaking in Simmons, pp. 84-85.

3. See Simmons, Chapter 4, and Darrin Scot, *"Ride the High Country," American Cinematographer*, July 1962, for more details.

4. Dialogue from *The Wild Bunch*.

Chapter Four

1. (Bloomington, Ind., 1969), p. 139.

2. In Simmons, p. 138.

3. Descriptions of the missing scenes vary somewhat. For further information, see Kitses, op. cit., pp. 139-40, and Simmons, pp. 138-39.

4. A term borrowed from Hitchcock, where the nature of the object of everyone's pursuit is irrelevant.

5. *Horizons West*, p. 144.

6. Speaking in John Cutts, "Shoot!" *Films and Filming* (October 1969), p. 6.

7. As quoted in Simmons, p. 131.

8. As quoted in Simmons, p. 136.

Chapter Five

1. Katherine Anne Porter, " 'Noon Wine': The Sources," in Cleanth Brooks and Robert Penn Warren, eds., *Understanding Fiction* (New York, 1959), p. 620.

2. As quoted in Stephen Farber, "Peckinpah's Return," *Film Quarterly*, 23 (Fall 1969), 11.

3. As quoted in Ernest Parmentier, ed., *"The Wild Bunch,"* *FilmFacts*, 12 (No. 10, 1969), 219.

4. Peckinpah, as quoted in Farber, p. 9.

5. As quoted in John Cutts, "Shoot!" *Films and Filming*, 16:i (October 1969), p. 8.

6. As quoted in Simmons, p. 189.

7. Simmons, p. 170.

8. As quoted in Richard Whitehall, "Talking with Peckinpah," *Sight and Sound*, 38 (Autumn 1969), 175.

9. Simmons, p. 192.

10. As quoted in Joel Reisner and Bruce Kane, "Sam Peckinpah," *Action*, May / June 1970, p. 27.

Chapter Six

1. For more on this, read Max Evans's account of the production, *Sam Peckinpah: Master of Violence*, (Vermilion, S.D., 1972).

Chapter Seven

1. See also Ardrey's *The Social Contract* (New York, 1970).

2. *The Territorial Imperative* (New York, 1966), p. 334.

3. Simmons, p. 232.

4. Quoted in William Murray, "Playboy Interview: Sam Peckinpah," *Playboy*, August, 1972, p. 68.

5. Peckinpah, as quoted in Murray, p. 68.

6. Ibid., p. 66.

7. Simmons, p. 227.

8. As quoted in Simmons, p. 228.

9. Quoted in Murray, p. 68.
10. As quoted in Simmons, p. 239.
11. Simmons, p. 241.

Chapter Nine

1. As quoted in Simmons, p. 276.
2. Simmons, p. 275.
3. Described by Kevin Thomas (*Los Angeles Times*), in Ernest Parmentier, ed., *"The Getaway," FilmFacts*, 15 (No. 24, 1972), 627.

Chapter Ten

1. Rudolph Wurlitzer, *Pat Garrett and Billy The Kid* (New York, 1973), p. v.
2. Recorded in Stephen Farber, "Peckinpah's Return," *Film Quarterly*, 23 (Fall 1969), 10.

Chapter Eleven

1. Quoted in Simmons, p. 338.

Chapter Twelve

1. *"The Killer Elite," Monthly Film Bulletin*, 43 (No. 506, March 1976), 55.
2. Information provided by L. Garner Simmons in conversation with author, June 1978.
3. See also Pauline Kael, "Notes on the Nihilist Poetry of Sam Peckinpah," *New Yorker*, January 12, 1976, for more on this private aspect of *The Killer Elite*.

Chapter Thirteen

1. As it appears in the American-release version, the scene is particularly frustrating because of two shots of another "ravaged" woman in the barn with Zoll and the woman he has with him. Obviously, an accounting for what this other woman is doing there is part of what has been cut. A friend who saw the film in Berlin reports that she has been ravaged by another platoon member. Other cuts in the film seem to have been made to eliminate some additional graphic violence in combat(!).
2. The quotation attributed to Brecht is as follows: "Don't rejoice in his defeat, you men. For though the world stood up and stopped

the bastard, the bitch that bore him is in heat again." Steiner's final weary expletive is heard as the quotation fades and the end credits begin.

3. For instance, the philosophical "subplot" between the two officers, Brandt and Kiesel, is a particular area for further investigation.

Chapter Fourteen

1. As quoted in Jan Aghed, *"Pat Garrett and Billy the Kid," Sight and Sound*, 42:ii (Spring 1973), 66. (Neider's book was the original basis for Marlon Brando's *One-Eyed Jacks*.)

Chapter Fifteen

1. *Sam Peckinpah: Master of Violence*, p. 1.
2. August 1972, p. 66.
3. Simmons, p. 293.
4. August 1972, p. 66.
5. "Notes on the Nihilist Poetry of Sam Peckinpah," *New Yorker*, January 12, 1976, p. 70.
6. Simmons, p. 75.
7. As quoted in Simmons, p. 210.
8. As quoted in *Time*, July 4, 1977, p. 73.
9. As quoted in Simmons, p. 135.
10. ". . . They wanted to die like William Holden": Peckinpah, as quoted in P. F. Kluge, "Director Sam Peckinpah, What Price Violence?" *Life*, August 11, 1972, p. 53.
11. Peckinpah, as quoted in *Playboy*, August 1972, p. 72.
12. Ibid.

Selected Bibliography

1. Books

Ardrey, Robert. *African Genesis*. New York: Atheneum, 1961.

–––. *The Social Contract*. New York: Atheneum, 1970.

–––. *The Territorial Imperative*. New York: Atheneum, 1966.
While all three of Ardrey's books are significant, *The Territorial Imperative* is breathtaking; engagingly readable, the book is compelling beyond its covers, concluding that human behavior is directly linked to animal behavior through an analysis of ideas of property, and that man is not nearly as unique an animal as we might prefer to think. Peckinpah agrees with Ardrey acutely.

Evans, Max. *The Hi Lo Country*. New York: Dell, 1975 (orig. pub. 1961). A novel for which Peckinpah has written a script and has long wanted to film; reading it, one can easily appreciate why. Other writers have refused to alter Peckinpah's script for it; hopefully, he'll get to make it.

–––. *Sam Peckinpah: Master of Violence*. Vermilion, S.D.: Dakota Press, 1972. A novelist and longtime friend of Peckinpah's, Evans played the part of "shotgun" on the stage in *The Ballad of Cable Hogue*. Aside from the book's unfortunate and misleading title, it is a warm and revealing account of the making of that film, invaluable for the impressions it gives of Peckinpah and some of his work methods, and a colorful, good "read" besides.

Garrett, Pat F. *The Authentic Life of Billy, The Kid*. Introduction by J. C. Dykes. The Western Frontier Library. Norman, Okla.: Univ. of Oklahoma Press, 1954. Originally published in 1882, the book's introduction is well documented, stressing the ambiguous nature of many of the "facts" on the Kid's life. In view of the cutting of Peckinpah's film, the book is extremely valuable in providing a background to Peckinpah's treatment of the story.

Kaminsky, Stuart M. *Don Siegel: Director*. Curtis Film Series. New York: Curtis Books, 1974. A fascinating career biography of Siegel, well researched with many interviews, and with an afterword, "Don Siegel and Me," written by Peckinpah.

249

KITSES, JIM. *Horizons West*. Cinema One Series. Bloomington, Ind.: Indiana Univ. Press, 1970 (orig. pub. London, 1969). A valuable study of the Western genre as contained in the work of Anthony Mann, Budd Boetticher, and Peckinpah. In part, a brief but insightful study of Peckinpah through *The Wild Bunch*; intriguing analysis and excellent suggestions. Highly recommended.

NACHBAR, JACK, ed. *Focus on the Western*. Englewood Cliffs, N.J.: Prentice-Hall, 1974. An excellent collection of essays on the genre; its bibliography is a required reading list for students.

SIMMONS, LOUIS GARNER. *The Cinema of Sam Peckinpah and the American Western: A Study of the Interrelationship between an Auteur / Director and the Genre in Which He Works*. Ph.D. thesis, Northwestern Univ., Evanston, Ill., 1975. (Available through University Microfilms International, Ann Arbor, Mich.; Order No. DAH75-29751.) Simmons's thesis is an invaluable book on Peckinpah, as well as an intriguing analysis of the Western genre. A labor of love, heavily detailed and fully documented, Simmons interviewed practically everybody remotely connected with Peckinpah, and his book is full of the results of those interviews. Objective and revealing, Simmons's book is critical to a deeper understanding of the director and his work, with much more contained than the title implies. It also includes a complete television filmography in detail, and an extensive bibliography.

WURLITZER, RUDOLPH. *Pat Garrett and Billy the Kid*. New York: Signet Film Series, New American Library, 1973. A script version of the film, by Wurlitzer's account somewhere between the original script and the finished film. The author's introduction is of interest, giving an impression of how some things came about, as well as something about the author's dissatisfaction with the changes Peckinpah made in his script.

2. Periodicals

AGHED, JAN. "*Pat Garrett and Billy the Kid*." *Sight and Sound*, 42,ii (Spring 1973), 64-69. An interesting article written during production of the film; includes some analysis and background to the work.

ANDREWS, NIGEL. "Sam Peckinpah: The Survivor and the Individual." *Sight and Sound*, 42,ii (Spring 1973), 69-74. An engaging analysis of Peckinpah's films through *The Getaway*.

KAEL, PAULINE. "Notes on the Nihilist Poetry of Sam Peckinpah." *New Yorker*, January 12, 1976, pp. 70-75. An intriguing analysis of *The Killer Elite* as a personal allegory of Peckinpah.

MACKLIN, F. ANTHONY, ed. *Film Heritage*, 10,ii, Winter 1974-75. An entire issue devoted to Peckinpah; includes Garner Simmons's account of Peckinpah's television work and television filmography.

McArthur, Colin. "Sam Peckinpah's West." *Sight and Sound*, 36,iv (Autumn 1967), 180-83. Interesting genre analysis of Peckinpah's first three films.

Miller, Mark Crispin. "In Defense of Sam Peckinpah." *Film Quarterly*, 28,iii (Spring 1975), 2-17. Probing, enthusiastic consideration of Peckinpah, mainly discussing *Bring Me the Head of Alfredo Garcia*.

Milne, Tom. "*Bring Me the Head of Alfredo Garcia*." *Monthly Film Bulletin*, 42 (No. 493, February 1975), 29. A very thoughtful review.

– – –. "*The Killer Elite*." *Monthly Film Bulletin*, 43 (No. 506, March 1976), 55-56. Likewise, penetrating.

Parmentier, Ernest, ed. "*The Wild Bunch*." *FilmFacts*, 12 (No. 10, 1969), 217-21.

– – –. "*Straw Dogs*." *FilmFacts*, 15 (No. 1, 1972), 1-5.

– – –. "*Junior Bonner*." *FilmFacts*, 15 (No. 17, 1972) 410-13.

– – –. "*The Getaway*." *FilmFacts*, 15 (No. 24, 1972) 627-30.

– – –. "*Pat Garrett and Billy the Kid*." *FilmFacts*: 16 (No. 4, 1973), 86-89.

– – –. "*Cross of Iron*." *FilmFacts*, 20 (No. 9, 1977), 203-205. Release information, credits, synopses, and review summaries. Parmentier & Co. deserve medals; not perfect, but very reliable.

Pechter, William. "Film Favorites: William Pechter on *The Wild Bunch*." *Film Comment*, 6,iii (Fall 1970), 55-57. Some spirited and convincing arguments in favor of the film.

Reisner, Joel, and Kane, Bruce. "Sam Peckinpah." *Action*, May / June 1970, pp. 24-27. Introductory article on Peckinpah, with insightful and engaging quotes from associates.

Ross, T. J. "*Straw Dogs*, Chess Men, and War Games." *Film Heritage*, 8,i (Fall 1972), 1-6. An interesting appraisal of *Straw Dogs*, in answer to some criticism of the film.

Scot, Darrin. "*Ride the High Country*." *American Cinematographer*, July 1962. A technical account of the filming, but you'd hardly know that Peckinpah had anything to do with it.

Simmons, Garner. "*Bring Me the Head of Alfredo Garcia*." *Take One*, 4,vi (July-August 1973; pub. Nov. 1974), 25-26. A thoughtful and revealing review of the film.

"Truckin' with the Big Iguana". *Time*, July 4, 1977, pp. 73-74. Some interesting impressions and reporting from the production of *Convoy*, on location.

3. Interviews with Peckinpah

Callenbach, Ernest. "A Conversation with Sam Peckinpah." *Film*

Quarterly, 17,ii (Winter 1963-64), 3-10. An engaging early interview, covering work through *Ride the High Country*.

CUTTS, JOHN. "Shoot!" *Films and Filming*, 16,i (October 1969), 4-8. An excellent, thoughtful interview, while *The Wild Bunch* was in release. Good background details on Peckinpah's early career.

FARBER, STEPHEN. "Peckinpah's Return." *Film Quarterly*, 23,1 (Fall 1969), 2-11. An interesting interview done prior to *Cable Hogue's* release; some interesting Peckinpah comments on violence.

KLUGE, P. F. "Director Sam Peckinpah, What Price Violence?" *Life*, August 11, 1972, pp. 47-54. Peckinpah interviewed during production of *The Getaway*; additional impressions of the author, and a *Life* picture spread.

LEYDON, JOSEPH. "James Coburn: His Life and *Hard Times*." *Take One*, 4,xii (July-August 1974; pub. Dec. 1975), 7-8. A revealing interview, with Coburn's comments on *Pat Garrett*.

MURRAY, WILLIAM. "Playboy Interview: Sam Peckinpah." *Playboy*, August 1972, pp. 65-74, 192. An influential piece, widely quoted and misquoted. Conducted during production of *The Getaway* and somewhat argumentative, it covers a broad range of topics.

WHITEHALL, RICHARD. "Talking with Peckinpah." *Sight and Sound*, 38,iv (Autumn 1969), 172-75. A good background interview done after completion of *The Wild Bunch*, with particular information on Peckinpah's television experience.

Filmography

THE DEADLY COMPANIONS(A Carousel Production, distributed by Pathé-America, 1961) Re-released in 1965 by Motion Picture Investors, under the title TRIGGER HAPPY.

Producer: Charles B. FitzSimons

Production Manager and Assistant Director: Lee Lukather

Screenplay: A. S. Fleischman, based on his novel (published as *Yellowleg*)

Cinematographer: William H. Clothier (Panavision, Pathé-Color)

Music: Marlin Skiles (conducted by Raoul Kraushaar)

Song: "A Dream of Love," by Marlin Skiles and Charles B. FitzSimons, sung (over the credits) by Maureen O'Hara

Sound: Robert J. Callen and Gordon Sawyer

Costumes: Frank Beetson, Sr., and Sheila O'Brien

Makeup: James Barker

Special Effects: Dave Kohler

Editor: Stanley E. Rabjohn, assisted by Leonard Kwit

Filmed on location in and around Old Tucson, Arizona

Cast: Maureen O'Hara (Kit Tildon), Brian Keith (Yellowleg), Steve Cochran (Billy), Chill Wills (Turk), Strother Martin (Parson), Will Wright (Doctor), Jim O'Hara (Cal), Peter O'Crotty (Mayor), Billy Vaughan (Mead)

Original Running Time: 90 minutes, cut to 79 minutes

American Release: June 1961

16mm. rental: None currently; available for TV from UPA

RIDE THE HIGH COUNTRY(Metro-Goldwyn-Mayer, 1962) (British title: GUNS IN THE AFTERNOON).

Producer: Richard E. Lyons

Assistant Director: Hal Polaire

Screenplay: N. B. Stone, Jr. (uncredited: William S. Roberts and Sam Peckinpah)

Director of Photography: Lucien Ballard (CinemaScope, Metrocolor)

Art Direction: George W. Davis and Leroy Coleman

Set Decoration: Henry Grace and Otto Siegel
Music: George Bassman
Recording Supervisor: Franklin Milton
Makeup: William Tuttle
Editor: Frank Santillo
Location work in California, and in Inyo National Forest
Cast: Randolph Scott (Gil Westrum), Joel McCrea (Steve Judd),
    Mariette Hartley (Elsa Knudsen), Ron Starr (Heck Longtree),
    Edgar Buchanan (Judge Tolliver), R. G. Armstrong (Joshua
    Knudsen), Jenie Jackson (Kate), James Drury (Billy Hammond),
    L. Q. Jones (Sylvus Hammond), John Anderson (Elder Ham-
    mond), John Davis Chandler (Jimmy Hammond), Warren Oates
    (Henry Hammond)
Original Running Time: 94 minutes
American Release: June, 1962
16mm. rental: Films, Inc. (Scope available)

MAJOR DUNDEE(Jerry Bresler Productions, distributed by Co-
    lumbia Pictures, 1965)
Producer: Jerry Bresler
Assistant to the Producer: Rick Rosenberg
Assistant Directors: John Veitch and Floyd Joyer
Second Unit Director: Cliff Lyons
Mexican Assistant Director: Emilio Fernandez
Production Manager: Francisco Day
Screenplay: Harry Julian Fink, Oscar Saul, and Sam Peckinpah,
    based on a story by Harry Julian Fink
Director of Photography: Sam Leavitt (Panavision, Eastman Color by
    Pathé, print by Technicolor)
Art Director: Al Ybarra
Music: Daniele Amfitheatrof
Title Song: "Major Dundee March," music by Daniele Amfitheatrof,
    lyrics by Ned Washington; sung by Mitch Miller's Sing Along
    Gang; Song: "Laura Lee," by Liam Sullivan and Forrest Wood
Sound: Charles J. Rice and James Z. Flaster
Costumes: Tom Dawson (uncredited: Gordon Dawson and Eric
    Seeley)
Special Effects: August Lohman
Makeup: Ben Lane and Larry Butterworth
Editors: William A. Lyon, Don Starling, and Howard Kunin
Location work done in Mexico, studio work at Churubusco
Cast: Charlton Heston (Major Amos Dundee), Richard Harris (Capt.
    Benjamin Tyreen), Jim Hutton (Lt. Graham), James Coburn
    (Samuel Potts), Michael Anderson, Jr. (Tim Ryan), Senta Berger
    (Teresa Santiago), Mario Adorf (Sgt. Gomez), Brock Peters

(Aesop), Warren Oates (O. W. Hadley), Ben Johnson (Sgt. Chillum), R. G. Armstrong (Rev. Dahlstrom), L. Q. Jones (Arthur Hadley), Slim Pickens (Wiley), Begonia Palacios (Linda).
Original Running Time (as released): 134 minutes
American Release: April 1965
16mm. rental: Corinth Films (Scope)

NOON WINE (Television production) (Talent Associates, for ABC-Stage 67, 1966)
Producer: Daniel Melnick
Associate Producers: James Clark and Lois O'Connor
Teleplay: Sam Peckinpah, from the novella by Katherine Anne Porter
Production Design: Walter Scott Herndon
Music: Jerry Fielding
Editors: Art Schneider and Lou Lombardo (uncredited)
Cast: Jason Robards (Royal Earle Thompson), Olivia De Havilland (Mrs. Thompson), Per Oscarsson (Olaf Helton), Theodore Bikel (Mr. Hatch), Ben Johnson (Sheriff Barbee), L. Q. Jones (Mr. McClellan)
One-hour, color, videotape, and film
Original broadcast: November 23, 1966
(Available for viewing at the Museum of Broadcasting, New York)

THE WILD BUNCH (A Phil Feldman Production for Warner Bros.-Seven Arts, 1969)
Producer: Phil Feldman
Associate Producer: Roy N. Sickner
Second Unit Director: Buzz Henry
Assistant Directors: Cliff Coleman and Fred Gammon
Production Manager: William Faralla
Screenplay: Walon Green and Sam Peckinpah, based on a story by Walon Green and Roy N. Sickner
Director of Photography: Lucien Ballard (Panavision 70, Technicolor)
Art Director: Edward Carrere
Music: Jerry Fielding
Music Supervision: Sonny Burke
Sound: Robert J. Miller
Wardrobe Supervisor: Gordon Dawson
Special Effects: Bud Hulburd
Makeup: Al Greenway
Editor: Louis Lombardo
Associate Film Editor: Robert L. Wolfe
Filmed entirely on location in Mexico
Cast: William Holden (Pike Bishop), Ernest Borgnine (Dutch Engstrom), Robert Ryan (Deke Thornton), Edmond O'Brien

(Freddy Sykes), Warren Oates (Lyle Gorch), Jaime Sanchez (Angel), Ben Johnson (Tector Gorch), Emilio Fernandez (Mapache), Strother Martin (Coffer), L. Q. Jones (T. C.), Albert Dekker (Harrigan), Bo Hopkins (Crazy Lee), Dub Taylor (Mayor Wainscoat), Paul Harper (Ross), Jorge Russek (Lt. Zamorra), Alfonso Arau (Herrera), Chano Urueta (Don Jose), Rayford Barnes (Buck), Aurora Clavell (Aurora), Sonia Amelio (Teresa), Fernando Wagner (Mohr)
Original Running Time: 148 minutes; later cut to 135 minutes
American Release: June 1969
16mm. rental: Twyman Films (Scope, "long version")

THE BALLAD OF CABLE HOGUE (A Latigo-Phil Feldman Production for Warner Bros.-Seven Arts, 1970)
Producer: Sam Peckinpah
Executive Producer: Phil Feldman
Co-Producer: William Faralla
Associate Producer: Gordon Dawson
Assistant Director: John Gaudioso
Screenplay: John Crawford and Edmund Penney
Director of Photography: Lucien Ballard (Technicolor)
Art Director: Leroy Coleman
Set Decorator: Jack Mills
Music: Jerry Goldsmith, orchestrated by Arthur Morton
Songs: "Tomorrow Is the Song I Sing," music by Jerry Goldsmith, lyrics by Richard Gillis; "Wait For Me, Sunrise," music and lyrics by Richard Gillis (both sung by Richard Gillis); "Butterfly Mornings," music and lyrics by Richard Gillis
Music Supervision: Sonny Burke
Sound: Don Rush
Costumes for Miss Stevens: Robert Fletcher
Makeup: Gary Liddiard and Al Fleming
Special Effects: Bud Hulburd
Unit Production Manager: Dink Templeton
Dialogue Supervisor: Frank Kowalski
Property Master: Robert Visciglia
Editors: Frank Santillo and Lou Lombardo
Titles: Latigo Productions (Peckinpah's company)
Location work done in Valley of Fire, Nevada, and Apache Junction, Arizona
Cast: Jason Robards (Cable Hogue), Stella Stevens (Hildy), David Warner (Rev. Joshua Sloane), Strother Martin (Bowen), Slim Pickens (Ben Fairchild), L. Q. Jones (Taggart), Peter Whitney (Cushing), R. G. Armstrong (Quittner), Matthew Peckinpah (Matthew)

Running Time: 121 minutes
American Release: March 1970
16mm. rental: Audio Brandon Films

STRAW DOGS (An ABC Pictures Presentation; a co-production of Talent Associates Films and Amerbroco Films, distributed by Cinerama Releasing Corporation 1971)
Producer: Daniel Melnick
Associate Producer: James Swann
Assistant Director: Terry Marcel
Assistant to Director: Katy Haber
Screenplay: David Zelag Goodman and Sam Peckinpah, based on the novel *The Siege of Trencher's Farm*, by Gordon M. Williams
Director of Photography: John Coquillon (Eastman Color)
Production Designer: Ray Simm
Production Design Consultant: Julia Trevelyan Oman
Art Director: Ken Bridgeman
Set Decorator: Peter James
Music: Jerry Fielding
Sound: John Bramall
Sound Editor: Garth Craven
Wardrobe: Tiny Nicholls
Makeup: Harry Frampton
Special Effects: John Richardson
Continuity: Pamela Davies
Production Supervisor: Derek Kavanagh
Property Master: Alf Pegley
Editors: Roger Spottiswoode, Paul Davies, and Tony Lawson
Editorial Consultant: Robert Wolfe
Location work done in St. Ives, Cornwall, England; interiors at Twickenham Studios
Cast: Dustin Hoffman (David Sumner), Susan George (Amy Sumner), Peter Vaughan (Tom Hedden), T. P. McKenna (Major Scott), Del Henney (Charlie Venner), Ken Hutchison (Norman Scutt), Colin Welland (Rev. Hood), Jim Norton (Chris Cawsey), Sally Thomsett (Janice Hedden), Donald Webster (Riddaway), Len Jones (Bobby Hedden), Peter Arne (John Niles), David Warner (uncredited) (Henry Niles).
Original Running Time: 118 minutes; cut to 113 minutes for U.S.
American Release: December 1971
16mm. rental: Films, Inc.

JUNIOR BONNER (A Joe Wizan-Booth Gardner Production in association with Solar Productions, for ABC Pictures, distributed by Cinerama Releasing Corp., 1972)

Producer: Joe Wizan
Associate Producer: Mickey Borofsky
Production Manager: James C. Pratt
Production Assistants: Raymond Green, Betty J. Gumm, and Katy Haber
Second Unit Director: Frank Kowalski
Assistant Directors: Frank Baur, Malcolm R. Harding, and Newt Arnold
Screenplay: Jeb Rosebrook
Director of Photography: Lucien Ballard (Todd-AO 35, color by Movielab)
Art Director: Edward S. Haworth
Set Decorator: Gerald F. Wunderlich
Music: Jerry Fielding
Songs: "Bound to Be Back Again," words and music by Dennis Lambert and Brian Potter, sung by Alex Taylor; "Arizona Morning," "Rodeo Man," words, music, and sung by Rod Hart
Costumes: Eddie Armand
Makeup: Donald W. Roberson and William P. Turner
Special Effects: Bud Hulburd
Property Master: Robert Visciglia
Editors: Robert Wolfe and Frank Santillo
Title Design: Latigo Productions
Technical Advisor: Casey Tibbs
Filmed on location in Prescott, Arizona
Cast: Steve McQueen (Junior Bonner), Robert Preston (Ace Bonner), Ida Lupino (Elvira Bonner), Ben Johnson (Buck Roan), Joe Don Baker (Curly Bonner), Barbara Leigh (Charmagne), Mary Murphy (Ruth Bonner), William McKinney (Red Terwiliger), Dub Taylor (Del), Sandra Deel (Nurse Arlis), Charles Gray (Burt), Matthew Peckinpah (Tim Bonner)
Original Running Time: 100 minutes
American Release: June 1972
16mm. rental: Films, Inc. (Scope)

THE GETAWAY (A Solar / Foster-Brower Production for First Artists Production Co., distributed by National General Pictures, 1972)
Producers: David Foster and Mitchell Brower
Associate Producer and Second Unit Director: Gordon Dawson
Assistant Directors: Newt Arnold and Ron Wright
Assistant to the Producer: Joie Gould
Screenplay: Walter Hill, based on the novel by Jim Thompson
Director of Photography: Lucien Ballard (Todd-AO 35, Technicolor)
Art Directors: Ted Haworth and Angelo Graham
Set Decorator: George R. Nelson

Music: Quincy Jones; harmonica solos by Toots Thielemans
Sound: Charles M. Wilborn, Garth Craven, Richard Portman, Joe von Stroheim, and Mike Colgan
Costumes: Ray Summers
Makeup: Al Fleming and Jack Petty
Special Effects: Bud Hulburd
Property Master: Robert J. Visciglia
Editors: Robert Wolfe and assistants Mike Klein and William G. Lindemann
Editorial Consultant: Roger Spottiswoode
Title Design: Latigo Productions
Filmed on locations throughout Texas
Cast: Steve McQueen (Doc McCoy), Ali MacGraw (Carol McCoy), Ben Johnson (Jack Benyon), Sally Struthers (Fran Clinton), Al Lettieri (Rudy Butler), Slim Pickens (Cowboy), Richard Bright (The Thief), Jack Dodson (Harold Clinton), Dub Taylor (Laughlin), Bo Hopkins (Frank Jackson)
Original Running Time: 122 minutes
American Release: December 1972
16mm. rental: Swank Motion Pictures (Flat only)

PAT GARRETT AND BILLY THE KID (A Gordon Carroll-Sam Peckinpah Production for Metro-Goldwyn-Mayer, 1973)
Producer: Gordon Carroll
Second Unit Director: Gordon Dawson
Assistant Directors: Newt Arnold and Lawrence J. Powell
Screenplay: Rudolph Wurlitzer
Director of Photography: John Coquillon (Panavision, Metrocolor)
Art Director: Ted Haworth
Set Decoration: Ray Moyer
Music: Bob Dylan
Sound: Charles M. Wilborn and Harry W. Tetrick
Wardrobe: Michael Butler
Makeup: Jack P. Wilson
Special Effects: A. J. Lohman
Unit Production Manager: Jim Henderling
Mexican Production Manager: Alfonso Sanchez Tello
Mexican Assistant Director: Jesus Marin Bello
Property Master: Robert John Visciglia
Editors: Roger Spottiswoode, Garth Craven, Robert L. Wolfe, Richard Halsey, David Berlatsky, Tony De Zarraga
Filmed on location in and around Durango, Mexico
Cast: James Coburn (Pat Garrett), Kris Kristofferson (Billy the Kid), Bob Dylan (Alias), Richard Jaeckel (Sheriff Kip McKinney), Katy Jurado (Mrs. Baker), Slim Pickens (Sheriff Baker), Chill Wills

(Lemuel), Jason Robards (Gov. Lew Wallace), R. G. Armstrong (Ollinger), Luke Askew (Eno), John Beck (Poe), Richard Bright (Holly), Matt Clark (J. W. Bell), Rita Coolidge (Maria), Jack Elam (Alamosa Bill), Emilio Fernandez (Paco), Paul Fix (Pete Maxwell), L. Q. Jones (Black Harris), Rudolph Wurlitzer (O'Folliard), Sam Peckinpah (Will), and uncredited in the American release version: Aurora Clavell (Ida Garrett), Barry Sullivan (Chisum), Elisha Cook, Jr. (Cody), Dub Taylor (Josh)
Original Running Time: 123 minutes, recut by MGM to 106 minutes for release
American Release: May 1973
16mm. rental: Films, Inc. (Scope; 106 minute version)

BRING ME THE HEAD OF ALFREDO GARCIA (An Optimus-Latigo-Estudios Churubusco Co-Production for United Artists, 1974)
Producer: Martin Baum
Executive Producer: Helmut Dantine
Associate Producer: Gordon Dawson
Executive Production Manager and Assistant Director: William C. Davidson
Assistant to the Director: Katherine Haber
Screenplay: Gordon Dawson and Sam Peckinpah, from an original story by Frank Kowalski and Sam Peckinpah
Director of Photography: Alex Phillips, Jr. (Eastman Color)
Art Director: Augustin Ituarte
Set Dresser: Enrique Estevez
Music: Jerry Fielding
Songs: "Bennie's Song" by Isela Vega, "A Donde Ir" by Javier Vega, "Bad Blood Baby" by Sam Peckinpah, "J.F." by Arturo Castro
Sound: Manuel Topete, Mike Colgan, Harry W. Tetrick
Wardrobe: Adolfo Ramirez
Makeup: Rosa Guerrero
Special Effects: Leon Ortega, Raul Fabmir, Federico Farfan
Property Master: Alf Pegley
Unit Production Manager: Carlos Terron Garcia
Mexican Assistant Director: Jesus Marin Bello
Dialogue Director: Sharon Peckinpah
Supervising Editor: Garth Craven
Editors: Robbe Roberts, Sergio Ortega, Dennis E. Dolan
Titles Designed by Latigo Productions
Filmed on location in Mexico in collaboration with Churubusco Studios
Cast: Warren Oates (Bennie), Isela Vega (Elita), Robert Webber (Sappensly), Gig Young (Quill), Helmut Dantine (Max), Emilio Fer-

nandez (El Jefe), Kris Kristofferson (Paco), Donnie Fritts (John), Chano Urueta (Old Man), Janine Maldonado (Theresa), Don Levy (Frank), Jorge Russek (Cueto)
Original Running Time: 112 minutes
American Release: August 1974
16mm. rental: United Artists 16

THE KILLER ELITE (An Arthur Lewis-Baum / Dantine Production of An Exeter / Persky-Bright Feature, distributed by United Artists, 1975)
Producers: Martin Baum and Arthur Lewis
Executive Producer: Helmut Dantine
Production Manager: Bill Davidson
Second Unit Director: Frank Kowalski
Assistant Directors: Newton Arnold, Ron Wright, Jim Bloom, Cliff Coleman
Production Assistant to the Director: Katherine Haber
Screenplay: Mark Norman and Stirling Silliphant, based on the novel by Robert Rostand
Director of Photography: Philip Lathrop (Panavision, Color by De-Luxe)
Production Designer: Ted Haworth
Set Decorator: Rick Gentz
Music: Jerry Fielding
Sound: Fred Brown, Charles M. Wilborn, Richard Portman
Wardrobe Designer: Ray Summers
Makeup: Jack Wilson and Jack Petty
Special Effects: Sass Bedig
Property Master: Robert J. Visciglia
Supervising Editor: Garth Craven
Editors: Tony De Zarraga and Monte Hellman
Cast: James Caan (Mike Locken), Robert Duvall (George Hansen), Arthur Hill (Cap Collis), Bo Hopkins (Jerome Miller), Mako (Yuen Chung), Burt Young (Mac), Gig Young (Lawrence Weyburn), Helmut Dantine (Vorodny), Matthew Peckinpah (Mat)
Original Running Time: 130 minutes
American Release: December 1975
16mm. rental: United Artists 16 (Note: 16mm. prints are flat only and looped for TV-acceptable dialogue; the scanning is fair)

CROSS OF IRON (A coproduction of Anglo-EMI Productions [London], Rapid Film [Munich], and Terra Filmkunst [Berlin]; An ITC Entertainment, distributed by Avco-Embassy [U.S.], 1977)
Producers: Alex Winitsky and Arlene Sellers

Executive Producer: Wolf C. Hartwig
Associate Producer: Pat Duggan
Production Supervisor: Dieter Nobbe
Second Unit Director: Walter Kelley
Assistant Directors: Cliff Coleman and Bert Batt
Production Assistant to the Director: Katherine Haber
Screenplay: Julius Epstein, Walter Kelley, and James Hamilton, based on the book by Willi Heinrich
Director of Photography: John Coquillon (Technicolor)
Production Designer: Ted Haworth
Art Director: Veljko Despotovic
Music: Ernest Gold, orchestration by Gerard Schurmann
Sound: David Hildyard, Bill Rowe, Jerry Stanford, Rodney Holland
Wardrobe Supervisors: Kent James and Carol James
Makeup: Colin Arthur
Special Effects: Sass Bedig, Richard Richtsfeld, Zdravko Smojver
Property Master: Robert Visciglia
Stunt Arranger: Peter Brayham
Military Advisors: Major A. D. Schrodek and Claus Von Trotha
Editors: Tony Lawson, Murray Jordan, and Michael Ellis
Filmed on location in Yugoslavia
Cast: James Coburn (Cpl. Steiner), Maximilian Schell (Capt. Stransky), James Mason (Col. Brandt), David Warner (Capt. Kiesel), Klaus Lowitsch (Kruger), Senta Berger (Sister Eva), Arthur Brauss (Zoll), Vadim Glowna (Kern), Roger Fritz (Lt. Triebig), Dieter Schidor (Anselm), Burkhard Driest (Maag), Michael Nowka (Dietz), Veronique Vendell (Marga), Slavko Stimac (Russian Boy Soldier)
Original Running Time: 130 minutes, later cut to 119 minutes for U.S.
American Release: March 1977
16mm. rental: Swank Motion Pictures

CONVOY (EMI Films, distributed by United Artists, 1978).
Producer: Robert M. Sherman
Executive Producers: Michael Deeley and Barry Spikings
Second Unit Directors: Walter Kelley and James Coburn
Assistant Directors: Tom Shaw, Richard Wells, Pepi Lenzi, John Poer, Cliff Coleman, Newton Arnold, Ron Wright
Production Managers: Tony Wade and Tom Shaw
Screenplay: B. W. L. Norton, based on the song by C. W. McCall
Director of Photography: Harry Stradling, Jr. (Panavision, Color by Deluxe)
Production Designer: Fernando Carrere
Art Director: J. Dennis Washington

Set Decorator: Francis Lombardo
Music: Chip Davis; supervision and lyrics by Bill Fries
Sound: Bill Randall, Don Mitchell, Bob Litt, Steve Maslow
Costumers: Kent James and Carol James
Makeup: Steve Abrums and Jim McCoy
Special Effects: Sass Bedig, Marcel Vercoutere, Candy Flanagin
Property Master: Robert J. Visciglia
Stunt Coordinator: Gary Combs
Supervising Editor: Graeme Clifford
Editors: John Wright and Garth Craven
Filmed on location in New Mexico
Cast: Kris Kristofferson (Rubber Duck), Ali MacGraw (Melissa), Ernest Borgnine (Lyle Wallace), Burt Young (Pig Pen), Madge Sinclair (Widow Woman), Franklin Ajaye (Spider Mike), Brian Davies (Chuck Arnoldi), Seymour Cassel (Gov. Haskins), Cassie Yates (Violet), Walter Kelley (Hamilton)
Original Running Time (as released): 110 minutes
American Release: June 1978
16mm. rental: United Artists 16

Index